"This detailed, insightful, and unsparing study of Franklin Pierce's storm-tossed presidency sharpens our understanding of one of the most crucial chapters in American history. Drawing upon his own original research and a sophisticated examination of the rich secondary literature on the troubled 1850s, Gara has produced a book of genuine interest to specialists and general readers alike."—Richard H. Sewell, author of *Ballots for Freedom: Antislavery Politics in the United States, 1837-1860*.

"This book skillfully recreates not only the events of the period but also the spirit of the age."—Ira V. Brown, author of *Lyman Abbot, Christian Evolutionist*.

"During Pierce's administration the Jacksonian party system ruptured and disappeared, Kansas erupted in violence, and the sectional conflict steadily worsened. Gara devotes considerable attention to these developments and also provides an important discussion of American expansionism and diplomacy during these years."—William E. Gienapp, author of *The Origins of the Republican Party, 1852-1856*.

"Gara's portrayal of Franklin Pierce as a tragic and complex figure is skillfully done. His major contribution, however, lies in his analysis of American politics and foreign policy during the 1850s. Especially compelling is his analysis of 'young America's' obsession with Central America and the Caribbean—an obsession that not only illuminates our past and our present, but, God forbid, our future."—Richard O. Curry, author of *The Border States during Reconstruction*.

Larry Gara is professor of history and chair of the Department of History at Wilmington College. He is the author of *The Liberty Line: The Legend of the Underground Railroad*, *Westernized Yankee: The Story of Cyrus Woodman*, *The Baby Dodds Story, as told to Larry Gara* (the autobiography of an early New Orleans jazz musician), and *A Short History of Wisconsin*.

The Presidency of
FRANKLIN
PIERCE

AMERICAN PRESIDENCY SERIES

Donald R. McCoy, Clifford S. Griffin, Homer E. Socolofsky
General Editors

George Washington, Forrest McDonald
John Adams, Ralph Adams Brown
Thomas Jefferson, Forrest McDonald
James Madison, Robert Allen Rutland
John Quincy Adams, Mary W. M. Hargreaves
Martin Van Buren, Major L. Wilson
William Henry Harrison & John Tyler, Norma Lois Peterson
James K. Polk, Paul H. Bergeron
Zachary Taylor & Millard Fillmore, Elbert B. Smith
Franklin Pierce, Larry Gara
James Buchanan, Elbert B. Smith
Andrew Johnson, Albert Castel
Rutherford B. Hayes, Ari Hoogenboom
James A. Garfield & Chester A. Arthur, Justus D. Doenecke
Grover Cleveland, Richard E. Welch, Jr.
Benjamin Harrison, Homer E. Socolofsky & Allan B. Spetter
William McKinley, Lewis L. Gould
Theodore Roosevelt, Lewis L. Gould
William Howard Taft, Paolo E. Coletta
Warren G. Harding, Eugene P. Trani & David L. Wilson
Herbert C. Hoover, Martin L. Fausold
Harry S. Truman, Donald R. McCoy
Dwight D. Eisenhower, Chester J. Pach, Jr., & Elmo Richardson
Lyndon B. Johnson, Vaughn Davis Bornet

The Presidency of

FRANKLIN
PIERCE

Larry Gara

UNIVERSITY PRESS OF KANSAS

© 1991 by the University Press of Kansas
All rights reserved

Published by the University Press of Kansas (Lawrence, Kansas
66045), which was organized by the Kansas Board of Regents and is
operated and funded by Emporia State University, Fort Hays State
University, Kansas State University, Pittsburg State University,
the University of Kansas, and Wichita State University

Library of Congress Cataloging-in-Publication Data

Gara, Larry.
The presidency of Franklin Pierce / Larry Gara.
p. cm. — (American presidency series)
Includes bibliographical references (p.   ) and index.
ISBN 0-7006-0494-4 (cloth : alk. paper)
1. Pierce, Franklin, 1804–1869. 2. Presidents—United States—
Biography. 3. United States—Politics and government—1853–1857.
I. Title. II. Series.
E432.G37 1991
973.6′6′092—dc20   91-8367
[B]   CIP

British Library Cataloguing in Publication data is available.

Printed in the United States of America
10 9 8 7 6 5 4 3 2 1

For
Robin, Chris, and Sarah
Brian and Falguni

CONTENTS

FOREWORD

The aim of the American Presidency Series is to present historians and the general reading public with interesting, scholarly assessments of the various presidential administrations. These interpretive surveys are intended to cover the broad ground between biographies, specialized monographs, and journalistic accounts. As such, each will be a comprehensive, synthetic work which will draw upon the best in pertinent secondary literature, yet leave room for the author's own analysis and interpretation.

Volumes in the series will present the data essential to understanding the administration under consideration. Particularly, each book will treat the then current problems facing the United States and its people and how the president and his associates felt about, thought about, and worked to cope with these problems. Attention will be given to how the office developed and operated during the president's tenure. Equally important will be consideration of the vital relationships between the president, his staff, the executive officers, Congress, foreign representatives, the judiciary, state officials, the public, political parties, the press, and influential private citizens. The series will also be concerned with how this unique American institution—the presidency—was viewed by the presidents, and with what results.

All this will be set, insofar as possible, in the context not only of contemporary politics but also of economics, international relations, law, morals, public administration, religion, and thought. Such a broad approach is necessary to understanding, for a presidential administration is more than the elected and appointed officers composing it, since its work so often reflects the major problems, anxieties, and glories of the nation. In short, the authors in this series will strive to recount and evaluate the record of each administration and to identify its distinctiveness and relationships to the past, its own time, and the future.

The General Editors

PREFACE

Who was Franklin Pierce? Why in the world would anyone write about his presidency? I have had to respond to those questions repeatedly as I pursued this study. If any president approaches oblivion in the American memory it is Pierce. Textbooks usually skip over much of his administration, but when he is remembered—after nearly a century and a half—it is often with disapproval. Some years ago an Ohio historian, visiting the Pierce home in Concord, New Hampshire, asked the guide why the state does not publicize more vigorously the home of its only president.

"Folks here," answered the guide, "don't think much of Mr. Pierce. The Kansas-Nebraska Act, you know."

Pierce remained loyal to the Democratic party even when it was tarred with the brush of treason during the Civil War—a war he refused to support—and he was himself accused of Confederate sympathies. That was enough to destroy his later reputation.[1]

Controversy over Franklin Pierce broke out anew in 1966 when the only house he ever owned was threatened by urban renewal. Despite his reputation, there were still some Pierce admirers in New Hampshire, who formed the Pierce Brigade, named for the army unit Pierce commanded during the Mexican War. One of the brigade's objectives was to save the Pierce Manse, given that name to distinguish it from two other houses he and his family had occupied in Concord. The Pierce Brigade raised money by "begging, borrowing and bake sales," and the state legislature provided the final $20,000 from a sesquicentennial fund derived from the sale of bourbon whiskey in commemorative bottles. In light of Pierce's drinking habits, it was a fitting contribution.

Attorney David Epstein took a different tack, organizing the Friends of Franklin Pierce, whose goal was "to rescue him from the obscurity he so richly deserves" and to present, in a *Washington Post* article, a bit of revisionist history. That prompted Harold F. Yeaton, president of the Pierce Brigade, to accuse Epstein not only of repeating all the stories that Pierce's opponents had circulated during the campaign of 1852, but of casting "further aspersions on his character and administration by twisting the facts." Even a distant relative, faced with having to sell a desk once used by Franklin Pierce, consoled himself with the thought that Pierce "was not one of our best presidents."[2]

Historians who participate in the presidential rating game agree that Franklin Pierce, while not himself a strong president, held the office during a significant, even critical, time in our national life. It was what happened during those years that makes the administration worth careful study. During the Pierce presidency the political system began to unravel and north-south polarization reached new dimensions. The Kansas-Nebraska Act and its aftermath made civil war more likely, if not inevitable. Other nations had abolished slavery without the trauma of war, and historians still disagree about whether that was possible in the United States. But there is no question that by the mid-fifties it was no longer possible to persuade northern voters to accept a program of further slave extension. Yet that is precisely what Pierce tried to do. Moreover, it would have taken political genius to persuade the South to relinquish not only slavery itself but the power disproportionate to the southern voting population which derived from slavery. Franklin Pierce was no genius. Indeed, the ordinary demands of the office were often beyond his ability. He was a politician of limited ability, and instead of growing in his job, he was overwhelmed by it.

While the years of the Pierce presidency were critical ones for the future of the Union, it was also a time of far-reaching developments in American foreign policy. Opening Japan to the West had momentous consequences. The expansion of American trade and influence brought disputes with France and Great Britain, and the obsession to acquire Cuba nearly precipitated a war with Spain. With the Gadsden Purchase Treaty the present borders of the continental United States were established. There was also serious discussion—in some cases more than mere discussion—about acquiring Alaska, Nicaragua, the Hawaiian Islands, Formosa, the Dominican Republic, the guano islands in the Pacific, even Canada. The Pierce years contributed an important chapter to the history of American imperialism.

Several matters of public policy that were prominent during the Pierce presidency continue to plague Americans in the late twentieth century. There are echoes of Young America meddling in the internal affairs of Nicaragua and of the activities of William Walker in the Central American policies of recent administrations. In domestic issues, Pierce's determination to limit the scope of government involvement in human services has contemporary overtones, and the debate goes on today.

Of course, viewing the nation's history from the White House has its limitations. Many Americans in the 1850s were not at all interested in the president or in what he was doing, and some important developments were unrelated to national politics. Some people, like the followers of John Humphrey Noyes, dropped out of the mainstream of society to attempt a more egalitarian and moral social order in the Oneida Community. It was during the Pierce years that German pietists of the Amana Community found in the United States a haven for their efforts to create a perfect Christian society. Many others worked to improve their country by joining organizations dedicated to world peace, temperance, or the abolition of slavery. While the reform groups sometimes worked through such traditional political organizations as the Free Soil party, more often than not theirs were attempts to influence change outside the electoral process. And they made their influence felt. Agitators like William Lloyd Garrison increased public awareness of issues long before politicians were willing to confront them, as did the women at Seneca Falls, New York, in 1848, who started a movement for equal rights.

Moreover, many events of the Pierce years which had little relationship to the presidency profoundly influenced the lives of later Americans. Certainly that was true of the industrial revolution, which contributed, among other things, to the growing urbanization of the country. That revolution made possible a higher material standard of living for many, along with unspeakable working conditions and pollution of the environment. Some small private ventures also had impacts that their promoters could not have foreseen. Such was the introduction of the English sparrow into the United States in 1853. The imported bird was supposed to end a plague of canker worms and other pests then infesting trees in Brooklyn. But the sparrows, preferring a vegetarian diet, found a good supply of seeds in the readily available horse manure on city streets. The little brown birds soon became common in every American city, town and village, another legacy of the Franklin Pierce years.[3]

Since this book is an interpretive synthesis, I am profoundly indebted to the many scholars whose works I have drawn upon. I wish also to thank Wilmington College for granting me a leave to write, and for several research grants. The staff of the S. Arthur Watson Library at Wilmington College has been generous and helpful in locating research materials and in borrowing books and articles not found in the local collection. I owe a special debt of gratitude to editors of the American Presidency Series, whose careful and penetrating reading of the manuscript has improved it immeasurably in both accuracy and style.

Finally, there are no words to express adequately my gratitude to Lenna Mae Gara, my life partner, for her help with this book. Without complaint, and without benefit of word processor, she edited my prose and put it into graceful English, then typed the entire manuscript. She set aside her own writing plans to help this book along, and when the outlook was dark, her loyal encouragement kept the project alive.

Larry Gara

Wilmington, Ohio
July, 1990

1

★ ★ ★ ★ ★

THE AMERICAN
LANDSCAPE: 1852

In 1852—the year Franklin Pierce was elected president—the United States was a sprawling, sparsely populated country. Most of its people—more than twenty-three million—lived on farms, the rest in small towns and a few cities dotting an expanse of magnificent natural beauty. Large sections of the interior, still heavily wooded, provided habitat for thousands of species of birds and animals, some of them now extinct. Thousands of immigrants from Europe came primarily to gain independence through land ownership or to acquire wealth by exploiting the natural resources of the New World. History often emphasizes those who came to escape religious or political oppression or to avoid military service; in fact, they were the minority, and even they often defined freedom in terms of material betterment.

If the abstractions of liberty were of secondary importance to most of those who sought a new life in a new world, the beauty of the natural environment was similarly uninteresting. A historian writing in 1736 referred to the land as a "hideous wilderness." Although breathtakingly beautiful in many places, it was an impediment to personal ambition. To succeed it was necessary to transform the land and make it livable. Forests were a formidable obstacle to be cut down or burned as quickly as possible. When the trees were destroyed, the bird population reduced, and the wild animals trapped and killed, the land, by nineteenth-century standards, was considered "improved." Said a historian of pioneer Wisconsin agriculture: "The lands of any country are important for the human opportunity they represent." To create farms, towns and cities from the natural areas was "progress," a matter of faith with those whose lives and thought had been influenced by the Enlightenment, with its assurance that human intelligence could solve all problems. Moreover, change was the destiny of humanity, and its inevitability constituted a secular determinism reminiscent of Calvinism without its divine aspect. Rational thought, science, and technology were replacing or in some cases coexisting with the God of Jonathan Edwards.[1]

To outsiders, the Americans seemed unduly obsessed with the pursuit of money. Lacking a hereditary aristocracy, Americans quickly developed an aristocracy based on wealth and talent. Because the population included various ethnic groups, generalizations about nine-teenth-century Americans must always be suspect. They had a variety of languages, customs, religions, and dress. Their emphasis on the rights and importance of the individual led to factionalism in every section. When they organized churches, lodges, reform groups, even colleges, they tended to subdivide over issues and personality disputes. A transplanted Maine Yankee summed it up in 1839 after he moved to Cincinnati: "Of the people I can say truly they are a motley crew. We have Germans and Dutch, English and French, Irish and Scotch, Yankees and Buckeyes, and lordly Virginian and the chivalrous Ken-tuck, the bowie bearer from the lower country and the Hoosier from Western land, all with their peculiar habits and sectional prejudices, but all agreed upon one thing: viz the acquisition of wealth." By 1852 that one thing was probably even more evident.[2]

Yet the pursuit of wealth had as many variations as the people involved. Opportunities depended on many factors: the nature of the soil, the terrain, proximity to the ocean or other bodies of water, the climate, desirable natural resources, and the degree of civilization as indicated by the number of inhabitants and the length of time since the area had been a wilderness. There was not yet a nation in the modern sense, but rather a combination of states, regions, and sections. Neither government nor business was centralized. People were concerned primarily with local problems and issues. Wherever they settled, Ameri-cans took pride in their local communities. In a town this was often a reflection of the views of the founder, usually a land speculator and booster whose interest it was to combine local pride with the desire to profit from continued settlement and growth. The location of a county seat, a canal, railroad, or military post seemed more important than national affairs. The federal government in Washington, referred to as the General Government, was of little interest except when policies immediately affected local inhabitants. From time to time such issues as the tariff, land policy, land subsidies for internal improvements, and eventually Free Soil stimulated an interest in national politics.

Although travel was still limited, an amazing number of Americans moved to new locations looking for the fame or wealth that they could not attain in older, more crowded parts of the country. For thousands this meant moving west, and eventually the people of the Northeast and Southeast created two new sections, the Northwest and Southwest. Farmers, doctors, lawyers, would-be political leaders, artisans, slave-holders, all seemed to find in the western country opportunities lacking in their original homes. While they were making changes in life and work, momentous changes were taking place in the young country that would also affect its political life.

To nineteenth-century Americans, farming was much more than an economic pursuit. It was a way of life, a source of independence, and the basis for a well-constructed political philosophy best exemplified by the popular version of the Jeffersonian myth. Jefferson's vision of the future was a land dotted with small farms, individually owned and worked by all members of the family. Cities would be few and far apart, and the limited industry would be related to agricultural pursuits. It was the farm of the mythical pioneer who raised most of the family's food and traded extra crops for items not produced in the home. It was an ideal seldom realized and not universally shared. Some entertained a vision of fortune gained through trade or land speculation, while in the southern states the man of success was a planter with large holdings and many slaves to work the fields and serve the family. Yet success in those terms was highly selective. Large numbers of those who worked the land did so either as farm laborers or as tenants whose dream of ownership never became a reality. Moreover, to the southern slave, success for the planter meant only a lifetime of unpaid labor without even the freedom to leave the plantation without permission.

Except for the slaves, nearly all those who engaged in agriculture shared the urge to speculate in land. There was something special— almost mystical—about land ownership, and virtually all who had excess capital to invest put at least some of it in land. From the poorest squatter to the wealthiest absentee landowner, speculation was a favorite activity. Every landowner tried to keep some of his holdings for future sale. Speculators were everywhere. Some worked individually, while others organized land companies, often sending agents into unsettled areas to pick off the land most likely to increase in value. Such agents, often transplanted eastern lawyers, combined land speculation with collection of debts and other business activities, usually charging what the traffic would bear. In Wisconsin one such agent, criticized for

3

charging a ten percent commission for collecting a debt, grudgingly reduced the fee with the comment: "You will hardly suppose that we settled here *on the backside of creation,* for the pleasure of doing business for nothing." Nor was speculation in western land limited to farmers: early Wisconsin land records reveal Daniel Webster, Edward Everett, Caleb Cushing, and Ralph Waldo Emerson as absentee landowners in the territory.[3]

When the lands were cleared and settled, farming took on whatever aspect seemed most profitable for the area. Even the earliest settlers grew more than they could use or kept an orchard and raised cattle and hogs for sale. By 1850 the trend was toward larger farms and a greater emphasis on commercial agriculture. The staples wheat and corn were grown in the northwestern states and shipped to eastern cities as grain, or in cattle and hogs to feed the growing numbers of city dwellers who had to import their food. As farming became increasingly commercial, farmers became less independent, and the dream of a self-sufficient homestead quickly faded. Such matters as world prices, transportation costs, tariff policy, the availability of credit, and the appearance of an ever-growing number of new farm machines affected farm income. Although the new John Deere plows and McCormick reapers helped farmers produce more per acre with less muscle power, the wonders of American ingenuity did not reduce the long work day. Neither did the popular sewing machines ease the work load of farm women, whose numerous chores included virtually all food preparation and preserving, taking care of the infants who appeared with startling regularity, nursing the sick, and often helping with field work. For women, farm life was monotonous, back breaking, endless. For those who had married tyrants, it was almost unbearable.

The new machinery was also expensive. Greater acreage meant a larger output of cash or credit, and the scramble for profit caused much consolidation of farm holdings, with many of the poorer farmers losing out. Before the era of the industrial robber barons there was the era of the bonanza farm owners of the prairie states, such as Michael Sullivant, who raised purebred cattle on five thousand acres near Columbus, Ohio. In 1852 he began purchasing land in Illinois, soon owning eighty thousand acres and hiring a hundred farm workers. By 1857 Sullivant's Illinois farms had three thousand acres in corn, somewhat less in wheat. Cattle raising also attracted the wealthy capitalist. B. F. Harris of Urbana, Illinois, kept about five hundred head of cattle and six hundred hogs each year. Bigness was often a goal in itself. When successful, such operations, which posed considerable risk, also resulted in hefty profits.[4]

Nearly all who commented on mid-nineteenth-century American farming noted its wastefulness. In Europe a severe shortage of good farmland encouraged experiments in soil replenishment and a judicious use of the land. In the United States there seemed to be an unlimited amount of land, although some of it had to be deforested or drained before it could be used for agriculture. But the tendency was to work the soil until it was no longer able to produce, especially in the tobacco-growing areas of the South. Instead of troubling to rotate crops and restore nutrients to the soil, most farmers sold their worn-out land and moved on.

Of course, there were exceptions. Farm scholars reported on European practices and urged the use of the farm manure and guano, a fertilizer derived from sea bird dung, to keep the soil healthy. Farm groups also requested aid from the federal government in the form of tariff protection for hemp, cotton, and wool, funds for distributing experimental seed crops, better weather information, retaliation against Peru for the excessive cost of guano, and, most important of all, free land for those who would work it. Although the desirability of limited government was the accepted wisdom, American farmers, like other citizens, assumed that their own interests required governmental attention and support.

The special interests of southern agriculture were slavery and the widespread cultivation of cotton. It is true that slaveholders constituted only a small percentage of the southern population, a fourth or less, and that most of those who claimed slave ownership had relatively few slaves. Still, the small minority of large-scale slaveholders and owners of large plantations tended to dominate southern politics and, through that, the South's economic and social policies. No southern congressman came near being a Free Soiler. Nearly all of them upheld the interests of the slaveholders, a policy that led northern critics of slavery to discern a slave power with influence in national affairs far beyond its numbers.

Southern agriculture, like its northern counterpart, was strikingly diverse, as was the economic status of its practitioners. Besides large-scale planters, there was a small class of very poor and a very large group of middle-class or yeoman farmers who owned few or no slaves and who grew tobacco, wheat, corn, and sweet potatoes, in addition to cotton, and kept livestock. A considerable portion of the food consumed in the South was produced there, on farms ranging from a hundred to two hundered acres. There were also oversized plantations specializing in rice and sugar production. These required the most difficult labor and took the greatest toll from the slaves who worked their fields. A common form of punishment for runaway slaves was to be sold and sent to the dreaded rice and sugar plantations of lower Georgia and Louisiana.

Of all Americans, southerners were the most suspicious of the federal government, fearing that any expansion of power at that level might ultimately be used to disrupt what they preferred to call the "peculiar institution." Yet they, too, looked to Washington for support when their interests demanded it. A majority of Louisiana sugar growers supported the Whig party's policy of a protective tariff for their crop. Southern farmers joined their northern counterparts in urging Congress to break Peru's monopoly of guano, and in 1829 South Carolina's rice farmers urged the War and Navy departments to purchase rice for the military, and urged the State Department to persuade England and the German states to import more American rice.

The most pervasive southern demand on the federal government concerned the fugitive slave issue. Owners of escaped slaves often assumed that northern abolitionists had encouraged them to run away and had given them refuge and aid in reaching Canada. A constitutional provision requiring the return of fugitive slaves was largely a dead letter by 1850, when a new, more stringent fugitive slave law was part of that year's sectional compromise. The new legislation placed all responsibility for the return of fugitives on the federal government, thus greatly enhancing its power. The law, weighted in favor of the owners, created new federal commissioners and obligated all American citizens to help return runaway slaves. Southerners demanded that the government protect their property, which in this case meant their labor force. Many citizens in the North felt no obligation to return a fugitive slave to southern bondage. That the section which most emphasized states' rights should now urge extension of federal power was a paradox lost on most of those who overlooked the constitutional principle in the name of self-interest. Some, however, recognized the danger. "If Congress can legislate at all between the master and slave in a State, where can its power be stayed?" asked delegates to an 1851 southern convention. "It can abolish slavery in the States," they warned. The fiery editor of the *Charleston Standard* agreed. "It might be well for us to consider," he said, "whether we have not, in fact, made a concession more fatal to our separate and distinct political existence than even the founders of the Constitution themselves were prepared to make."[5]

Beyond the constitutional questions, the industrial revolution, a force soon to dominate much of northern life, posed a serious threat to the system of southern slave labor. The *New York Tribune* referred to it as "a great though silent revolution in our National Industry [which] has for forty years been in progress." The industrial revolution, which substituted first water power, then steam power for the older muscle power in the manufacture of consumer goods and machine tools, began in England but quickly took hold in the New World. There, a growing market, seemingly unlimited natural resources, an energetic and skilled work force, and a steady supply of domestic and foreign capital, including California gold, encouraged growth and development. Many viewed this, too, as progress, though the craft workers whose skills were made obsolete by the new machinery saw it in a different light. Increasingly, items used in the home were produced in factories rather than in small shops. Americans contributed such vital elements as the use of interchangeable parts, perfected by the United States arsenal at Springfield, Massachusetts, and promoted by Eli Whitney, Samuel Colt and others, and the invention of a great variety of machine tools used to produce such diverse items as wooden clocks and textiles.[6]

The new industry was heavily concentrated in the Northeast, where labor was plentiful and agriculture often difficult. Merchants began investing their extra capital in manufacturing, viewing labor as just another element in the cost of doing business. With industrialism came a new working class composed of factory laborers who worked long hours, usually in sanitation and health conditions that, in later times, would be considered barbaric. The textile mills at Lowell, Massachusetts, were regarded as a model operation, hiring mostly young, unmarried women whose paternalistic employers required them to be in their boarding houses by ten at night, to attend church, and to refrain from foul language and improper behavior. Infractions were duly reported. Laborers worked from dawn until 7:30 in the evening, for which the women were paid $2 and the men $4.20 a week in addition to their board, which cost the company 17½ cents a day for the women. Young farm men and women found jobs in these and other, even less attractive workplaces. By 1850 the Lowell mills had seriously deteriorated, with ownership in the hands of absentee capitalists who preferred to hire immigrant workers under even less humane conditions. Such conditions became more common as the trend toward corporate ownership accelerated.[7]

It was a system that worked perfectly for those whose major objective was to reap the largest profit possible. There were some rags-to-riches examples, like Amos and Abbott Lawrence, who went to Boston with only a few dollars and founded a business that soon made them Boston's leading merchants. Illness ended Amos's business career, but Abbott went on to serve several terms in Congress and to promote a new industrial town which took his name.

The Lawrence brothers were the exception, however. The majority of new capitalists were scions of families whose wealth was already well established. Successful merchants often added manufacturing, mining or railroad promotion to their endeavors, or else shifted completely. Some, like A. T. Stewart, continued to lend energy and talent to merchandising, which remained an important component of the new economic order. Increasingly, bright and talented young men turned to business rather than politics. The business of the United States was already becoming business.

Yet while some were piling up fortunes from industry, merchandising, mining, and railroading, others were dropping lower on the social and economic scale. Artisans not only lost control of their workplace, they also lost much of the status they had earned over the years. With the industrial revolution came periods of depression and unemployment. What had been small pockets of poverty became a major feature of American urban life. The poverty and miserable conditions of many northern workers and the unemployed came to the attention of journalists and authors who often tended to castigate the poor for their own plight. Many writers saw it as a moral issue and put the blame on the shoulders of the poor. Apologists for slavery frequently contrasted the lot of poorer northern workers with a highly idealized view of the condition of southern slaves.[8]

Some of the workers tried to fight back by organizing unions or engaging in work strikes, boycotts, and demonstrations. They were usually the more skilled of the workforce—printers, bricklayers, bakers—whose tradition of organized effort predated the new era. Sometimes they made gains, only to lose them in times of economic distress. Opposing all such effort was the power and influence of businessmen, who viewed labor organizing as a violation of their property rights, if not a prelude to social revolution. Factory owners sometimes took political office in addition to their business activities or found officeholders who would represent their interests. Laissez-faire was a matter of faith with American politicians, and that faith included opposition to organized labor. Employers often worked together to crush labor groups, frequently forming their own associations, which circulated blacklists of ''undesirable troublemakers.'' At the Middlesex mill in Lowell, seventeen women quit when the company cut wages in violation of their contract. When the women looked for other jobs they discovered they had been blacklisted. In a petition to the legislature they explained: "Some of us went to work for other companies, but these companies soon received our names and we were immediately turned off. Some of us applied for work where hands were wanted, but were informed that they could employ 'none of the turnouts from the Middlesex.'" The sordid episode, reported in a Mobile, Alabama, newspaper in 1850, made excellent grist for the southern propaganda mill.[9]

Such practices, however, were generally accepted as necessary to the successful expansion of American industry. Another important factor in that expansion was the multitude of American inventions. There is no better index of Yankee ingenuity than the gadgets, tools, and machines produced by people whose training and experience were acquired on the job. Some inventions—the sewing machine, vulcanized rubber, reapers and improved plows, the telegraph, Colt revolvers—laid the basis for new and thriving industries. Visitors to the industrial exhibition at London's Crystal Palace in 1851 were strongly impressed with the display of American products. One proud American observed that his country's "handled axes, hay-rakes, grain cradles, scythes and snathes, three-tined hay-forks, solid steel hoes, road-scrapers, posthole augers, fan-mills, smut-mills, sausage cutters, sausage stuffers, tin-man's tools, currycombs, corn-brooms, portmanteaus and trunks, ice-cream freezers, aletrees, paintmills, and many other things of universal use here, but in the shape of conveniences which we have given them utterly unknown in Europe, established for our industry a character independent of and unlike that of any other nation." The London Exhibition also provided Britons the first opportunity to see American sewing machines, the Otis elevator, and the very popular McCormick reaper.

Despite the prevailing laissez-faire philosophy, American inventors had welcomed the protection of the United States Patent Office ever since the first effective patent legislation in 1836. The service became increasingly important. In the decade of the 1840s the government office granted an average of 650 patents a year, a number that jumped to 2,500 in the next decade. Those inventions affected every aspect of economic life. Some, like Robert Stevens's T-rail, which led to standardization of railroad tracks throughout the world, were never patented. Since many inventions extended or improved on the work of others, many who claimed credit and the profit that went with it were involved in lengthy and bitter lawsuits, such as Eli Whitney's dispute over the cotton gin and Cyrus McCormick's over the reaper. Some innovations were simply a new or improved process, such as the introduction of interchangeable

THE PRESIDENCY OF FRANKLIN PIERCE

parts, the assembly line procedure used by Cincinnati meat packers, and the concept of the factory itself, which was used first in 1814 to manufacture cotton cloth in Waltham, Massachusetts.[10]

While manufacturing and transportation provided Americans with their greatest source of wealth, the economic health of the new nation also depended heavily on foreign trade. Ships constructed in New England's ports carried a variety of goods throughout the world and were the source of some of the early great fortunes. Some trade was very lucrative, such as that with China dating from 1784 when the *Empress of China* carried its cargo of more than forty tons of ginseng to the Celestial Kingdom. Soon American ship captains began to carry furs as well as ginseng to China and the East Indies, bringing back tea, silk, coffee, pepper, and spice. Merchants were constantly seeking new markets for American agricultural and manufacturing products, which included everything from wooden pails to firearms, carpeting, leather goods, and clocks. If a market could be identified or created, the Americans would search it out. One of the most exotic trade products was ice from northern ponds, first sent to Martinique in 1806. It was the brainchild of Fredric Tudor, who shipped the first batch from his father's Lynn, Massachusetts, pond. Eventually, storage methods improved, and the trade expanded. New England ice went to the southern states, Latin America, Australia, and Asia. By 1846 New England ports were shipping out seventy-five cargoes of ice totaling 65,000 tons, with more than double that amount exported a decade later.[11]

Trade, no matter how lucrative, was always subject to the uncontrollable forces of foreign wars, economic cycles, and the trade policies of other nations. The importance of foreign trade demonstrates the narrowness of any view depicting the United States of the nineteenth-century as isolationist and helps explain the considerable space American newspapers devoted to foreign political events. Repeal of the protective British Corn Laws in 1846 had a powerful effect in the United States by opening up the British market to northern producers of wheat and other grains. Great Britain was the United States' most valuable trading partner, a fact that helped defuse political tensions between the two countries. Cotton, wheat, and tobacco remained the most important exports to the British Isles, with such manufactured goods as textiles and iron heading the list of British imports. The thriving overseas trade was carried on primarily by freighters built for their capacity to carry bulky items rather than for speed or aesthetics. But by the 1850s the sleek American clipper ships were carrying gold seekers to California and Australia, and furs and ginseng to China. Soon the clipper, another marvel of American design, would be outstripped by British steamships.

Whatever the design of the vessels, however, the importance of trade went beyond its economic impact. The search for markets contributed to the opening of Japan and had profound effects on United States military policy and on the way Americans thought about faraway places.

Equally important as foreign trade to the emergence of the United States as a modern industrialized and commercial nation was the revolution in transportation. In the early period of the Republic, goods and people traveled over mostly poor roads, sometimes no more than forest clearings built on Indian trails. Often muddy and impassable in summer, they were icy and dangerous in the winter. Still, the major characteristic of those thoroughfares was their local nature. Usually short and unconnected to other roads, they nevertheless served a useful function and were heavily used for travel and transporting of all kinds of goods. The fact that all adult, able-bodied males did road work for a required number of days each year underlines the importance of these roads to the communities they served.[12]

Because land transportation was slow and difficult, early Americans preferred to travel on waterways—rivers, lakes, and the ocean. And when there was no available waterway, they built new ones. The completion and immediate success of the Erie Canal in 1825 sparked a craze for constructing such artificial rivers throughout the settled parts of the land. By 1840 there were 3,326 miles of operating canals in the United States. Canals made possible the rapid settlement and development of Ohio, the first state to be carved out of the Northwest Territory.

Canal construction, however, was costly. Although New York proved that a canal could be built with private and state funding, pressure on Congress to help finance a network of canals was too strong to resist, and later canals were subsidized in part with federal money. Canals connecting rivers with lakes and other rivers reduced the time required to ship the produce of Ohio farmers to eastern cities and in turn greatly reduced the cost. Canals quickly became essential, thriving instruments of trade and travel, but they had drawbacks as well. Upkeep and maintenance were excessively costly, and both flooding and drought could stop their operation. They filled with silt and snags, and in severe winters a cover of ice could shut them down for several months.

Though the canals were important, it was a new and much more revolutionary transportation device that laid the basis for a viable national market. The steam railroad made possible, for the first time, efficient, fast, and reliable transportation over large masses of land.

Although some early lines connected one waterway to another, from the beginning the railroads were competitors rather than partners with the river and canal interests. The change from waterway to railway was stunning. By the time of the Civil War the canal system, which had been built with such enthusiasm and optimism, was doomed. More than a hundred miles had already been abandoned, and many of the smaller canals were operating at a heavy loss. One exception was the St. Mary's canal, which opened in 1855 and made practicable the exploitation of the rich iron and other ore of the Lake Superior region. Unfortunately, the preservation of the older canal system as a competitor to the railroads did not seem desirable or possible, and before long the same western settlers who had begged and sometimes mortgaged their farms for a railroad found themselves at its mercy.[13]

Building a railroad was even more costly than construction of a canal, but the very thought of a huge nation crisscrossed by railroads seemed to bring a new meaning to the concept of progress. The minority who had reservations or who actually opposed railroad construction was usually those whose own interests were threatened by the change—the canal people, the politicians who had staked their careers on canals, and land speculators and town boosters who feared that the new era would leave them out. Only a few Americans, such as Henry David Thoreau, considered the environmental cost of the new system or questioned whether greater speed necessarily meant greater progress.

Beginning in 1850 the railroads enjoyed the larges of the federal government in the form of land grants ultimately involving millions of acres. These subsidies reached their peak during construction of the great transcontinental lines after the Civil War. Land-grant subsidy was only one of several devices used by friendly congresses to help the railroads. From time to time the government lent its engineers to survey proposed railroad routes. For thirteen years a reduction of the tariff on imported iron resulted in a six-million-dollar saving for the private railroads. Forty-five roads in ten states received nearly four million acres in the federal land grants of 1850, 1852, 1853, 1856, and 1857. State, county, and local governments also helped the railroads by allowing generous interpretations of the right of eminent domain, land for rights-of-way, immunity from tax, the right to issue securities without supervision, the purchase of stocks, the granting of monopoly privileges, and even permission to operate banks or lotteries. In addition, many legislatures were virtually controlled by railroad interests. New Jersey's alliance between railroads and politics was so notorious that editors attacked what they referred to as the "monopoly swindle." Even in Congress, Representative William Bissell of Illinois asked, "Why, is the

State of New Jersey itself anything except a railroad company? Or a sort of fixture or attachment to such a company? I believe her entire sovereignty is kept by the railroad company, or the directors thereof.''[14]

A number of legislatures in northern states fell under similar suspicion. While some observers deplored what they perceived as corruption, others viewed a close alliance of private business interests and public policy as a contribution to the general good. Since the South soon lagged in railroad construction, it was ironic that a line running for 136 miles out of Charleston, South Carolina, in 1833 constituted the longest railroad anywhere under one management. There were plenty of southern promoters and would-be railroad builders, but it was in the northeastern and later the northcentral states where most lines were built. Gradually, the focus shifted westward. While Boston was briefly the country's leading railroad center, it was soon outdistanced by Chicago, which by 1855 was served by more than one hundred trains a day.

While southern railroad lines failed to create a viable transportation network, northern railroads were connecting eastern port cities with western centers of trade. The east-west connection had momentous consequences for both economic development and politics, for the railroads were creating the basis for a sectional alliance that seemed to pose a threat to the South and its interests. It was the groundwork for a self-conscious North embracing both the East Coast and the growing western regions as the newer system replaced the old north-south route via the Mississippi River. While Ohio and Illinois farmers and settlers had many differences with eastern bankers, laborers, and businessmen, their common interest in expanding mutual trade minimized and sometimes overshadowed those differences.

At the same time that the transportation revolution was creating the basis for a truly national market—and eventually for a more unified nation—other forces were having a similar impact in other areas of American life. Of those, none was more influential than religion. Most of the seventeenth-century Europeans who came to the United States were part of the Protestant Reformation. They brought with them a suspicion and fear, even hatred, of the Catholic Church, a sentiment that translated into prejudice and represented a mean-spirited aspect of nineteenth-century American life. Of course, there were Catholic settlers, but they were few in number, and seldom was their right to religious and political freedom honored by their Protestant neighbors.

Religious differences became even more divisive with the influx of

German and Irish Catholic immigrants. Vicious anti-Catholic literature found a receptive audience in the 1830s, some of it written by Samuel F. B. Morse, who became better known as an artist and the inventor of the telegraph. Morse described "Popery" as "opposed in the very nature to Democratic Republicanism" and therefore "opposed to civil and religious liberty, and consequently to our form of government." In order to protect the country from falling prey to the "Catholic conspiracy," Morse proposed legislation that would deny suffrage to any foreigner who came into the country after the law was passed.[15]

Despite the fact that Americans gave lip service to the idea of separation of church and state, Protestant churches had a strong influence on American life and morals. Shunning establishment of an official church was a pragmatic necessity in a land of so many denominations, but it did not prevent religionists from trying to influence private morals. The American system of voluntary religion was in some ways as effective a control as the state-sponsored religions of Europe. Alexis de Tocqueville observed in 1833 that by avoiding direct political involvement, the American clergy gained power and supervised the manners and morals of many communities. He found that virtually all citizens he came in contact with were convinced that Christianity was an essential ingredient for republican government. If their influence waned, the pastors held huge evangelical gatherings, or camp meetings, to effectively put the fear of the Lord in the people. After three years in the United States, the English writer Frances Trollope was convinced that "a religious tyranny may be very effectually exerted without the aid of government." She learned that in Cincinnati, for example, one had to affiliate with a religious group in order to be "well received in society." And having joined a church, the convert must give "unqualified obedience to the will and pleasure of [the] elected pastor," or risk excommunication. Heresy trials for ministers and church leaders were also common.[16]

Such observations, however, may have painted a misleading picture. Many early Americans were not church members, and those who were often had beliefs unacceptable to evangelical Protestants. The French Revolution and the European Enlightenment, while spreading ideas of political liberty and equality, had also promoted a religion compatible with reason. Deism, with a faith in a creator God and an emphasis on good works and ethical behavior, made a significant impact on some of the better educated Americans, including many of those who became known as the Founding Fathers. Though deism never became institutionalized, many of its basic concepts were included in Unitarianism and Universalism, both considered heresy by more orthodox

Christians. The same was true for transcendentalism, with its reliance on intuition and its emphasis on individualism and human effort. Both deism and transcendentalism emphasized human relationships rather than the fine points of theological interpretation, or biblical truth. To evangelical Protestants the large number of unbelievers was a challenge. Especially concerned about the people going west, they organized a major campaign that included missionary work, the distribution of tracts and Bibles, and huge, emotional camp meetings that promoted the conversion of sinners. Without the control of religion the West, they believed, would become a secular cancer that might well destroy the healthier parts of the body politic.

Evangelical Christians worked not only to lead others to personal salvation, but to reform society itself. Many believed that poverty in the United States was unacceptable, even though they believed the poor were partially responsible for their own plight. The idea of Christian charity was also an aspect of the religious community, as was concern for the victims of alcohol, for abused children, for prisoners, and for the several million Afro-American slaves, who were at the complete mercy of their masters. It was evangelist Charles G. Finney who clearly defined the doctrine of Christianity as being a "higher law" than the Constitution, a doctrine later accepted by many other church leaders and eventually by Free Soil politicians. There was a strong urge to remake society along Christian lines. Mark Hopkins, president of Williams College, predicted a time when "wars, and intemperance, and licentiousness, and fraud, and slavery, and all oppression," would end "through the transforming influence of Christianity." Revivals emphasized the doctrine of "disinterested benevolence," and evangelists frequently included "selfishness" among the sins they so roundly condemned. To hasten the day when the social order would be totally Christian, evangelicals founded such organizations as the American Bible Society, the American Sunday School Union, the American Tract Society, the American Temperance Society, and the American Peace Society. Some supported the American Antislavery Society until abolitionist William Lloyd Garrison's condemnation of American churches as a bulwark of slavery led them to find other antislavery channels for their zeal.[17]

While elimination of slavery was the objective of many northern Protestants, many clergy in both the North and the South found the "peculiar institution" to be wholly consistent with Christianity. They claimed biblical justification for slavery, pointing out that by bringing African pagans into contact with Christian "truth" they were not only saving them from eternal doom but also elevating their way of life.

These same ministers saw northern abolitionists as anti-Christian atheists who rejected God's word. Said one New Orleans pastor: "We defend the cause of God."[18]

Although most northern churchmen toned down their attacks on slavery and adamantly refused to accept Garrison's view that slaveholders and defenders of slavery should be cast out of the church, even moderate criticism stung their southern brothers and sisters. The issue refused to go away. Divisions caused by the slavery debate, combined with doctrinal and personality clashes, proved stronger than the ideal of one nation, under God. Before 1850 the Methodists, Presbyterians, and Baptists had all split over slavery into northern and southern churches. Of the major Protestant denominations, only the Episcopal Church escaped division, a division that seriously eroded the fabric holding the nation together.

And that fabric had always been thin. While Americans were proud of their Revolution and their achievements in creating a government built on the will of the people, there was stubborn resistance to the acceptance of federal power as a force in everyday life. The states continued to be very powerful. During the War of 1812, many New Englanders had opposed all measures that would involve them deeply in the conflict. A minority even talked of secession. When Congress created the second Bank of the United States in 1816, its power to do so was challenged in the courts by Maryland and Ohio, whose taxation of the bank's notes amounted to a kind of nullification. Increasingly, southerners, with slavery at the center of their labor system, saw themselves challenged by the economic, political, and social interests of the North. But provincialism was not restricted to the South. Citizens of each section felt first loyalty to their own states, then to the nation. Governors wielded as much power and had as much influence as United States senators. The federalism that had made the Constitution of 1787 possible was to plague the nation until the issue was settled by force in 1865.

2

★ ★ ★ ★ ★

DARK HORSE
FROM THE GRANITE STATE:
THE ELECTION OF 1852

The presidential election of 1852 was removed from the ratification of the Constitution by sixty-four years, and only seventy years earlier the Americans had won their independence from Great Britain. To establish a government with an elected executive and legislature was a truly radical move, one the European powers considered dangerous and subversive. Many European heads of state regarded the horrors of the French Revolution and military expansionism under Napoleon as bitter fruits of the American Revolution. That various Central and South American governments patterned their constitutions on that of the United States was further proof of its diabolical nature. Ordinary people, thought the autocrats, were to be governed, not consulted, and certainly should not be enfranchised.

Such disapproval did not disturb Americans, who were proud of their experiment in self-government. They viewed Europe as chained to an old, decadent, monarchical system, and they encouraged any move on the Continent toward self-government. They boasted of their success, growth, and freedom made possible by an unbelievable bounty of natural resources and vast amounts of unoccupied land. The Revolution had kindled a sense of nationhood, and the ratification of the Constitution deepened it. At times, politics took center stage in American life. Election days were major social events as well as moments of political decision. Since the early 1840s, presidential elections had involved parades, rallies, mass meetings, long speeches, and much pageantry. Newspapers, usually allied with a political party, reprinted the speeches, thus reaching hundreds of thousands who were unable to be there in person. Since the days of Andrew Jackson, presidential campaigns had been theatrical performances on a national stage.

Ironically, those performances played to a limited electorate. In the earliest days, religious and property qualifications in many states restricted the number of voters, and even when those obstacles were removed, voting was generally limited to adult, white males. Although slaves were counted in calculating congressional representation or direct taxation, no one seriously considered giving them the vote. Even in the North, black citizens were often disfranchised, as in Ohio, by state constitutions. Native American tribes, whose cultures were rapidly being destroyed by the success of the United States, were first considered to be nations whose grievances were accommodated by treaties. Later, Native Americans were treated as wards of the nation. In any case they were not citizens and had no direct voice in the government that was to determine their fate.

Moreover, political power was exclusively a masculine prerogative. Half the adult white population was thereby excluded from even the limited power that came from voting. Most women were conditioned to think of their status as "morally superior" but unfit for the dirty world of politics. Even those who met at Seneca Falls, New York, in 1848 to launch the modern women's movement found too controversial for unanimous agreement a resolution stating that "it is the duty of the women of this country to secure to themselves their sacred right to the elective franchise." A cautious minority considered the voting demand a major strategic error. Indeed, it was primarily the suffrage resolution that male opponents targeted to discredit and ridicule the gathering. Women were deeply involved in church politics and the many reform movements of the day, especially abolition and temperance. In the antislavery movement women organized petition drives and set up sewing circles to make clothes for fugitive slaves and occasionally broke new ground by speaking in public. Some women even participated in traditional politics by attending rallies and writing for and supporting candidates. One of the arguments used in James Buchanan's bid in 1852 for the presidential nomination was the large number of women who supported his candidacy.[1]

In addition to those who were refused admittance to the mainstream political process there were some who chose not to participate. Fiery abolitionist William Lloyd Garrison urged his followers to refrain from voting because, he said, the constitution itself was a proslavery document. Garrison was following the advice of John Humphrey Noyes, a communitarian and proponent of Bible Communism, who envisioned an alternative political and social order and refused to have anything to do with the United States government. That was also the position of thousands who chose life in the Shaker communities and those who lived in other nineteenth-century socialistic communities. While most reformers wanted to change the social order in one way or another, the communitarians chose to build a new society as a model for others to follow. They were the dropouts of their time. For them, voting was meaningless.

Similarly, voting was meaningless when none of the candidates seemed worth supporting or when the issues failed to excite the voters. While presidential elections in the nineteenth century usually attracted a much larger percentage of eligible voters than would be true in the twentieth century, there were still times when some who were eligible chose not to vote. Sometimes the choice of candidates was limited and unappealing. A segment of both northern and southern Whigs who could not stomach their party's candidate in 1852 simply stayed home on election day.

By that time the modern, national political party system had been created through a series of developments unforeseen by the signers of the Constitution. Many, such as George Washington, viewed parties as divisive impediments to order and stability in government. Presidents, they assumed, would be chosen on the basis of special qualification from among the more affluent and better educated class. Early presidents shared common political and economic values. They tended to be above party concerns and tried to avoid self-interest. They were an elite with a deep sense of responsibility for public service. Washington, Jefferson, Madison, and other presidents from southern states were also owners of large slave plantations. Political differences in those years revolved around personal following and sectional interests.[2]

When followers of Jefferson formed first a faction, then a new political party, the basis for the political system was established. But it was not until the time of Andrew Jackson that modern parties began to take the shape that would dominate national political life. Along with modern political parties came the emergence of a federal bureaucracy, and with the expansion of white male suffrage in the 1820s came a new opportunity for party growth. Yet personality also played an important part in the choice of presidents, who continued to be men of established reputation in government service or military life. The new element was the role of political parties. With the refinement of the party system under Jackson, men gave their loyalty to the party rather than to a particular candidate. From then on, with the exception of the so-called Era of Good Feeling, national politics functioned on the basis of two major political parties, with minor parties playing important roles from time to time. From the presidency of Jackson to the administration of Franklin Pierce the two major parties were the Democrats and the Whigs. Party leaders devised programs with popular appeal in order to sell the ticket, and patronage—the distribution of jobs and economic favors—became the glue holding the various pieces of each party together.[3]

Ironically, the new political system attempted to choose a person for an office that was virtually impossible to fill in all its aspects. Like European monarchs, the president was expected to be the symbol of the nation, a role requiring proper appearance at public ceremonies and public statements on questions of the day. As administrator and head of his party, the president appointed cabinet officers and government job holders, supervised federal patronage, and was responsible for the workings of the federal government. He was commander-in-chief of the nation's armed forces and the chief diplomat, whose power over foreign affairs equaled if not exceeded that of Congress. Finally, despite the separation of powers clause in the Constitution, the president had the responsibility to propose legislation and to veto any bills passed by Congress that he believed to be unconstitutional. To choose a person qualified in so many areas who was also acceptable to an enlarged electorate was no easy task.[4]

Above all, the president had to be loyal to established values and to the economic and political system as it was. While some candidates were presented to the public as having risen from poverty, if not actually born in a log cabin, most were of substantial middle-class or wealthy backgrounds. Popular expectations of a well-educated president worked to eliminate the sons of poor or working-class parents. More than that, party leaders tended to choose candidates who were conservative on the major questions of the day.[5]

Perhaps because of that conservatism, ideas and programs seldom played an important role in national elections. During the heat of campaigning, Whigs and Democrats seemed to be advocating totally different programs, but once a man was in office, differences tended to blur, and there was continuity between administrations. The Whigs generally supported internal improvements, some kind of United States bank, and use of paper money, but they were seriously divided between the Free Soil "conscience Whigs" of the North and the proslavery "cotton Whigs" of the South. The party originated as a coalition of all groups opposed to Andrew Jackson, and opposition to whomever the Democrats were running became their chief characteristic. Democrats opposed a high tariff, a national bank, and a federally-funded system of internal improvements, and they strongly supported states' rights. But they, too, were divided along sectional lines and were interested primarily in getting their candidates elected. Despite the heat of political controversy, American elections were chiefly a struggle for power, and its attraction virtually became an obsession with would-be American politicians. There was always a generous supply of men interested in holding office who believed they were qualified to lead the nation as its highest elected official.[6]

In 1852, with sectional differences threatening to disrupt the Union, a candidate had to be acceptable to all sections. Southern interests in a slave economy were creating a sense of southern nationalism. Free Soil sentiment in the North had expressed itself in 1848 in a Free Soil presidential campaign with ex-President Martin Van Buren as the candidate. Although the Free Soilers were able to garner only 291,263 votes, the split they caused in New York's Democratic party contributed substantially to the Whig victory of Zachary Taylor and Millard Fillmore. The Free Soil Democrats who split from the party were labeled "Barnburners" by those who claimed they were willing to burn down a barn to get rid of the rats. The Barnburner split in New York and other northern states created bitter memories that would have momentous consequences for future political campaigns.[7]

Two years later the nation was granted a brief, but deceptive respite from sectional warfare when Congress enacted the Compromise of 1850, a compromise more in name than in spirit. The legislation grew out of Senator Henry Clay's efforts to put the slave question to rest by resolving the most dangerous of the issues dividing the country. Clay, joined by his Whig colleague in the Senate, Daniel Webster, proposed an omnibus bill that would admit California to the Union as a free state, organize the rest of the land taken from Mexico into territories without any restriction on slavery, settle a hotly contested border dispute between New Mexico Territory and Texas by granting the disputed land to New Mexico while the federal government assumed the public debt of Texas, abolish the slave trade but not slavery in the District of Columbia, and pass a stronger fugitive slave law. Clay's proposal met stiff opposition from many southerners, led by the aged and ill John C. Calhoun, as well as from antislavery congressmen such as William H. Seward of New York. President Taylor, who insisted that California be admitted without slavery and without reference to other sectional issues, also opposed the bill and threatened a veto.

When all hope of passing Clay's measure had disappeared, procompromise leadership fell to Stephen A. Douglas. The Illinois Democrat devised a plan to separate the proposal into five bills, thus ensuring support for each measure from different factions. Time worked in Douglas's favor. A southern convention called to oppose any compromise measures met in Nashville but failed to endorse extremist proposals, issuing instead a moderate defense of southern rights. On 9 July, President Taylor died suddenly, and Millard Fillmore, his successor, was willing to sign the compromise measures into law. Although the legislation passed, it did not represent a spirit of compromise in Congress.

During the debates on the compromise, speeches of Free Soilers on one hand, and southern fire-eaters on the other, had clearly revealed the depths of the division. More than any of the other bills, the Fugitive Slave Act kept the sectional controversy brewing until it erupted in 1854. An earlier law, which put the burden of returning runaway slaves on the states, was rendered virtually useless after 1842 when the Supreme Court in *Prigg* v. *Pennsylvania* made the federal government responsible for returning fugitives. The new law was harsh and unfair, and it greatly expanded the power of the federal government. A slaveholder's oral or written claim to ownership was sufficient to cause the fugitive's arrest. The law created the office of a commissioner to decide the facts of the case. If the commissioner decided for the owner his fee was ten dollars; if he declared the suspect free, the fee was half that. The suspected runaway could not testify in court and was denied all due process. Furthermore, the law obligated all citizens to assist in the return of fugitives, and anyone who helped a slave escape would be heavily penalized. Northern sentiment against enforcing the statute quickly assumed the tone of sectional pride. Abolitionists called it "an enactment of Hell," and it became a test of the compromise itself.

Yet that compromise, which grew out of Clay's original proposal, had strong support from Daniel Webster and was passed under the Whig administration of Millard Fillmore. It received the necessary support from leaders of both parties. Since antislavery sentiment had influenced more northern Whigs than Democrats, it was the latter who gave the strongest unqualified approval to the settlement. Leaders of both parties were deeply concerned about the future of the Union should the slavery question reopen. Important as parties had become by 1852, there was a flurry of interest in creating a Union ticket with both a Democrat and a Whig as candidates. A few politicians gave the proposal serious consideration, but ultimately, party loyalty triumphed.

Still, it was clear that the candidate of either party would have to accept all parts of the compromise settlement if he were to become a serious contender for the presidency. A number of prominent Democrats were willing to give the compromise their stamp of approval, thus underscoring the view that political acrimony over slavery was a thing of the past. Two of them, James Buchanan and Stephen A. Douglas, had begun their bids for the White House as early as 1850. Other would-be contenders were Lewis Cass of Michigan, William Marcy of New York, William O. Butler and Lynn Boyd of Kentucky, Samuel Houston of Texas, Thomas Benton of Missouri, and Levi Woodbury of New Hampshire.

Each Democratic hopeful represented a section of the country, and each had his personal following. Except for Douglas, all had lengthy careers in public service, and each had his share of enemies. They represented the old leadership of the party, with several of them part of the original Jackson machine. Two of the most important factions of the Democratic party were the "Barnburners," who had left the party to support Van Buren's Free Soil bid in 1848 but were now back in the Democratic fold, and the "Hunkers," who, according to their critics, would accept anything that helped elect Democrats. Hunker leaders, who had decided to unite the party under the compromise, urged rejection of either a Free Soil or a southern states' rights emphasis. Such an approach was suggested in their newspaper, the *Washington Union*, which, since April 1851, had been edited by Andrew Jackson Donelson. His mission was to revive the old Jacksonian party of unity and strength. Another Hunker tactic was to align the party with compromise senti- ment by sponsoring a resolution of finality to both houses of Congress. Yet even with Whig cooperation, Senate Democrats were unable to agree on a resolution of endorsement. After considerable political maneuvering the House finally accepted a resolution recognizing "the binding efficacy of the compromises of the Constitution" and declaring its intention to sustain enabling legislation, including the provision for the delivery of fugitive slaves. The resolution deplored "all further agitation of questions growing out of that provision . . . and of ques- tions generally connected with the institution of slavery, as unnecessary, useless, and dangerous."[8]

Despite division in the ranks, Democrats were hopeful of recaptur- ing the presidency in 1852 if only they could choose the right person as their standard-bearer. New York's Hunker leader, Daniel S. Dickinson, as well as other party leaders, saw Lewis Cass as that person. Cass, then nearly seventy years old, had been defeated in his 1848 bid for the presidency. His long public career in the military, and as governor of Michigan, secretary of war under Jackson, minister to France, and United States senator, combined with his popular prejudice against the Indians, the British, and European tyranny, made him an acceptable candidate. His supporters thought him a fitting representative of the

Northwest, with its growing importance in national affairs, though he was challenged by the much younger Stephen A. Douglas, who was from the same section.

Soon Cass's weaknesses as a candidate began to outweigh his strengths. He seemed only half-hearted about the possible nomination, and some of his backers used his name only as a front for other candidates they hoped to introduce after the Cass movement had collapsed. Then there was his appearance. A poorly-fitting wig, his obesity, slow-moving manner, and poor speaking ability prompted Horace Greeley, editor of the *New York Tribune*, to characterize him in 1848 as "that pot-bellied, mutton-headed cucumber Cass." His support for popular sovereignty, or the right of citizens of a territory to decide for themselves whether to have slavery, made him unacceptable to those southerners who refused to consider any plan that might keep slavery out of new territories. Except for southern unionists, he had little support in that section, and no important state had come out for him. When the convention opened, the *New York Times* named Cass "the man most distinctly marked out to be cheated. His friends will make a noise at first, ballot for him once or twice and then desert." As it turned out, the prediction was close to the mark.[9]

In contrast to Lewis Cass's indifference was the burning ambition of Pennsylvania's James Buchanan. He opened his campaign for the nomination in the fall of 1850 when he sent a letter to Democrats meeting in Philadelphia, attacking the continued agitation of the slavery question and urging obedience to the Fugitive Slave Act. Charging "radical abolitionists" with "infinite mischief," he made a strong plea for the Union, "the grandest and most glorious temple which has ever been erected to political freedom on the face of the earth." The sixty-two-year-old Buchanan had also had a long and distinguished public career. He started with a term in the Pennsylvania legislature and went on to serve in Congress, as minister to Russia, as United States senator, and as secretary of state under Polk. Although he was from Pennsylvania, Buchanan did not represent the growing industrial element, and that was one of his problems. Simon Cameron, ironmaster, newspaper magnate, banker, and railroad promoter who had supported Buchanan early in his career, broke with him over Cameron's demand for a high, protective tariff and Free Soil policies. Buchanan and Cameron became involved in a hotly fought battle for control of the Keystone State's Democratic party machine.[10]

To Buchanan, party loyalty was a matter of faith. He had served the party and the nation well, and his reward, if all went according to plan, would be the presidency. He maintained a voluminous correspondence with allies throughout the land, including Alabama's Senator William R. King, wealthy New York banker August Belmont, Virginia's Henry A. Wise, and Louisiana's John Slidell, who tried without success to enlist the support of William L. Marcy in New York. Much of Buchanan's strength lay in the South, where his popularity increased with his strong defense of southern rights and his repudiation of the Cass-Douglas program of popular sovereignty. Reluctantly he supported the compromise, though he would have preferred extending the Missouri Compromise line to the Pacific. Despite Cameron's opposition, which hurt politically, the Pennsylvania convention endorsed Buchanan. His followers then went to the national convention with that endorsement as well as the support of numerous delegates from south of the Mason-Dixon line.[11]

Such maneuvering was not unique to Pennsylvania Democrats. The many factions of the party struggled everywhere for control, because political parties were essential vehicles to power. Indeed, party battles sometimes took on a life of their own, removed from the practical matters that would face leaders once they had gained power. Nowhere was this more evident than in New York State, which had been pivotal in the 1848 defeat. By 1852, John Van Buren had led former Barnburners back into the Democratic fold to join the Hunkers. Some of the latter, labelled "hards" and led by former Senator Daniel S. Dickinson, were determined to punish the Barnburners for their apostasy and to nominate Cass. The "soft shells," who included William L. Marcy and Horatio Seymour, favored reconciliation with the Barnburners in the interest of party unity and electoral victory.

The candidate of the soft shells was Marcy, probably the best qualified for the presidency of all available Democrats in 1852. He had served the party well since the days of Andrew Jackson, holding various state and federal offices, including a three-year term on the state supreme court and three terms as governor. A loyal partisan who made no apologies for the role of patronage, Marcy was best known for his statement that "to the victor belong the spoils." He had been secretary of war under Polk and was widely commended for his administration of the department during the Mexican War. He had considered himself retired from public life until friends tempted him with the possibility of becoming the unity candidate in the impending election. Some who supported Cass but doubted that he could be nominated planned to support Marcy when the Cass boom collapsed. Marcy had supporters in his home state and agents working for him in several southern states and in Congress. Increasingly they argued that their man was right on the compromise and was a trustworthy and available second choice. Yet

Marcy, like the other leading candidates, met with determined opposition, such as Daniel Dickinson, who worked to defeat the Marcy bid for the presidency. The division in the New York delegation—twenty-four for Marcy, eleven for Cass—did not bode well for the former New York governor.[12]

Still another serious division among party ranks affected Democrats throughout the nation. That division was symbolized by the "Young America" program based on prejudice against old leadership, impatience with what was perceived as a "no policy" party, and an itching for government jobs and federal aid for numerous economic interests. Young Americans thought the party was dominated by what they called old fogeys, which included all but one of the possible presidential candidates. Lewis Cass, James Buchanan, William Marcy, and Sam Houston were all fifty-eight or older. It was Stephen A. Douglas of Illinois who became the candidate of Young America, both on the grounds of his youth—he was thirty-nine—and his espousal of the faction's doctrines. Douglas was a champion of western expansion, railroad construction, government land for homesteaders, and, most important of all, an aggressive foreign policy.

It was the latter that gave the Young America movement its special flavor, though that movement could not claim exclusive rights to it. Since the administration of Thomas Jefferson, exporting American revolutionary ideals to the Old World had been at least an implied goal of foreign policy. But pride in American political institutions, which many viewed as a model for the rest of the world, became a major ingredient of the new nationalism. Along with that nationalism went a drive for expansion of national boundaries. The concept of Manifest Destiny was extended to include lands beyond North America, lands not necessarily contiguous with the United States.

Economic, racial, nationalistic, and military factors fueled the urge to expand. As early as 1795 John Adams had declared the United States "destined beyond a doubt to be the greatest power on earth." Americans, with agricultural and manufactured products to export, looked to their government for help in the search for new markets and for protection of trade. Such a policy required an effective navy, which in turn suggested new places for conquest or trade. When Secretary of the Navy Abel P. Upshur requested a 50 percent increase in funding for the Navy in 1851 he said: "Commerce may be regarded as our principal interest because, to a great extent, it includes within it every other interest." No party or section held a monopoly on such views. Even some of the Free Soilers took satisfaction in the conquest of Mexico through a war they opposed only because they were convinced it would open up new land to slavery. Salmon P. Chase, Ohio Free Soil senator, thought the American occupation of Mexico in 1848 should lead to the "establishment of a Mexican Government under [American] auspices and protection to prepare the way for the gradual incorporation into [the] American Union, and thus extend [the U.S.] Boundary to the Isthmus." And although Whig Free Soiler William H. Seward opposed the southward expansion of slavery, he favored exercising "a paramount influence in the affairs of the nations situated in this hemisphere."[13]

To make an aggressive foreign policy the heart of a political program was the contribution of the Young Americans, and for such a program they could find no better candidate than Stephen A. Douglas. The principal foreign adversary of the United States was Great Britain, and Douglas opposed any thaw in relations between the two countries. In an effort to settle Anglo-American differences in Central America, the Fillmore administration negotiated the Clayton-Bulwer Treaty. The agreement provided for the joint control and protection of any canal that might be constructed across the isthmus and pledged that neither nation would occupy, fortify, colonize, or gain dominion over any part of Central America. Douglas opposed it in the Senate: "Its objects and provisions were at war with all those principles which had governed all my actions in relation to the affairs of this continent," he said. It was "truckling to Great Britain."[14]

Douglas also spoke frequently and in strong terms about an American role in encouraging and aiding European countries warring against outside occupation. He demanded self-determination for Hungary and Ireland, and he outdid all other politicians in giving verbal support to the Hungarian patriot-nationalist Louis Kossuth when he visited the United States. His defiance of European monarchs included a vague threat to send military aid to the Hungarian uprising. Such rhetoric was popular with many immigrant groups, especially the Germans, who shared the Little Giant's hatred of Old World despotism. And George Sanders, editor of the *Democratic Review* and principal promoter of Douglas, was even more deeply committed to the cause of Hungarian independence. Sanders, who had earlier worked in the U.S. Patent Office, joined businessman-speculator George Law in an unsuccessful scheme to sell the Hungarians 144,000 muskets that had been discarded by the War Department. The two saw nothing wrong with making private profit and advancing desirable foreign policy goals at the same time. The lack of judgment behind the scheme was all too characteristic of George Sanders, who was to become one of Douglas's major obstacles to the nomination.[15]

It was Douglas who had helped Sanders get the editorship and find underwriters for the *Review,* a move he lived to regret. The pages of the journal were full of praise for Douglas and for the ideals of Young America. But Sanders's enthusiasm outran his common sense when he began attacking all the other potential candidates as old fogeys. As the paper's editorial virulence increased, Sanders antagonized Democrats in all parts of the Union. Douglas tried unsuccessfully to distance himself from Sanders's irresponsible behavior. There were other negatives, too. While flag-waving speeches in support of European republican movements were generally popular, some southerners feared that such a policy could open the way for European interference with American interests, including slavery. Moreover, many, like Andrew Johnson, regarded Douglas as the candidate of opportunists determined to profit personally from public office, a mixture of "adventurers, politicians, jobbers, lobby-members, loafers, letter writers, and patriots which call themselves 'Young America.'" Johnson saw Douglas as a "mere hotbed production, a precocious politician warmed into and kept in existence by a set of interested plunderers that would in the event of success disembowel the treasury, disgrace the country and damn the party to all eternity that brought them into power." Johnson spoke for many Democrats, but the ambitious Douglas was undaunted. He was determined to gain the nomination.[16]

Such factionalism posed serious impediments to a Democratic victory at the very time when the party seemed to be in a winning position. Yet a successful candidate had to be acceptable to all sections, and each of the prospects had major problems. The scent of power was a strong motivation, but who could bring matters to a successful conclusion? The South had no strong representative. Many supported Thomas Benton, but he refused to run. Sam Houston had too many strikes against him, including a questionable association with Free Soilers that destroyed what southern support he might have received. It appeared that what was needed was a northern man acceptable to the South. Lewis Cass was very old and carried the taint of his 1848 defeat, and his squatter sovereignty doctrine met with considerable southern opposition. William Butler of Kentucky had little personal appeal and had shared Cass's losing ticket in 1848. Buchanan, Marcy, and Douglas all faced bitter rivals who spread the fear that neither could win enough votes to carry the presidency. All the while, Young America was promoting prejudice against the old leadership and demanding a larger role in policy-making and a greater share of patronage. Should convention delegates fail to agree on a standard-bearer it could be 1848 all over again. Party leaders were determined not to let that happen. A likely choice would be one of the minor candidates or a dark horse, like James K. Polk in 1844.

Increasingly, party leaders turned to Levi Woodbury of New Hampshire as that possible dark-horse candidate. New England Democrats believed the time had come for another president from their section. Since New Hampshire had voted consistently for Democrats since the days of Jackson, party leaders believed their state deserved the honor of uniting the party and heading a victorious ticket. Woodbury had had a long public career as jurist, cabinet member, and United States senator. He was a loyal Jacksonian and a strong supporter of states' rights, insisting that the issue of slavery be decided by individual states. He was backed by the "Concord Cabal," a group of New Hampshire railroad lawyers, including his friend and former student Franklin Pierce, and had important support in Massachusetts and Maine as well. Woodbury had few political enemies and was acceptable to the South. His unexpected death in September 1851 sent party leaders searching for another unifying figure.[17]

Woodbury's death gave new hope to the backers of Sam Houston, but the flurry of interest in the Texan quickly died down. For a while it looked as though Senator William O. Butler might fill the gap, but he made an unpardonable mistake, alienating all northerners with even moderate Free Soil sentiments, when he released a letter supporting a resolution of the Kentucky Democratic Convention that affirmed the right of slaveholders to carry slaves into any territory of the United States. These developments encouraged a small group of political operators whose candidate was New Hampshire's Franklin Pierce. He had been considered for second place on a Butler-Pierce ticket, but more and more there was behind-the-scenes talk of a presidential nomination for Pierce.[18]

Franklin Pierce, born 23 November 1804 in Hillsborough, New Hampshire, became a party leader with very little effort of his own. His main assets were family background, total loyalty to the Democratic party, a willingness to be a party hatchet-man, and, above all, his charm and striking appearance. More than any of the others, he looked like a president. Handsome and well-groomed, he influenced others by a pleasing habit of appearing to agree with whomever he was conversing. His father, Benjamin Pierce, had served as a general in the Revolutionary War and then for two terms as governor of New Hampshire. When the elder Pierce was elected for the second time, Franklin went to the state legislature, having graduated five years earlier from Bowdoin

College. In college Pierce had been known more for his social assets than his scholarship. At one point he was last in his class, but he improved until he graduated fifth in a class of thirteen. After practicing law briefly, he joined his father in the New Hampshire government. When he was only twenty-eight, his charm and family connections helped him become speaker of the house. Then followed two terms in Congress and, in 1837, election to the United States Senate.

During his congressional career Pierce was more a follower than a leader, always adhering to the strict party position. He supported the gag rule, voted against internal improvement measures, spoke often in support of party issues, and did yeoman service on committee assignments, especially the Senate Committee on Pensions. He was rebuked by the great John C. Calhoun himself, who read in the Senate an article from a New Hampshire abolitionist newspaper which charged that Pierce had lied in saying that not one in five hundred in New Hampshire sympathized with abolition. The humiliating experience taught Pierce the danger of angering those who defended southern rights. In 1842, under pressure from his wife, he resigned from the Senate and returned to the practice of law.

His winsome ways and likable personality helped Pierce as a trial lawyer to bring juries to his point of view. In Washington, Pierce made valuable contacts with influential colleagues, and back home he continued to enlarge his circle of friends. Politics was in his blood, however, and he campaigned for others during every election year. He also accepted the role of party disciplinarian, publicly chastising and withdrawing party support from John P. Hale for his acceptance of Free Soil views and opposition to the annexation of Texas. When the Democrats scratched Hale's name from their list of congressional candidates, he fought back, helping to organize a coalition of Whigs and Free Soil Democrats, which succeeded in preventing the regular Democrats from controlling the legislature, their first defeat in New Hampshire since 1828.[19]

When the Mexican War broke out Pierce volunteered as a private but was later appointed colonel and then brigadier general. In Mexico, Pierce led a column of twenty-five hundred men from Vera Cruz to Mexico City, a trek of 150 miles through hostile territory where his men warded off six attacks. Nevertheless, military glory eluded him. While Pierce led an attack on a camp near Mexico City his horse, frightened by artillery fire, jumped suddenly and threw him. Pierce fainted from the pain of a pelvic injury and a severely wrenched knee, but after medical treatment he found another horse and resumed fighting until late at night. When General Winfield Scott ordered him out of action and back to the base at San Agustin, Pierce refused, saying he must lead his troops in the last great battle of the war. But his injuries made him worthless. The next day, while wading through a swampy thicket, he twisted his injured knee and again fainted from the pain.[20]

Pierce's Mexican War experiences were only part of a series of unlucky breaks that tended to offset his advantages as a presidential candidate. Trouble seemed to follow him. Fortunately for his public career, most of his bad luck affected only his private life, though the two could not always be separated. He was an alcoholic at a time when the nature of that malady was a total mystery. Washington's social life, which depended heavily on the consumption of alcohol, placed a terrible temptation in front of anyone with Pierce's problem. To avoid excessive drinking was one of the reasons he resigned from the Senate, and he made a serious attempt to conquer his weakness. For a brief time in the 1840s he even joined the temperance crusade. But misfortune stalked him, and he never became a total abstainer as his father had done in the last years of his life. Although it is impossible to fully document Pierce's heavy drinking and its effect on his faculties, rumors appeared again and again in political gossip. Some of the very qualities that made him popular in the Washington social scene contributed to the problems in his personal life, and those problems explain in part his ambivalence about political position. While he enjoyed the status and power of public office, he dreaded the temptations that it inevitably brought. In part for that reason he declined appointment as United States attorney general under President Polk, refused to accept appointment to the United States Senate in 1848, and turned down a move to nominate him for governor of New Hampshire. His mixed feelings about the 1852 presidential nomination almost cost him the honor.[21]

Pierce's family life constituted another tragic story. In 1834 he married Jane Means Appleton, the daughter of a Congregational minister and president of Bowdoin College, who died when Jane was thirteen. Her family environment provided a good general education, and she had a special interest in literature, though she cloaked everything in a stern Calvinism with its heavy emphasis on guilt. Jane Pierce was of slight build and suffered physical and psychological problems most of her life. She was tubercular and seldom enjoyed good health. She considered Pierce and his Democratic family inferior to her Federalist forebears, and above all, she despised politics and politicians. Considering the effect of political life on her husband's drinking habits, one can understand the tension in the Pierce household.

Yet for the most part, the two got along well. Pierce made many adjustments to his near-invalid wife's well-being. He hired a couple to live with her while he was in Washington, and when she objected to living in Hillsborough he agreed to move to Concord. His correspondence reveals his love for Jane and solicitude for her fragile health. Jane Pierce hated Washington, and for most of Pierce's time in Congress she remained in New Hampshire. Even the joy of raising children was denied the couple. Their first child, Franklin, died in infancy. A second son, Frank Robert, died of typhus at age four, and their third child, Benjamin, died at age eleven, in a train wreck just before Pierce's inauguration as president. Bennie's death cast a deep cloud over the Pierce presidential years and virtually destroyed what was left of Jane's health and mental stability.[22]

Franklin Pierce's candidacy was first suggested by the Concord cabal, which began wooing him after Levi Woodbury's death. After his military service in Mexico, Pierce had again entered politics, leading a movement to force John Atwood, the Democratic candidate for governor, to renounce his criticism of the Fugitive Slave Law. Before the election Atwood was repudiated as the party standard-bearer, and Pierce's strong support for the compromise, including the much-hated Fugitive Slave Law, received favorable notice in the South. One of his rewards was consideration for the vice-presidency. When New Hampshire Democrats met to nominate a governor early in 1852 they suggested his name "as worthy . . . of high place among the names of the eminent citizens who will be conspicuously before the national convention." The aim was to strengthen Pierce's chances for the vice-presidential nomination, although the office was not mentioned. When word reached Pierce he was personally torn, but Jane convinced him to nip the movement in the bud. He wrote a friend that the use of his name before the nominating convention would be "utterly repugnant" to him. Seemingly that was the end of a Pierce nomination, certainly a stumbling block to those who had worked for it.

Of those, none was more active on Pierce's behalf than Edmund Burke, whose many political contacts stemmed from his years in Washington as congressman, commissioner of patents, and a year as joint editor of the *Washington Union*. Burke hoped that the election of a New England president would help him to return to Washington as senator. Burke made several trips to Washington to test the water and solicit support for his candidate. But first he had to convince Pierce to cooperate with efforts to get him the nomination. Pierce reluctantly agreed, assuming it was a long shot with little chance of success. He answered two letters asking for his views on the compromise, underlining his enthusiastic support. Privately he agreed to accept the nomination should it come. But he insisted that his name not go before the convention unless it was clear that none of the others could win. In addition to New Hampshire friends, Burke got the support of Caleb Cushing of Massachusetts, who had served with Pierce in the Mexican War. Democrats who had commanded brigades in that war were organized for Pierce by Gideon Pillow, a Tennessee lawyer and politician who became active when it looked as though the Whig choice would be his old enemy, Winfield Scott. Pillow hated Scott because of a falling out and court martial during the war. The veterans, members of the Aztec Club, hoped, among other objectives, to have Pillow chosen as the vice-presidential candidate. For weeks before and during the convention Burke and Pierce's men were active behind the scenes, promoting their invisible candidate and planning to make him visible at the appropriate time.[23]

Preconvention maneuvering also occupied Congress, whose business was set aside for political rhetoric. "President-making is still the only serious occupation in Congress," commented the New York Times in March. In February, Washington lawyer Edwin Stanton wrote his law partner, Benjamin Tappan, in Ohio: "Besides the Presidential agitation there is nothing of any interest in Washington. There is no one in either branch of Congress that a person wishes to hear speak; neither is there any question of importance under discussion." Even the compromise, he said, was "worn out."[24]

When the six hundred Democratic delegates met from June 1 to 4 in Baltimore's heat, it was clear to most observers that, barring a miracle, none of the leading contenders would win the prize. Achieving such a miracle would have meant breaking the rule that required a two-thirds vote of all delegates for a nomination. Yet there was virtually no support for getting rid of the rule. Although Chairman John W. Davis called on the convention to "cultivate harmony, conciliate compromise—everything for principles, nothing for me," the various contenders and their supporters ignored his words.

The factional maneuvering continued until the third day, when balloting began. With 288 approved voting delegates in attendance, a candidate needed 197 votes to win. Each of the leading contenders had his forces ready to push his name over the top with appeals, deals, and arm twisting. Yet ballot after ballot failed to choose a nominee. At the outset, Lewis Cass was in the lead, but as voting continued Buchanan, Douglas, and Marcy all seemed, from time to time, to be within sight of the goal. Finally, in desperation, the Buchanan forces decided to divide, supporting others in order to demonstrate that no one could win alone and that a rally for their man would be wise. The plan was for some to support Pierce, some Marcy, and some Butler, while a contingent kept Buchanan's bid alive by continuing to support him. They tried to include Dickinson, who was Cass's manager, but in the interest of good faith he refused to cooperate. Meanwhile the Burke-Pierce forces were hard at work convincing delegates that their man would unite the party and win the election, that he was for the compromise and, just as important, that he would dole out patronage to all factions that supported him.

Burke's strategy was successful on the forty-ninth ballot, when North Carolina's James C. Dobbin started a snowball effect for Pierce with an impassioned speech, casting his state's vote for Pierce. Delegation after delegation joined the boom. Announcing the results the chair noted: "Cass 2, Douglas 2, Butler 1, Franklin Pierce of New Hampshire (God bless him) 282 votes." Word of the result went by telegraph to New Hampshire, where Pierce and his family were returning from a trip to Mt. Auburn. A friend met their carriage with the news. Pierce found it hard to believe, and Mrs. Pierce fainted. When Bennie heard about the nomination he wrote his mother: "I hope he won't be elected, for I should not like to live in Washington and I know you would not either."[25]

On Friday afternoon, 4 June, the last session of the convention, Buchanan's forces were appeased by the nomination of Alabama's William R. King for vice-president. King, like others who had worked hard for their candidates, expressed his disgust with the convention system, which, he said, allowed a wild mob to pass over men of experience and nominate one with little experience or national reputation. The only other remaining convention business was to pass on the platform, which was duly presented to a dwindling group and approved without comment. The platform restated what had become orthodox party doctrine: the federal government had limited power, it did not have the power to promote and administer internal improvements, it should practice rigid economy, it had no power to charter a national bank, and government money should be separated from banking institutions. Congress, it insisted, had no power under the Constitution to interfere with or control the "domestic institutions of the several States," and it warned that abolitionist efforts to persuade Congress to legislate slavery questions would bring "alarming and dangerous consequences." The platform pledged the Democrats to faithful execution of the compromise measures, including the Fugitive Slave Law. Moreover, the party would resist all further agitation of the slavery question. The document neatly avoided the question of the finality of the compromise, but that gave no solace to Democratic Free Soilers who favored repeal or modification of the Fugitive Slave Law.[26]

What mattered now was party unity, and no one provided a more convincing symbol of that unity than Franklin Pierce. Quite literally, he was everything to everybody, and his rivals for the nomination were the first to enlist in the campaign. Stephen A. Douglas campaigned vigorously, predicting that "Illinois will give Franklin Pierce a larger majority than any other State in the union." William Marcy wrote a friend: "Strange as you may think, I really rejoice. . . . Pierce is a fine fellow." Both southern Democrats and northern Free Soilers found Pierce acceptable. A delegate from the South who had hoped for a Jefferson Davis nomination for the vice-presidency commented: "All admit that Pierce is as sound on all Southern questions as any Southern man." Yet Free Soiler David Wilmot, who feared the "mighty interests of slavery," supported Pierce, confident that he would oppose southern aggressions. Even the Young Americans considered Pierce their man. George Sanders described Pierce in the *Democratic Review* as one "whom a great nation has sought out in the valleys of the White Mountains, to lead its youngest and greatest generation to the battle for the world's liberty, and to the fulfillment of its magnificent destiny."[27]

There were second thoughts, of course. One New Englander was later said to have commented that in New Hampshire, "where everybody knows Frank Pierce, and where Frank Pierce knows everybody, he's a pretty considerable fellow, I tell you. But come to spread him all over this whole country, I'm afraid he'll be dreadful thin in some places." In truth, Pierce was virtually an unknown outside his native region, and it was important for the Democrats to respond quickly to Whig chants of "Who's Frank Pierce?"

No less than half a dozen campaign biographies provided answers. The most notable was written by an old college friend, Nathaniel Hawthorne, who volunteered for the job even though he needed more time than was available, "in order to produce anything good." Although inferior to his best literary work, Hawthorne's short book helped sell the candidate. In it he outlined Pierce's public career, which proved what he could do. Concerning the slave question, Hawthorne wrote that ever since Pierce's days in Congress, he had recognized "the rights pledged to the South by the Constitution." He had not swerved from that position even after antislavery agitation made it difficult, nor did he shun the "obloquy that sometimes threatened to pursue the northern man who dared to love that great and sacred reality—his whole, united, native country—better than the mistiness of a philanthropic theory."

Hawthorne claimed that his countrymen had seen in Pierce's public life "evidences of patriotism, integrity, and courage," and because they also recognized in him the "noble gift of natural authority," they would summon him to the presidency. The *New York Times* characterized Hawthorne's book as "a violent and extremely biased political tract intended solely for electioneering effect." The *Times* was right, of course, yet Hawthorne was convinced of the potential for greatness that his candidate possessed. After Pierce's election Hawthorne wrote a friend: "I have come seriously to the conclusion that he has in him many of the chief elements of a great ruler. . . . He is deep, deep, deep."[28]

With the nomination of Pierce, Democrats had restored their well-organized political machinery. Their opponents, however, were in disarray. Misfortune haunted the Whig party. Their only elected presidents had both died in office. Interparty wrangling and unreconciled divisions between Union Whigs of both sections and the conscience and cotton Whigs presented a serious handicap. Moreover, their few well-known national leaders were elderly, and two of them—Henry Clay and Daniel Webster—were near death. Yet despite his failing health Webster was determined to become president. The other two contenders were the incumbent Millard Fillmore, who had succeeded to the presidency when Zachary Taylor died, and Maj. Gen. Winfield Scott, the hero of the Mexican War. Webster's entire political life had been geared toward receiving the nation's highest honor. At a time when presidential candidates were presented as reluctantly accepting a nomination because the voters demanded it, his obvious ambition defied the tradition. A few days after Webster lost his final bid for the White House, a friend asked why he had wanted the office. He had asked himself the same question, said Webster, but persisted because he considered the presidency "the greatest office in the world; and I am but a man, sir, I want it, I want it."[29]

While Webster made no attempt to be coy about the nomination, Millard Fillmore was just the opposite. In late 1851, a year and a half after becoming president, Fillmore confided to a friend that he had no intention of running for another term, asserting that he had made the decision at the time he assumed the presidency. He had not made his feelings known, he said, because he did not want to be seen as a lame duck officeholder. Fillmore represented the Union Whigs, willingly signing the various 1850 compromise bills that Zachary Taylor, his predecessor, had so strongly opposed. Increasingly, the Union Whigs were looking to Fillmore to unite all factions and demonstrate their party's ability to hold the presidency for more than one term. Elder statesman Henry Clay, near death, made an impassioned appeal for Fillmore: "He has been tried in the elevated position he now holds, and I think that prudence and wisdom had better restrain us from making any change without the necessity for it—the existence of which I do not perceive." Eventually, Fillmore himself came to agree with Clay, deciding to stay in the race primarily to defeat Scott, who was generally perceived as the choice of William Seward and the other Free Soilers in the party.[30]

The Whig convention was nearly as riotous an affair as that of their rivals. They, too, met in steamy Baltimore. When the voting began it was clear that the choice was between Fillmore and Scott. Webster did not even have all of New England behind him, and southern delegates turned to Fillmore. Although Webster never got more than thirty-two votes, his supporters were loyal, and he stubbornly refused to ask them to withdraw his name. Finally, after forty-six ballots and a weekend adjournment, Webster agreed to drop out, assuming that his supporters would then vote for Fillmore. Instead, enough of them transferred their votes to Scott so that he was nominated on the fifty-third ballot. The result did not seem to bother Fillmore, but it was a bitter pill for the ailing Webster. "How will this look in history?" he asked. Despising the thought of a Scott presidency with Seward calling the shots, Webster advised his friends to vote for Pierce.[31]

Many southern Whigs considered Winfield Scott untrustworthy. If not himself a Free Soiler, his administration would be dominated by them. Some southerners supported Pierce while others vowed to sit out the election. Yet the Free Soilers, except for Seward and his friends, were far from satisfied with Scott's record. He was a slaveholder, and he fully accepted the procompromise platform, which pledged "strict enforcement" of the Fugitive Slave Act and other compromise measures, and he deprecated "all further agitation of the question thus settled, as dangerous to our peace." His stand was appealing to Americans, who were weary of a decade of sectional strife and welcomed the respite provided by the compromise. With Whig agreement on the pressing issue, both parties found common ground in a determination to avoid the most explosive question of the day.[32]

The ensuing campaign, having little of substance to debate, was conducted with an excess of mudslinging and fulsome rhetoric. Superior organization and temporary unity benefited the Democrats, who circulated thousands of speeches as well as campaign biographies in several languages. They had better and more energetic writers and speakers, and their rallies drew the largest crowds. They organized "Granite Clubs" and set up "Hickory Poles to the honor of Young Hickory of the Granite Hills." But since both parties were determined to evade the central issues, the contest boiled down to one of personality. On this the Whigs took the offensive, portraying Pierce as the "fainting General," the "hero of many a well-fought bottle." They charged as well that Pierce was anti-Catholic, an abolitionist, a do-nothing in Congress, and pro-British. Democrats fought back with attacks on Winfield Scott, "Old Fuss and Feathers," who disliked "firing on the rear" and whose election would bring a "Reign of Epaulets." They claimed he was anti-Catholic and hostile to foreigners, pompous, and argumentative. The latter charge had some validity, though most of the others on both sides were cut from whole cloth or gross distortions of isolated incidents.

All of this combined to make for one of the least exciting campaigns in presidential history. Gamaliel Bailey's Free Soil paper, the *National Era*, commented: "In our recent travels in New York and New England we should not have known from any indication of popular feeling, that a Presidential election was pending." Others echoed similar sentiments. As the campaign progressed it became increasingly clear that the Whigs were in deep trouble. Much of it was of their own making. Scott was not popular with many of the party faithful. Before the convention opened, Horace Greeley had told Indiana Whig Schuyler Colfax: "I suppose we must run Scott for president, and I hate it." Despite such feelings, Greeley was able to support Scott himself, but not the procompromise Whig platform. "We defy it, execrate it, spit upon it," he said in a well-publicized editorial.

With even the party faithful in such a mood, enticing others to support Scott was a major undertaking. The unpopular candidate broke tradition when he decided to speak on his own behalf, as he did during a trip to Kentucky. He should have followed tradition, for his speeches got him more deeply in trouble. In Cleveland he said, "I love that Irish brogue—I have heard it before on many battlefields, and I wish to hear it many times more." On another occasion he spoke of the "mellifluous accent" of the Germans. Being there in person apparently boosted Scott's popularity, but his blundering speeches and impulsive comments canceled out any advantage he may have gained. Some Whigs were horrified by his performance. The Democrats, who kept their man out of sight, grew more confident. A party loyalist told Pierce's campaign manager: "Scott's person and personal appearance is doing something for him, when he says nothing, but when he talks he is sure to be . . . a damn fool."[33]

Not all voters were willing to accept such a low level of campaigning. Some demanded that the electorate face real issues. Free Soil-antislavery activists, like many reformers of the 1850s, were turning increasingly to political action to achieve their goals. Most of them had backed the earlier Free Soil party, and they were unwilling to support a party that endorsed the hated Fugitive Slave Law or a candidate whose Free Soil credentials were weak at best. While many in the South considered Scott a pawn of William Seward, northern Free Soilers were not sure that he would be fair to northern interests. Instead, they helped reorganize their old party, now called the Free Democratic party, with John P. Hale as candidate. A minuscule antislavery faction followed radical abolitionist Gerrit Smith in forming a new Liberty party with a ticket headed by William Goodell, antislavery editor and reformer. Both minor parties rejected compromise. The Free Soilers wanted slavery confined within its present boundaries. Liberty party policy went further, demanding that Congress move to abolish slavery. It also called for an end to racial discrimination in the North, a position deliberately avoided by Free Soil leaders. Once persuaded to accept the Free Democratic nomination, Hale led a vigorous campaign. Free Soil ranks had diminished sharply since 1848, but the two minor parties fulfilled an important function by raising issues that the major parties avoided but that could not permanently be set aside. The total number of votes they received was small, but since many of Hale's followers came from the Whig party, his campaign had a bearing on the outcome of the election.[34]

As election day approached, the Democrats worked to get out a heavy vote. In state elections in the fall, only Vermont went to the Whigs, with nine states for the Democrats. The presidential election proved to be the Whig disaster that journalist Thurlow Weed and other party leaders had feared. Pierce carried the electoral vote in all but four states: Massachusetts, Vermont, Kentucky, and Tennessee. He got 254 electoral votes to Scott's 42. Although the election made a shambles of the Whig party, the Democratic victory was not as great as it would seem at first glance. Scott got 1,386,580 popular votes, Pierce 1,601,474, but 156,667 cast ballots for Hale, and even the deceased Daniel Webster got 7,000. With more than three million voters casting ballots, Pierce had fewer than fifty thousand more votes than his combined opponents. The number of eligible voters who actually voted in the 1852 election declined from an estimated 77.1 percent in 1848 to 75.3 percent. Most who chose not to vote were in the South, where there was no extremist party to parallel the Free Soil option available in the North.[35]

For a variety of reasons the Whig strategy had failed. While some

Whig Free Soilers supported Scott, many stayed home, and still others voted for Hale or Pierce. Many of the party's traditional Protestant supporters were alienated by Scott's appeal to Catholics, while nativists, who had previously supported the Whigs, were angry because Scott had abandoned his earlier nativist stand. Yet Scott's appeal to Catholics failed to win members of that faith from the Democrats, who succeeded in getting many German and Irish votes. Moreover, while developments outside the realm of politics had influenced the election, party issues also had their effect. The open feud between Millard Fillmore and William Seward hurt the Whig effort. For some loyal Whigs the 1852 defeat was the party's death knell. Lewis Campbell, congressman from Ohio, commented: "We are slayed—the party is dead—dead—dead!" While a majority of northern Whigs still hoped to revive the party, more and more were seeking a new political vehicle, one that would represent the interests of the North. Massachusetts Free Soiler Charles Sumner told Seward: "Out of this chaos the party of freedom must arise." Events proved Sumner correct.

As for the Democrats, the sweet taste of victory overpowered the bitter fruit of political reality. They had unified themselves in order to elect a president, but that unity was temporary. The sharp differences among factions—Barnburners and Hunkers, followers of Buchanan, Marcy, Douglas, and others, southern states' rights advocates and unionists—soon reemerged. Each faction looked for a major share of the spoils and opposed any favors going to its rivals. The new president would soon learn that the narrow Democratic lead in Congress would give him far less cooperation than he had anticipated. Forces outside the political system were also destined to affect the presidency. The emotionally charged issues of immigration and the growth of Catholicism would look much larger in the coming years. Above all, the growth of a spirit of northern nationalism in confrontation with what many came to call the "Slave Power" would seriously affect administration policy. If support for the compromise meant sending escaped slaves back to bondage, there would be no quieting of that issue. Henry Clay and Daniel Webster, two of the nation's leading proponents of compromise, had died during the campaign. Their passing seemed to write the end of a chapter.

Nevertheless, the Democratic political machinery had done its job by electing Franklin Pierce, who had come up through the ranks by diligent performance of party and political functions. Whether he was capable of providing creative leadership at a time of change in so many areas of American life remained to be seen. One of his contemporaries found Pierce to be "shrewd, keen, and penetrating," with a "well-balanced mind, but not of the first order," and a "good knowledge of men." But Georgia's Robert Toombs, a Whig congressman, was far less sanguine: "The nation," he said, "with singular unanimity has determined to take a man without claims or qualifications, surrounded by as dishonest and dirty a set of political gamesters as even Catiline ever assembled, rather than the canting hypocrites who brought out General Scott." The four years of the Pierce presidency would reveal which assessment was correct.[36]

3

★ ★ ★ ★ ★

PRESCRIPTION FOR TROUBLE: THE ADMINISTRATION OF FRANKLIN PIERCE

Because of deepening sectional animosities, the years of the Franklin Pierce presidency called for the highest level of statesmanship from the White House. The nation required decisive leadership and wise policies that addressed the interests of all sections. The president needed to have a clear statement of policy, the ability to present that policy to the nation, and a sense of direction focused on the ultimate disposition of the slavery question. Early settlement of land recently taken from Mexico produced major growing pains. Questions of land distribution, Indian policy, railroad construction, territorial government with or without slavery, and enforcement of the new Fugitive Slave Law all called for attention. Foreign relations also required skillful decisions. A continued British presence in Central America worried American nationalists as well as trade and business interests. New England fishermen were demanding freer access to Canadian waters. The Young America policy of expansion in both the Caribbean and the Pacific had support from many segments of the population. With a background of general economic prosperity, a spirit of optimism greeted the new administration. It was Franklin Pierce's assignment to build on that spirit in providing a political environment to supervise the nation's rapid development.

His first task was to choose a cabinet, a process that demonstrated how much easier it was to assemble a political coalition to win an election than to follow up that victory by choosing a cabinet whose members satisfied all elements of the party. It was in the midst of that process that tragedy struck. Early in January the Pierce family, after a few days with friends in Massachusetts, boarded a train in Boston to return to Concord for last minute preparations before their departure for Washington. Scarcely a mile from the station an accident caused their passenger car to lurch violently and roll down an embankment. Before the horrified eyes of his parents, who were themselves uninjured, eleven-year-old Bennie was crushed to death in the wreckage.

The terrible experience turned anticipatory joy into shock and sadness, and laid on Pierce feelings of guilt that darkened his four years in office. It also strengthened his tendency toward indecisiveness. Putting together a cabinet in those circumstances was painfully difficult. His problem was compounded by the fact that the campaign had been fought on the question of support for the Compromise of 1850. Pierce might have consolidated such support by choosing men who had been strong unionists during and after the compromise fight. Instead, he assumed that the compromise itself had reflected a national spirit of accommodation and tried to assemble a cabinet that included all elements, including northern Free Soilers and southern states' rights advocates. He also meant to reward personal friends and include representation for all sections of the country. In short, Pierce tried to satisfy all elements. He ended by satisfying none.

Although cabinet members dealt with many issues affecting the lives of ordinary Americans—postal service, road construction, collecting tariff revenue, and land sales, among many others—they were chosen strictly on the basis of politics. It was assumed they would carry out their duties of supervision and service, whether or not they had had relevant experience. For the most part this worked better than might have been expected. For example, Pierce appointed William L. Marcy as secretary of state even though Marcy had had no experience in foreign policy. Yet historians have generally given Marcy good grades for his performance in that office.

Pierce's task was complicated by the many conflicting elements in the Democratic ranks and by his preoccupation with the recent family tragedy. He wrote his old friend, Jefferson Davis: "How I shall be able to summon my manhood to gather up my energies for the duties before me, it is hard for me to see." Worse, his original plans for a cabinet began to fall apart. Virginia's Senator Robert M. T. Hunter, who was to represent the extreme states' rights faction, declined the offer. New York Free Soiler John A. Dix, who was to balance the Hunter appointment, was unacceptable to so many Democrats that the president-elect finally withdrew Dix's name, promising him an important diplomatic appointment instead. Southern unionists were urging the appointment of

Georgia's Howell Cobb, while Lewis Cass and others wanted to see Indiana's Senator Jesse D. Bright included in the cabinet. Each faction and party leader proposed names for consideration. By the end of the year, Pierce had decided on his cabinet, though he had not yet matched each appointment with an office. All prospective cabinet members were required to read and approve Pierce's inaugural address.[1]

William L. Marcy was to head the State Department. Marcy had participated in several conferences Pierce held to work out details of his appointments. A longtime Democratic politician, Marcy was a soft-shell Hunker who favored reconciliation with the Barnburners of 1848. Thus he was opposed not only by those who still wanted to punish the defectors, but also by some Barnburners who continued to emphasize Free Soil ideas. Yet Marcy was a powerful figure in New York politics, a leader of the old Albany Regency. His career had included three years as justice of the New York State Supreme Court, a term as United States senator, five years as governor of New York, and secretary of war under President Polk during the Mexican War. Pierce decided to include Marcy in his cabinet after rejecting New York's Daniel Dickinson, a hard-shell Hunker who was later offered the collectorship of customs for the Port of New York.[2]

Caleb Cushing was to be attorney general. Although he was fifty-three, Cushing's ideas were very much in harmony with those of Young America. A former Whig, he espoused an expansionist foreign policy and defended the South in its claim to property rights in slaves. He had also been the first American minister to China and was the only member of the cabinet with experience in foreign affairs. Cushing was scholarly, humorless, and hardworking, a strong personality who became an important influence on the new president. The other leading member of the Pierce cabinet was Secretary of War Jefferson Davis, also influential in some matters though perhaps not as much so as previously believed. Davis, too, was a Mexican War veteran who had met Pierce, then a senator, in 1837 when Davis visited Washington. He literally had to be talked into accepting the cabinet post. The friendship between the two deepened considerably during the Pierce presidency. While Davis's appointment delighted many southern rights men it was anathema to unionists such as Howell Cobb, who got no reward for supporting the compromise that Davis had opposed.[3]

Forty-year-old James Campbell was named postmaster general. As leader of the Pennsylvania Catholic faction, Campbell had assisted Pierce during the presidential campaign. He was also backed by Buchanan, and thus opposed by the Simon Cameron faction. Campbell was responsible for much of the administration's patronage, with its thousands of post office positions throughout the country. Representing the other southern states was Kentucky's James Guthrie, sixty years old, a man whose great wealth came from real estate, railroads, and banking. He had served in several state offices and had presided over his state's third constitutional convention. Guthrie was better known as a businessman than as a politician when Pierce named him secretary of the Treasury. For secretary of the navy Pierce chose North Carolina's James C. Dobbin, whose impassioned speech at the Baltimore convention had sparked the stampede for Pierce. Dobbin, a slight man of thirty-nine years, was in poor health and had a tendency to overwork. He knew nothing of naval affairs at the time of his appointment. Pierce believed that Dobbin, a prounion southerner, would help balance the cabinet, only to learn later that Dobbin had opposed the compromise and supported the Nashville Convention in 1850. The cabinet member who represented the Northwest was Secretary of Interior Robert McClelland, who had the support of the Lewis Cass Democrats. Forty-five years old, McClelland had voted for the Wilmot Proviso when in Congress but later repented and gave strong approval to the Compromise of 1850.[4]

After the election a Pennsylvania Democrat wrote James Buchanan, "I doubt not, Gen. Pierce will select a good cabinet, and that he will have a brilliant Administration." One can only guess what he said after the cabinet members' names were announced some weeks later. About all that could be said for the appointments was that they provided good geographical representation and that they were all loyal Democrats. It was a disparate mix, with the three strongest personalities at odds over ideology. Both Cushing and Davis were brilliant but wholly incapable of understanding anyone with differing views. They never practiced give and take, and lacked virtually all political instincts. The most politically astute member, William Marcy, was assigned the post furthest removed from partisan strife. The others were known only locally before they joined the cabinet. Both the Douglas faction and the southern unionists were totally omitted. This cabinet was destined to be the focus of power in a new administration headed by an indecisive president.

The composition of the cabinet, and the way Pierce chose it—with little or no consultation with longtime party leaders—quickly led to disillusionment with the new administration. Francis Preston Blair, one of the Democratic elder statesmen, wrote Martin Van Buren of a conversation with Pierce in February 1853. "I told him," he reported, "that he had put in his cabinet his enemies—men who felt his nomination a blow to their ambitions and who certainly would avenge it on him unless he complied with their wishes in avenging it upon those honest men whose affections had been with him from his youth upwards."

Banker-politician August Belmont, severely disappointed, found the cabinet to be "not in some instances composed of such material as the *true* friends of the Administration and the party would have wished. The selection of Marcy & Cushing at the North & of Jefferson Davis at the South will not, in my humble opinion, be much calculated to harmonize the party."[5]

Just as Pierce tried to create harmony by including so many disparate elements in his cabinet, so did his inaugural address carry strong messages for both the Young America radicals and conservative supporters of the recent compromise. Inauguration day, 4 March 1853, was cold and blustery in Washington. Melting snowflakes fell on the president-elect as he solemnly affirmed rather than swore the required oath, which Chief Justice Roger B. Taney administered. After removing his overcoat, Franklin Pierce astounded his audience by delivering the entire address without a manuscript or note. He began with a reference to the recent family tragedy: "It is a relief to feel that no heart but my own can know the personal regret and bitter sorrow over which I have been borne to a position so suitable for others rather than desirable for myself." After that mournful opening, Pierce outlined in very general terms his presidential objectives. In foreign affairs his administration would harbor no "timid forebodings of evil from expansion." American interests and world position, he said, made further acquisition of new territory "eminently important" to national security, protection of commercial rights, perhaps even to world peace. "Should they be obtained," he promised, "it will be through no grasping spirit, but with a view to obvious national interest and security, and in a manner entirely consistent with the strictest observance of national faith." Still, he concluded, such pursuits were best attained by peace and were "entirely consistent with the tranquility and interests of the rest of mankind."

Turning to domestic affairs, Pierce pledged "devoted integrity in the public service, . . . rigid economy in all departments," and protection of states' rights. "If the Federal Government will confine itself to the exercise of powers clearly granted by the Constitution," he said, "it can hardly happen that its action upon any question should endanger the institutions of the States or interfere with their right to manage matters strictly domestic according to the will of their own people." Having promised no interference with slavery, Pierce extolled the Union, on which he had fastened his "best and dearest hopes."

Moreover, the laws of the Compromise of 1850 were strictly

constitutional and should be enforced, especially the Fugitive Slave Act. The Constitution, he proclaimed, recognized involuntary servitude as an "admitted right." "I believe," he said, "that the constituted authorities of the Republic are bound to regard the rights of the South in this respect as they would any other legal and constitutional right, and that the laws to enforce them should be obeyed, not with a reluctance encouraged by abstract opinions as to their propriety in a different state of society, but cheerfully and according to the decisions of the tribunal to which their exposition belongs." Promising to act on his convictions, he added his fervent hope that the slave question was at rest, "and that no sectional or fanatical excitement may again threaten the durability of our institutions or obscure the light of our prosperity." While Pierce was frequently interrupted by the cheers of the faithful and converted, his failure to recognize the complex issues involved in an expansionist foreign policy, of the growth and intensity of Free Soil sentiment, and his own total ignorance of the moral and religious dimensions of the controversy over slavery would soon dampen the enthusiasm of even his most ardent followers.[6]

While Franklin Pierce played the public role of head of state, his life as occupant of the White House was far less complicated. There was nothing that resembled presidential staffs of later years. Pierce had only one bodyguard, Thomas O'Neil, who had been his orderly sergeant during the Mexican War. He had one private secretary, young Sidney Webster, joined later by an assistant. Because of Jane Pierce's serious emotional problems, she had a companion, Mrs. Abby A. Means, a wealthy widow and longtime friend. Abby Means assumed the role of official White House hostess, presiding over the few social functions occurring during the early years of the administration. A gardener and a few household servants constituted the rest of the White House staff.

Life in the White House was very informal, as was indicated by Pierce's first night there. The inaugural ball had been canceled in deference to the first family's tragic ordeal, but there was a long, tedious reception. After the tiring day, when all the guests had departed, Pierce and Sidney Webster found that the living quarters were not yet ready for occupancy. Ascending the stairs by candlelight the two found beds where they could finally get some rest. Pierce often walked alone around Washington and once told a group of White House visitors: "You need no introduction to this house, it is your house and I am but the tenant for a time." It was a warm welcome to a cold household. When Mrs. Pierce finally joined the president, she spent much of her time alone, sadly writing letters to her departed son. In 1855 she began appearing at public functions, but her heart was not in any of it. "Everything in that mansion seems cold and cheerless," commented one visitor. "I have seen hundreds of log cabins which seemed to contain more happiness."[7]

President Pierce was often seen walking or riding horseback around the capital city, sometimes to visit friends. He and Mrs. Pierce were especially close to the Jefferson Davis family. Davis's youthful wife was a leader of Washington social life, which was dominated by southern groups. Jane Pierce was also very fond of their son, Samuel, virtually adopting him as a substitute for her own lost son. The Davis child's death just before his second birthday proved another terrible blow to her fragile health. The next Davis baby was born during one of the worst snowstorms in Washington history, and the difficult birth brought Varina Davis near death. Pierce, determined to comfort the family, fought the weather for nearly an hour to arrive exhausted at the Davis home.

A disquieting incident showed the dangers to the president of such casual disregard for security. One day a young man who had been drinking heavily greeted Pierce as he waited in the White House rotunda for his carriage. When Pierce declined the offer of a drink and began to enter his carriage the angry youth threw a hard-boiled egg at the president. The young man was arrested, attempted suicide in jail, and was later released without charge. While there was no harm to the president, his assailant might well have been armed with something more deadly.[8]

It was political pressure, however, that provided most of the stress in Pierce's job. His presidency began when federal employment was gaining prestige. Hordes of office seekers besieged members of the new administration. Wrote Democrat Gideon Welles to Pierce: "The power of the federal government is derived from the whole of the States & consequently the addition of every new state adds to its powers. . . . Every year the federal government more and more overshadows the States, and the people are more and more inclined to look to it as *the government*, and to regard the States as mere subordinate corporations." Despite the relatively poor conditions in federal employment, there was a rush for such jobs. "Washington is full of strangers," wrote a correspondent to James Buchanan. "It seems as if a resurrection had brought to life all our rotten fishy politicians." An estimated thirty thousand office seekers and their supporters besieged Pierce and his cabinet. The *National Intelligencer* reported that cabinet members "had to assume *roundabouts* to enable them to pass *from their offices to their boarding houses.*"

To dole out the patronage, Pierce and his cabinet met daily, with two considerations dominating the agenda: distribution among the factions and geographical representation. The latter was necessary for congressional approval. In May 1853 Secretary of Interior Robert McClelland announced that federal clerkships would be distributed among the states according to their seats in Congress. Apparently given the task of carrying out this policy, he wrote every department but the State Department, asking each to furnish him with "a statement, showing the number of Clerks from each state, in your Dept., and their salaries, similar to the one I have caused to be prepared in reference to this Dept." Congressmen expected to be consulted about patronage in their districts and were quick to chastise the administration if they were not.[9]

In winning some of the lesser appointments, Stephen A. Douglas's wing of the party fared better than it had in cabinet appointments. Douglas himself was satisfied with the patronage in his home state but disappointed in seeking jobs for constituents outside Illinois. The failure of those efforts was due, in part, to Senator Jesse D. Bright of Indiana, who worked against the Douglas suggestions in order to lessen the Little Giant's presidential chances in 1856. Pierce, however, tried to comply with Douglas's suggestions for territorial posts.

Factional rivalry that had so hurt the party in the past resurfaced in the scramble for favors. New York was again a special problem. Daniel S. Dickinson, still chafing over the appointment of his old enemy Marcy to the State Department, wanted no Barnburners nor anyone who had overlooked the Barnburner "heresy" to get the smallest share of postelection loot. Yet Pierce, still convinced that rewarding all factions was the best way to heal party wounds, named Dickinson to be collector of the Port of New York and Dickinson's opponent, John A. Dix, to be his assistant. Dix was promised a diplomatic post later. As an 1848 bolter from the party, Dix was highly controversial, and it looked for a time as though the Senate would reject him. He was finally confirmed, but eight senators, including six Democrats, voted against him. Several of Dix's opponents were powerful Democrats whose opposition to the new president was a preview of trouble to come. For his part, Dickinson refused to accept the Pierce plan and turned down the collectorship, which then went to another hard-shell Democrat, Greene C. Bronson.[10]

The New York headache soon became a migraine, partly because of Marcy's determination to discredit Dickinson. Marcy or one of his friends attacked Dickinson in a letter to the *Washington Union*. The letter revived bitter factional strife on the eve of the New York state party convention. The result was a Hunker-Barnburner split, with both factions writing platforms and naming candidates for minor state offices. When the Hunkers attacked Marcy, the Pierce administration took up his cause, demanding that Bronson stop appointing only Hunkers to the jobs under his jurisdiction. Secretary of the Treasury Guthrie also warned Bronson, then sent two chastising letters to him before he was fired and replaced with a new collector. Dix, who still expected a foreign assignment, resigned. The New York split deepened, no one was satisfied, and the Pierce administration reaped criticism from all sides. Wrote a party follower to Buchanan: "Nothing could have been more silly than the war on Dickinson, which has become a war with a powerful party." The Barnburners, too, attacked Pierce for trying to implement the questionable practice of rewarding all factions and were further alienated when the president informed Dix that because of continued opposition there could be no diplomatic post for him.[11]

Administration attempts to discipline Massachusetts Democrats were no more successful and revealed Attorney General Caleb Cushing's total lack of political finesse. He had long objected to the coalition of Democrats and Free Soilers in his home state, and when the coalition published its own list of candidates he responded with a letter to Richard Frothingham, editor of the *Boston Post*. Democrats who participated in the coalition, said Cushing, had abandoned a fundamental principle. "To support or vote for the Free Soilers of Massachusetts," he wrote, "is to give countenance and power to persons engaged avowedly in the persistent agitation of the Slavery question, and therefore hostile in the highest degree to the determined policy of the Administration." In near hysterical terms he defended the Pierce administration in its determination to crush "the dangerous element of Abolitionism," no matter how it presented itself. The letter was immediately dubbed "Cushing's Ukase" and, along with others he had written, made party unity in Massachusetts an impossible dream. The *Washington Union* applauded, as did other party loyalists and Hunkers, but the Barnburners and Free Soilers denounced it as abuse of executive power. At a rally of Free Soilers in Faneuil Hall, Charles Francis Adams called Cushing's letter "the most monstrous document that was ever presented to a free people." It was an ill-advised move and hurt the Democratic party both within Massachusetts and beyond.[12]

The New York and Massachusetts stories were repeated in Missouri and other states. Increasingly, Pierce was perceived as an inept administrator incapable of carrying out his own policies. Just as he had done years before in New Hampshire, he tried to use cabinet members to bring dissenters into line, but the tactic didn't work on the national scene. Many of his early supporters, including Edmund Burke, began attacking the administration for dictatorial tactics and ill-advised rewarding of party traitors. James D. Bowlin, a friend of Stephen A. Douglas, complained to Buchanan: "His efforts have entirely failed to unite the party. . . . It is torn into shreds and tatters."[13]

Faced with factional strife and widespread criticism in the press, the administration began efforts to improve its reputation. It was an age when newspapers played a large role in public relations. "Who can conceive the power of the press in a country like ours?" wrote a correspondent to Buchanan from a hotel where, he noted, even the servants read newspapers while they ate breakfast. "Everybody reads a paper, and if the proper popular cord is touched," he said, "the press can organize and lead the public mind in the bent of its inclining." The absence of a strong, effective administration newspaper proved to be a serious handicap. In addition, cabinet members seldom gave interviews or issued releases. Only Attorney General Cushing entered the public arena, and his views usually brought a negative reaction.[14]

The closest thing to an administration newspaper was the *Washington Union*, but it was poorly edited and never provided the kind of effective support that was needed. In midsummer 1853, Pierce succeeded in getting veteran journalist Alfred O. P. Nicholson to take over the newspaper and edit it with help from Harvey Watterson and John W. Forney. Caleb Cushing frequently contributed as well. Pierce could influence the newspaper's views, but it remained independent of administration control. Plans to establish a newspaper in New York, edited by Forney and charged with getting the true party position before the public came to nothing.

Much of the partisan Democratic press was highly critical of Pierce and his policies. In 1853 a group of prosouthern hard-shells established their own Washington newspaper, the *Sentinel*, with Beverly Tucker as editor. Its pages strongly defended slavery and constantly attacked Pierce as a Free Soiler under the influence of John Van Buren. Similar views were expressed in the *New York Herald*, edited by James Gordon Bennett, who had failed in his bid for a diplomatic post in France. A disappointed friend of Caleb Cushing, bitter at not getting a consulship, avenged himself on the administration as American correspondent to the London *Times*. All of this, of course, was nothing compared to the constant stream of vituperation from the *Washington National Intelligencer* and the many other Whig newspapers throughout the country. Near the end of 1853 William Seward, who had just seen the president, wrote: "He is care-worn, and the embarrassments of his Administration are obviously oppressing him and his ministers."[15]

Public appearances gave the president and his cabinet an opportunity to make a positive appeal to the nation. Public relations was another function of the cabinet, and when Pierce visited the first world's fair to be held in the United States—at New York's Crystal Palace in July 1853—he took with him Secretaries Guthrie, Davis, and Cushing. It was a rare chance for Americans to see the president and top officials, and it was a marvelous opportunity for Pierce to mend political fences. The official party stopped in Baltimore, Wilmington, Philadelphia, and in five places in New Jersey before reaching New York. Pierce was suffering from a cold, and the damp, chilly weather did not help him. His speeches, standard patriotic glorification of the Union, stressed the importance of states' rights, free trade, and American idealism. The cabinet members also made speeches. Jefferson Davis made five, painting in each a glowing picture of the country, predicting a time of domestic peace, expanded trade, and high prosperity, and praising President Pierce as a "glorious patriot" who knew "no North, no South, no East, no West" and who would "abide by all the obligations and enforce all the rights and privileges of the Constitution."

In his Philadelphia speech Davis struck a new theme in response to one of the most ambitious and daring projects to be proposed in the 1850s, the dream of connecting all parts of the nation with a network of railroads. First promoted by Asa Whitney in 1844 as a railroad to the Pacific—financed with generous land grants from the government—such a road would facilitate western settlement, expand internal trade, assure the economic future of various terminal cities, and enrich those involved in their construction and operation. Politician-businessman Robert J. Walker, California Senator William M. Gwin, Senator Thomas J. Rusk of Texas, and Missouri Senator Thomas Hart Benton were among those exerting strong pressure on the administration to support a Pacific railroad, though they by no means agreed about the route to be followed. Davis had to appease railroad promoters without violating the Democratic creed that opposed federal funding of internal improvements. To Davis the issue was simple: in matters of national defense and national unity, federal funds for privately-owned transportation facilities posed no problem. In his speech he described administration policy as federal aid for a defense project and reminded his listeners that a Pacific railroad would provide new markets for Pennsylvania iron and coal.

Davis's speech cheered Keystone State workers and their political leaders. Buchanan responded with approval for the railroad project. It was also during this visit to Philadelphia that Pierce convinced Buchanan to accept the post of minister to Great Britain.

Yet even though railroad prospects encouraged Americans, including many of the press, the trip failed to restore Pierce's reputation. John W. Forney, who accompanied the president for most of the trip, was disappointed, finding that Pierce fell far short of the mark set for one in that office. Forney wrote Buchanan that, though Pierce had had a fine reception, his habits were deplorable. "He drinks deep," said Forney. "The place overshadows him." Crushed by the great duties of his office, he sought refuge in alcohol. "His experience convinces me," wrote Forney less than a year into the new administration, "that a great mistake was putting him in at all."[16]

Nevertheless, for the most part the Pierce administration fulfilled its pledge to govern the country with integrity in public service and economy in all departments except the military, which expanded considerably under Davis and Dobbin. In the federal civilian service there were two groups of job holders. Most were subject to dismissal when the administration changed. The others, clerks with higher classification who had what amounted to job tenure, provided continuity and stability in the various departments. An 1853 act of Congress instituted a system of uniform pay for the departmental clerks and limited the size of the permanent clerical staff. The new legislation also attempted to prevent or limit any additional compensation government clerks might receive, but since the salaries stipulated were close to the subsistence level, clerks and agents found ways of evading that part of the law.

Another important step in improving government service was the introduction of a limited civil service examination system. The law, which affected just under seven hundred departmental offices, provided for examinations to assure that nominated persons were qualified for the position. It did not affect the patronage system since it applied only to those who had already been named. Some of the examinations were written, others were oral. When Secretary of Treasury Guthrie administered the exams he found nearly all of the clerks under his jurisdiction to be qualified. He was convinced that the new system greatly improved the effectiveness of the department and enabled him to appoint more capable men for the first class positions. Other Pierce cabinet members agreed. Although the process did not apply to the State Department, Marcy was so impressed by it that he recommended legislation to institute the system there as well. Such a law passed toward the end of Pierce's term but was repealed before it went into effect.[17]

Some of Pierce's appointments went further than the law prescribed in insisting on acceptable performance from the clerks. Guthrie introduced the practice of having an outsider inspect the books of the treasury collectors, a practice he found to be useful in detecting errors and omissions and in achieving a more responsible administration of revenue laws. Government jobholders were seldom removed for incompetence, but auditor William F. Phillips noted in his 1854 report that in so large an office employing so many workers, "it could scarcely be expected that none of them should fall into habits of dissipation and unfaithfulness to duty. During the year it has been my painful duty to report several such persons to you, as useless to the office, and they have been thereupon invariably removed from office." Whether those charged were at fault, they were removed, as many others had been removed for partisan reasons. There was no due process for government workers. Just as in the business world, the department or bureau head had absolute power. Any serious move toward labor organization, at least in the War Department, was nipped in the bud. When the bricklayers at work on the extension of the Capitol building attempted to create a closed shop, Davis got tough. He felt it his duty "to resist a movement so improper in itself, and so injurious to the public interests." He ordered the project superintendent to give all the workers due notice and fire any who persisted in their organizing. If other skilled workers were not available in Washington, he should hire men from outside the city.[18]

While every executive department provided jobs for eager party affiliates, the most coveted were assignments in the foreign service directed by Secretary of State William L. Marcy. It was a strange assignment for Marcy, who was the most skilled politician in the Pierce administration but had no experience whatever in the area of foreign relations. He had had a long record of public service and was well-read and hardworking. He presided over the State Department at a time when the expansionist plans of Young America were promoted by many United States diplomatic representatives, yet he had little use for such a policy. He strongly opposed several of the appointments and had a moderating influence on such men as Dan Sickles, secretary of the legation in London, George Sanders, U.S. consul in London, and especially on Pierre Soulé, the minister to Spain. Marcy's first task was to become familiar with the office and attempt to create order in a department that had suffered from neglect during Daniel Webster's illness and Edward Everett's brief tenure at the end of the Fillmore administration. Then there was the question of patronage. Those job seekers who did not call personally had their friends pester the secretary, both in person and by mail. At one point Marcy complained that the only applicants who deserved to be considered were those who stayed home. Yet most Americans serving abroad were replaced with loyal Democrats from various sections of the nation.[19]

Most of the diplomatic corps under Marcy were southerners or expansionist Democrats. An exception was the aged and experienced diplomat James Buchanan, who was finally persuaded to accept the position of minister to Great Britain. Yet even he shared the imperialistic creed of Young America, and his secretary of the legation, Daniel Sickles, was loud in his public promotion of republican virtues. London Consul George Sanders made his home a place of conspiracy against the European monarchies. At the urging of Jefferson Davis, and over the objection of Marcy, Louisiana's Pierre Soulé became minister to Spain. Soulé, a revolutionary exile from France, proved more committed to American expansion than to the accepted ways of diplomacy. He was an inappropriate choice for so sensitive an assignment. The last of the major European posts went to John Y. Mason of Virginia, who became minister to France. The new post of Central America went to Solon E. Borland, who had held several political offices and had fought with Pierce in the Mexican War. Another Jefferson Davis protégé, South Carolina's James Gadsden, was appointed minister to Mexico.

The best known of those getting lesser diplomatic assignments was Pierce's friend and biographer, Nathaniel Hawthorne, who was to be consul in Liverpool. Hawthorne's reluctance to accept the post subsided when he learned how lucrative it could be. He grumbled about his office, which was in a "shabby and smoke-stained edifice, . . . a plainer and uglier structure than was ever built in America." His attitude did not sweeten when Congress enacted reform legislation ending the payment of fees for American consuls. Hawthorne was not a popular diplomat, but while in Liverpool he found time to write. His one European novel, *The Marble Faun*, drew heavily on the notebooks he filled while in England and later in Italy.[20]

The entire State Department operation was conducted by Marcy in an ancient edifice called the Northeast Executive Building, near the White House. Here the secretary often worked well past midnight trying to juggle the many operations under his jurisdiction. In addition to foreign affairs, Marcy had to act as keeper of the rolls, supervise the territorial governments, and oversee all legal appointments. Even after he had transferred responsibility for pardons, judicial and legal appointments, and cases arising under extradition procedures to the attorney general, the job was still too much for one person. In addition to two assistants, Marcy had a staff of only forty-three, and that included ten laborers. Twenty-seven major diplomatic representatives serving outside the country, along with eighty-eight American consuls scattered throughout the world, all required his attention. Whether sending orders or suggestions to diplomats or writing well-researched and exhaustive reports, Marcy always seemed to be on top of things. Once, when asked how he kept his balance and good humor, he replied that each morning he had his secretary scan the newspapers to assign any critical comments to the wastebasket, leaving only complimentary stories for the secretary to read.[21]

During the years of the Pierce administration Congress made several attempts to reform the diplomatic and consular service. Such legislation was long overdue, and part of it was worked out in cooperation with A. Dudley Mann, Marcy's assistant secretary of state. One such law abolished the office of chargé d'affaires, but that proved to be a temporary change. Other reform measures abolished the grade of minister resident and required the president to raise all those holding that title to minister plenipotentiary. For the first time the issuing of passports was carefully regulated. There was also provision for supervising the activity of consuls and forbidding them from engaging in private business. Only American citizens were to be consular agents. These and other mandated changes were an attempt to bring order into the diplomatic corps, but some of the proposals met with opposition from the administration. Within a day after the bill was signed, Marcy wrote a stinging critique, alleging congressional invasion of executive power. He then sent a series of queries to the attorney general, who responded with a strong defense of executive privilege. Congress had no right to make changes in rank mandatory on the president, nor did it have a right to prescribe qualifications for diplomats. With Cushing's opinion to back him up, Pierce refused to implement some of the objectionable provisions. Yet this significant legislation and the act of 1856 that superseded it provided the legal grounds for the foreign service until the early twentieth century. In foreign affairs as in domestic policy the expanding government was forced to face questions of efficiency and order within the various departments.[22]

In terms of administrative style, Secretary Marcy is best remembered for his widely publicized "dress circular," which appeased a spirit of nationalism at home but stirred up trouble for diplomats abroad. The circular may have been a concession to Young America. It certainly was an expression of Marcy's democratic bias, a bias that also led him to oppose creating the rank of ambassador, which he believed too lofty and unrepublican, implying as it did that the person involved was the representative of the sovereign. On 1 June 1853 Marcy, who had no familiarity with the conventions of European courts, addressed all American diplomats with a circular encouraging them, as far as practicable and without impairing their usefulness, to appear at court "in the simple dress of an American citizen." Thus, by following the example of Benjamin Franklin, they would demonstrate the "spirit of our political institutions." The document, written in haste, was only a suggestion.

Several American diplomats rejected it entirely. Peter Vroom in Berlin thought it would be unwise to appear at the Prussian court in any other than the usual prescribed dress. Dan Sickles, secretary of the London legation, continued to wear his ornate New York State Guard uniform, which, on one occasion, nearly caused him to be mobbed by an angry crowd who mistook him for a member of the hated Austrian Imperial Household Guard. John Y. Mason, United States minister to France, found it discreet to wear the traditional dress when attending a ball at the Tuileries. That so angered Henry S. Sanford, the acting chargé at Paris, that he wrote a protest to Marcy and tendered his resignation. Because of the status of Anglo-American relations, it was the response of James Buchanan that received the greatest publicity. Although Buchanan had some concern that "this costume affair," as he called it, might prove an embarrassment, he accepted it with relish. When informed that traditional dress was required, Buchanan stayed away from public functions, even ignoring a command appearance for the opening of Parliament. Finally, taking the bull by the horns, he showed up at the Queen's levy in plain dress. He had appeared, he wrote Marcy, "in the very dress which you have seen me wear at the President's levees, with the exception of a very plain black-handled and black-hilted sword. . . . I have never felt prouder as a citizen of my country than when I stood amidst the brilliant circle of foreign Ministers and other court dignitaries 'in the simple dress of an American citizen.'" He reported, too, that Marcy's circular met with considerable public approval in England.

That was certainly true at home. In a private communication, Marcy reported to Buchanan that his action secured "quite a large stock" of popularity. "I heartily rejoice," he said, "that you have got along to your entire satisfaction with the 'Costume question.'" A Pennsylvanian wrote Buchanan that his handling of the costume business was "universally commended," and that nothing else he had done had given him "so great a hold on the masses of the people, of all parties." Needless to say, not all Americans thought the issue worth the attention it was getting. A writer for *Harpers* commented: "If it is foolish for a Court to require a certain dress and etiquette, it is certainly more foolish to lose the advantages of foreign social intercourse for no more serious a reason than the color of a cravat." The symbolism of American republican pride proved more effective than its substance in evaluating foreign policy under the Pierce administration.[23]

Symbolism was less important than effective administration to James Campbell, who headed the postal service under Pierce. Before his appointment as postmaster general, the forty-year-old Campbell had had only local political experience and was unknown to Pierce. He was also a protégé of James Buchanan and a Catholic, which contributed to his anglophobia. He was not flamboyant or adventuresome, and he put high priority on running a tight ship. The two-million-dollar annual deficit in his department was distressing to Campbell, and he was determined to reduce if not eliminate it. This helped make him one of the most unpopular members of the official team. Attempts to reduce costs of mail contracts angered those who looked upon government business as a form of legitimate subsidy for their operations. His stubborn efforts to eliminate fraud in the post offices irritated the postmasters. Recommending higher postal rates for newspapers sparked a flood of bitter and angry editorials. Still more explosive was the suggestion that the franking privilege should be abolished. Even Free Soil Congressman Horace Mann cherished that privilege, writing home in 1853 that he was glad it was still available. Campbell's attempts to work out a better postal agreement with Great Britain failed, as did most of his domestic recommendations. Congress did approve his setting up a system for registering mail and for requiring postal stamps on all mail, but his request for larger quarters was turned down by the Senate after House approval.

An incident concerning the Chicago post office illustrates Campbell's loyalty and Pierce's ineptness regarding patronage. Having received complaints about the Chicago office, Pierce wrote a letter to Senator Douglas and sent it over Campbell's name. The letter recited several problems, including robberies implicating two relatives of the postmaster, lack of diligence on the part of other employees, and the "loose and irregular" manner in which the office was managed. Pierce acknowledged the postmaster's personal integrity but wished him removed anyway, in the "least disagreeable" manner. Yet when the senator disagreed, the postmaster remained on the job. There were other occasions when Pierce seemed to act decisively in matters of patronage but backed down in the face of opposition. Together they gave the impression of a vacillating president.

Moreover, for all of Campbell's diligent service, little was accomplished in his department. Improved salaries for postmasters and a vastly expanded postal service—the new Mississippi River mail service and the doubling of railroad mileage involved in carrying the mail— made the department's deficit larger than ever. As for the franking privilege, he repeatedly asked for its abolition, but Congress, then or at any time since, would not give up something so useful. The postal service, with an annual deficit of nearly two million dollars, was essential to the economic and political growth of the nation, and there was no way it could operate in the black. Campbell's attempts to improve foreign mail service also failed. Great Britain, Mexico, and France, the major nations involved, rejected his suggestions. The postmaster general was frugal and determined, but the cost of the operation he oversaw, combined with the opportunities for huge profits for transportation interests and the privileges cherished by politicians, made his goal of ending the deficit only a dream.[24]

Honesty and strict accountability on the part of government workers contributed to efficiency but not to political effectiveness at a time when the national political parties were starting to disintegrate. Whether the nation could survive the tensions and uncertainties of rapid change without a stable party system remained to be seen. Just as Campbell's department operated with a new emphasis on public integrity, so did the Treasury Department under James Guthrie, who was determined to introduce into government service the same business practices that had brought him immense wealth. Guthrie, whose six-foot-tall figure topped with a black "Quaker" hat, sleepy appearance, and Kentucky drawl made him a Washington character, was also a hard-working administrator. He never took vacations, though he did some entertaining, probably as part of his official responsibilities. At the social gatherings Guthrie, a widower, had the help of his two daughters who acted as hostesses. These receptions were "large and lavish," but some who attended saw that his presence was "perfunctory rather than a pleasure."

When Guthrie assumed office three issues had to be confronted. While there was still a government debt, there was a large surplus in the Treasury. He managed to reduce the debt from more than $69 million to $31 million without permitting financiers to profit from the operation.

He also found that much government money had not been deposited in the National Treasury, a legal requirement under the Independent Treasury Act. This, too, he stopped, much to the annoyance of those bankers who had profited from the laxness of earlier secretaries. Then there were the widespread rumors of fraud. Guthrie moved swiftly against all those suspected of such activity. He ended the practice of allowing customs officers to keep part of the fines they collected and fired those whose fiscal honesty he found wanting. He brought order into the Treasury Department and reduced to a minimum the opportunity for graft. He became known as the "prairie plow," which may have had some popular appeal but brought angry groans from the nation's bankers as well as the workers in his department and their supporters in Congress.

One of Guthrie's recommendations, included in each of his reports, was a request for reducing the tariff. In his last report he included, at the request of Congress, a large amount of economic data, and the final bill reaching Pierce for his signature provided a modest reduction in the tariff. He also urged new procedures to improve the Independent Treasury system and suggested that if the nation's banks continued recklessly to issue excessive amounts of paper money a federal tax might be required to stem the practice. In addition to his strict policies for Treasury, Guthrie was known in the Pierce administration as the one who punished New York's collector, Greene C. Bronson, and as an ardent promoter of government aid for a Pacific railroad.[25]

Reform and honest administration also characterized the Interior Department headed by Robert McClelland, another stickler for rules and procedure. McClelland, who was personally low-keyed and unobtrusive, was brusque and demanding in his official capacity. He headed a department consisting of four important operations—land, Indian, pension, and patent bureaus—with offices scattered around the city. It was also a department where opportunities for graft abounded. Still, he did what he could to make its operation responsible. He was overworked and understaffed, and his was an almost impossible assignment. Although he introduced more orderly procedures and strict work rules within the department, the interests of land speculators and illegal settlers on public land, the thousands claiming a right to government pension, unscrupulous Indian agents, and greedy railroad promoters all worked to undermine McClelland's reforms.

Nevertheless, in his final report the secretary was able to outline some achievements. Under his supervision almost ninety-four million acres of public land had been distributed, with sixty-three million of those going to military bounty holders, to the states for railroad construction, or in grants for swampland. The entire Mexican cessions plus Oregon, Washington, Kansas, and Nebraska were placed under the government land system. The pension bureau doled out more than a million dollars a year. McClelland believed that many pensions were unnecessary and proposed that only those who were indigent should get federal pensions. The patent office noted that the number granted had increased from 2,522 for 1840–1853 to an average of more than four thousand a year. McClelland suggested revising the patent procedure. Indian bureau work had also doubled under his tenure. He and the Indian commissioner had negotiated fifty-two treaties involving 174 million acres at a cost of eleven million dollars. He had introduced the practice of requiring financial statements and checking the accounts of the agents. He recommended ending government cash annuities for the Indians, colonizing them instead, or isolating them on reservations and teaching them better work habits and Christian doctrine. He envisioned preparing the Indians for a new and, to him, better way of life. He failed to mention in his report that Commissioner George W. Manypenny, who had a more realistic knowledge of the situation, had told him of resistance and impending Indian wars in Washington Territory. Finally, the secretary told of introducing order in the department, which housed both the Indian bureau and land office in the same building with him. It was the proud report of a dedicated bureaucrat who failed to recognize the impact of his policies on the individuals they affected: western settlers, recipients of pensions, and especially the various Indian peoples.[26]

Most of the Pierce cabinet members were relatively low-keyed and inclined to stay out of public notice, but Jefferson Davis was the exception. The secretary of war was tall and handsome and walked with a military bearing acquired at West Point. He could be a charming entertainer, and many of the major social functions of the city took place at his home, where such a mix as his cabinet colleagues and Free Soil Whig Senator William H. Seward mingled on warm and friendly terms. While serving in the cabinet, Davis promoted the interests of the South but set aside temporarily his secessionist views. In his official role Davis was full of grandiose ideas seldom shared by others. He was arrogant and demanded obedience and was inclined to get into controversy. Certainly he was one of the president's most influential advisors, though he did not always get his way. It was Davis who was responsible for the appointment of James Gadsden to the important Mexican post, and probably that of Pierre Soulé as well. And it was Davis who for a time persuaded Pierce to overlook the soldiers of fortune known as filibusters, with their schemes for invading Cuba and parts of Central America. In all his dealings with the president, Davis presented a prosouthern view as the American view. Pierce would often slip away unseen at night to visit the Davis household, fearing that too much social contact in public would bring complaints that he favored the South. Yet no cabinet member was closer to the president. It was Davis whose name, along with that of President Pierce, was spelled out in fireworks when they and the rest of the cabinet went to Fortress Monroe to review the troops and enjoy a military-style holiday.[27]

Davis presided over the War Department when, except for the continuing wars of Indian resistance, the nation was at peace. Nevertheless, he was alarmed at the condition of the army and was determined to bring about much needed reform. West Point needed repairs and its academic program needed upgrading. The pay for officers and enlisted men was far too low, causing poor morale and a flood of desertions, especially from the dull, mostly routine service in the West. Without a railroad to the Pacific the transportation of men and supplies to the Far West was arduous and time-consuming. The military had its own ruling bureaucracy, which often challenged the policies of the War Department. Davis did not help matters when, as he frequently did, he neglected to exercise authority after having given general policy orders. Each of his annual reports repeated his proposals for reform of the military: higher compensation, streamlining the chain of command, increasing the staff personnel, reforming the field command, diversifying military duties, and establishing a list of retired personnel. Congress agreed to add four new regiments and to improve the coastal fortifications, but most of Davis's reform ideas met with a cold and negative response.

Davis was one of the most ardent of the Pacific railroad promoters in the Pierce administration, and he was determined that it should be built over a southern route. But improvements in transportation could not wait for the railroad. After a great deal of thought and study, he suggested as an interim measure that camels be used to transport goods across the Southwest. Camels were capable of carrying enormous loads considerably faster than horses over rough desert terrain where water was scarce. Congress allotted funds to purchase thirty-three camels representing six different species. The camel project made Davis the object of much ridicule, but official reports indicated that the experiment worked. Although Congress denied money to Davis's successor for an additional thousand camels, those already in service were used by the army until the outbreak of the Civil War and were later used by the Confederate postal service.[28]

The camel project illustrated Jefferson Davis's tendency to propose ideas with romantic appeal that sometimes lacked practicality. One problem with the camels was lack of expertise in handling them, and the preference of army personnel for horses and mules. Another of his grand schemes, the Crimean War Commission, also produced few practical results. Davis decided to create a commission of three military men to study and report on all aspects of warfare as it was then being conducted in Europe. After naming the commission and preparing specific instructions, he seemed to lose interest in the project and gave little support to commission members in their attempts to get permission from European governments to observe not only their military but actual battle conditions. Long-term, decisive leadership was not his forte.[29]

Even though the War Department under Davis had a reputation for integrity and fiscal responsibility, there were rumors of land speculation by army personnel in Kansas, and a more substantial exposé of the close relationship between Robert J. Walker's railroad plans and Davis's preference for a southern route along the thirty-second parallel. In matters concerning the administration of his department Davis was scrupulous about accountability, even to the point of refusing to permit his wife to accept any of the gifts that came to the White House as a result of the Perry expedition to Japan. However, when Pierce sent him a miniature Japanese dog named Bonin he accepted it as his personal pet, much to the vexation of his wife and the servants. For a number of reasons he resisted congressional pressure to close down the government armories and purchase all arms through contracts with private companies. In the matter of weapons, Davis modified his laissez-faire philosophy, arguing that the government could produce arms less expensively, that government manufacturing set a standard for cost, and that the government would be more likely than private firms to make improvements. Though he professed confidence in private arms manufacturing, Davis also renewed a request for Congress to fund a national foundry, a recommendation that got nowhere.[30]

Fighting Indians provided a considerable amount of the United States' early nineteenth-century military experience, and much of that activity occurred during the Pierce years. Before the 1840s, official policy had been to set aside large areas of land for the Indians' use and to separate them from the rest of the population. Much of the land west of the Mississippi River was considered unfit for agriculture or settlement and was designated for the Indians, who were moved there by force or the threat of force. Several developments required a change in Indian policy. A growing number of settlers moving to California or the Oregon country, the acquisition of new western land as a result of the Mexican War, and plans for a transcontinental railroad all contributed to the change. In 1841 the Indian bureau began negotiating new treaties with the western Indians. A policy first announced that year by Indian Commissioner T. Hartley Crawford involved removing most of the Indians from much of the western country and eventually creating two Indian colonies, a northern one in what became the Dakotas and a southern one in what is now Oklahoma. Between the Indian lands there would be white settlement.

A series of treaties made before and during the Pierce administration paved the way for the construction of one or more transcontinental railroads and for widespread settlement on the plains. Although the new policy meant the forced removal of Indians from their land, those who devised the policy believed it would benefit Indians as well as whites. The policy provided army protection for Indians who agreed not to harass or attack settlers and annual cash payments to the various tribes. Yet the treaties were made at gunpoint, and they provoked considerable Indian resistance on the plains, the West Coast, and in the Southwest. It was to President Pierce that Chief Seattle of the Duwamish people sent a statement of Indian rights and grievances that was to become a classic. "We are two distinct races with separate origins and separate destinies," said Chief Seattle. "There is little in common between us." His people would accept confinement to a reservation, he predicted. "It matters little where we pass the remnant of our days. They will not be many. The Indian's night promises to be dark." Still, insisted the chief, the Indians must be permitted to visit ancestral burial grounds. "Every part of this soil is sacred to my people. Every hillside, every valley, every plain and grove had been hallowed by some sad or happy event in days long vanished."

If Chief Seattle's eloquent words ever reached Franklin Pierce, they had little effect on policy, which continued to be one of Indian removal to reservations and harsh punishment for any tribes that resisted. It was Secretary of War Jefferson Davis who was responsible for carrying out that policy, even though the Indian bureau had been moved to the Department of the Interior when the latter was created in 1849. Davis had participated in the Black Hawk War—actually more a chase than a war—and that experience gave him respect for the Indians as fighters.

He objected to the shackling and exhibiting of Black Hawk, years later commenting that "the real heroes were Black Hawk and his savages." Yet as secretary of war he did not hesitate to send military expeditions to quell Indian resistance in virtually all of the western country. His four new regiments were designed for war against the Indians. Pierce himself called to Washington Gen. William S. Harney, who was experienced in Indian warfare, urging him to "assume the command and whip the Indians." The expedition in question was intended to punish the Sioux for attacking and destroying a U.S. military detachment.

Davis eventually became so obsessed with defeating the Indians that he ordered field commanders in Kansas Territory to give it a higher priority than policing the area. In his final report he suggested concentrating western troops in several large frontier outposts rather than scattering them over a large area. After an experiment with this strategy in Texas, Indian raids were substantially reduced. Although Davis admired Indian warriors and believed that the government had a responsibility to assist the Indians, he insisted upon their submission as a prelude to the building of a Pacific railroad. He certainly did not agree with Congressman Joshua Giddings of Ohio, who opposed military expeditions against the Indians and suggested that the United States use the money to furnish food for them rather than feeding an army to fight them. It could be done with a quarter of the funds the military required. "The best protection that has ever been afforded against Indian spoliations," maintained Giddings, "has been found in being just, generous, and kind to them, in making them our friends rather than our enemies."[31]

Besides subjugating the Indians the War Department was responsible for surveys to determine the best route for a western railroad. Indeed, direct military administration was only a part of Davis's responsibility. The Army Corps of Engineers and the Topographical Engineers were both under his jurisdiction. The project dearest to his heart and of greatest consequence to the nation was the work of the Topographical Engineers in conducting four extensive surveys for a Pacific railroad route. Congress had appropriated $120,000 for four surveying expeditions, a northern, St. Paul-to-Seattle route, a central, Chicago-to-St. Louis-to-San Francisco route, an upper southern route from Memphis to San Francisco, and a lower southern route from New Orleans to San Diego.

The project's stated purpose was to determine the "most practicable and economical route for a railroad from the Mississippi to the Pacific

Ocean,'' but for Davis the unstated goal was to cut through political smoke and pave the way for construction of a railroad along the thirty-second parallel, or the lower southern route. Such a road would increase the economic and political clout of the South. Although all four of the surveyed routes were eventually used for operating railroads, both the engineers' reports and Davis's follow-up strongly promoted the route along the thirty-second parallel. He stubbornly refused to accept a substitute, even the more practical route along the thirty-fifth parallel from Memphis to San Francisco, which had considerable congressional support. That refusal, along with allegations of collusion between the War Department and Robert Walker's Atlantic and Pacific Railroad Company, made it virtually certain that no road would be started during the Pierce years. It was another example of Jefferson Davis's uncompromising personality and political ineptitude.[32]

While the surveys failed to break a political logjam over railroad construction, they had other, positive results. Along with the engineers went more than a hundred artists, naturalists, geologists and other scientists whose observations and notebooks made a substantial contribution to knowledge about the American West. Although the data was collected in haste, the specimens sent to the Smithsonian made it one of the world's great museums, and the maps proved invaluable for future settlement and road construction. The thirteen-volume survey report provided much new information about plants, animals, and birds of the American West. Robert Baird, the Smithsonian director, mined the report and classified the bird skins sent him by the engineers to provide material for his *Birds of North America*, a groundbreaking study. Indeed, there was far more information on animal and bird life than on the Indians, though one author, Thomas Eubanks, included an appreciative essay on the Indians of the West.[33]

The role that Jefferson Davis played in the railroad survey project caused a major setback to the improvement of transportation, both for the nation and for the South. His tendency to become involved in personality disputes also demeaned him as a cabinet member. The most acrimonious and publicized of those disputes was with Gen. Winfield Scott, Commander of the Army. Earlier, while in the Senate and chair of the Committee on Military Affairs, Davis had tangled with Scott, who was also argumentative and demanding, when he opposed a bill to make Scott brevet lieutenant general. Scott, whose nickname, ''Old Fuss and Feathers,'' was well-earned, kept his headquarters in New York to avoid Davis. When Scott put in claims for an increase in pay and expenses, Davis again opposed the general. A lengthy and bitter argument followed, with both parties resorting to name-calling and personal attacks. Attorney General Cushing and President Pierce over-ruled Davis, but the dispute continued. In letters Davis called Scott "depraved" and Scott referred to Davis as an "enraged imbecile," behavior that did not add to the stature of the disputants nor to that of the Pierce administration.[34]

In spite of such petulance, Davis used his tenure at the War Department to increase the importance of the military in American life. Congress granted money for a larger army, for the construction of military roads in the territories, for West Point improvements, and for coastal defenses. Although the nation was at peace, except for the Indian wars, spending for the War Department increased from 20 percent of the national budget in 1854 to 28 percent in 1857.[35]

Secretary of the Navy James C. Dobbin also instituted improve-ments, for he found a navy much in need of reform. Having virtually no knowledge of naval affairs when he joined the cabinet, Dobbin soon acquired a wealth of information and became an effective advocate of a stronger navy at a time when naval power was considered the key to a nation's strength. Dobbin's style was in sharp contrast to that of Davis. A capable administrator, he was practical and popular with all who did business with him. Dobbin found the navy far too small, with low morale among the seamen. Congress honored his request for more ships and permitted him to have them built either in government navy yards or by private companies. He chose the navy yards. Dobbin also wanted to convert the navy to steam, which he considered "unquestionably the great agent to be used on the ocean, as well for purposes of war as of commerce." Many in Congress were skeptical. They had too much faith in the majestic Yankee clipper ships to abandon wind for steam power in the navy. His suggested reforms met with a mixed response. His proposal for a procedure to dismiss or retire incapacitated officers, to be administered by a naval board, was adopted in a weakened version. He successfully resisted a move to reintroduce flogging and instituted instead a well-devised system of rewards and punishment, but his proposal for promotion based on merit rather than seniority failed to win approval. Dobbin's other reform measures included making seamen a part of the regular naval force and raising their pay, reviving an apprenticeship program, and reducing the time of cruises from three to two years.[36]

Like the army, the navy had projects that would aid the nation's trade and business interests. It was under Dobbin's term as secretary that Commodore Matthew Perry completed his historic mission to

Japan. In 1853 Dr. Elisha Kent Kane led a two-year naval expedition to explore the arctic region, the second such expedition for the United States. Another naval expedition, traveling south, brought back sugar-cane cuttings to replenish the stock of Louisiana sugar planters. Naval interests strongly supported the acquisition of islands in the Pacific and the Caribbean, both for coaling stations and as places for American economic penetration. When Dobbin assumed his office the navy had about seventy ships, including a few that were steam powered. In his first report he deplored the weakness of the navy, which had only seventy-five hundred men, with many of the officers incompetent or elderly. He was able to institute important reforms and to persuade an economy-minded Congress to approve the construction of six additional steam frigates and five of the smaller sloops-of-war. Dobbin, who was not deterred by his small size and poor health, supervised the navy department with efficiency.[37]

One of the most influential of Pierce's cabinet members, Attorney General Caleb Cushing, did not have a department at all. Under new legislation, Cushing received an annual salary of $8,000, freeing him from the need to practice private law while carrying out his official duties. Taking on the legal responsibilities transferred from the State Department doubled his work load. Cushing was by far the most learned and well-traveled member of the cabinet, but his early public life as a Whig made him subject to criticism. Among the few Democratic politicians who trusted him was Franklin Pierce, who leaned heavily on his advice. Cushing often spoke for the administration. His daily editorials in the *Washington Union* reflected the shifts and turns in the president's views. He also wrote several of Pierce's proclamations and substantial sections of the presidential messages.

Cushing's impact on the office he held was also impressive. He worked assiduously to clear up a backlog of cases left from the former administration. At the request of the president he wrote a full description of the role and historical development of the office of attorney general, describing it as "the administrative head, under the President, of the legal business of the government." He suggested that the attorney general make periodic reports to the president and through him to Congress, prosecute all suits in which the United States was ultimately concerned, be given authority to grant pardons, and give all commissions of a judicial character. Cushing's analysis became the standard description of the office, but when he proposed much-needed expansion and reform of the federal judiciary, Congress turned him down. Undoubtedly there were several reasons for that, but opposition from those who feared that Pierce would appoint all prosouthern men to the new court openings was a major factor. When the judiciary was finally enlarged after the Civil War, most of Cushing's recommendations were adopted.[38]

As a congressman, Cushing had opposed the Gag Resolutions, which prevented petitions relating to slavery from reaching the floor. His opponents accused him of having Free Soil ideas, but none of his actions in the Pierce administration supported such a charge. He became increasingly prosouthern as he began to view the southern faction of his party as the law and order element, and their opponents as subversive. He and Davis were often on the same side in heated exchanges with Marcy. Cushing wrote an opinion supporting the right of southern postmasters to exclude abolitionist publications from the mails. He strongly defended the rights of the South to have slavery in the territories, and he emphasized the importance of states' rights. In a series of opinions he supported strict enforcement of the Fugitive Slave Act, and in one opinion he anticipated arguments used in 1857 to deny civil rights to the slave, Dred Scott. In a Faneuil Hall speech in 1857 Cushing condemned the abolitionists as "impracticable zealots," asserting that whites and blacks were "unequal by nature" and that no laws could make them "equal in fact."[39]

At times, Cushing had as much influence on foreign relations as the secretary of state. He was an ardent imperialist and a consistent foe of Great Britain. His opinions frequently influenced Pierce in matters of policy and treaty-making, although the president by no means followed Cushing's advice at all times. On some issues Cushing was opposed by Marcy, who always had a cooler head and favored a more cautious policy. At other times it was Jefferson Davis who differed with Cushing. Davis was more than willing to give secret support to American soldiers of fortune in Central America and the Caribbean, while Cushing viewed them as troublesome impediments to American expansionism. When he clashed with Davis on foreign policy, Cushing's was the cooler head. Since all three were expansionists, their arguments were over means, not ends. Sometimes it was primarily a matter of personality and power. These disputes further complicated the life of Franklin Pierce, who tended to follow the advice of the last person with whom he had met.[40]

Many of Cushing's opinions affected the course of American life for years to come. The consequences of his refusal to approve a patent for Dr. William G. Morton, a dentist who had discovered the use of ether as an anesthetic, extended far into the future. Morton had claimed a violation of his patent rights by the military, which also used ether for anesthesia. Cushing ruled the Morton patent invalid because a scientific discovery could not be patented for profit, although "specific instruments or methods of such application" might be.

The Morton patent issue illustrates the variety of questions that Caleb Cushing had to address as attorney general. He, too, was a hardworking member of the Pierce team. His official opinions fill three 700-page volumes. His influence on the president led some historians to characterize him as the Richelieu of the Pierce administration. Certainly he did nothing to dampen the administration's prosouthern bias, which grew in strength and blinded Pierce to demands for recognition of northern rights.[41]

In terms of effectiveness, the successes of the Pierce administration were mixed. It is hard to imagine a less unified group than those who made up his cabinet. However, virtually all of the departments were well run, and several were sufficiently reformed as to lay the basis for a modern, workable bureaucracy. Except for the hint of collusion between Jefferson Davis and railroad interests, there was little suggestion of scandal. Through prodigious efforts Caleb Cushing added prestige and influence to the office of attorney general. All members of the administration took their jobs seriously and worked hard at them. While Pierce asserted himself on some occasions, it was, for the most part, a government run by department heads. Yet the president visited each department personally as often as he could and involved himself in nearly all the matters they handled. He held regular cabinet meetings, which often became so rancorous as to spark threats of resignation. Yet there were none. For the first time, a cabinet remained intact during a full presidential term. The strongest personalities—Davis, Cushing, and Marcy—dominated the sessions and frequently clashed, with Marcy often working as a counterforce to the more bumptious of his colleagues. All of the departments, bureaus, and government offices had been established to govern the nation according to acceptable principles, yet the final result was a domestic record prosouthern enough to please Davis and a foreign policy of louder Young America rhetoric than its actions bore out.

4

SOURCES OF DIVISION: THE PRESIDENT AND CONGRESS

Franklin Pierce, as titular head of the Democratic party and of the administration that directed the government, was in fact the boss of neither. Democrats, whether in elective offices or working for the party, usually had their own legislative agenda. Congressmen and senators saw themselves as equal to the president and thought that defining administration policy was as much their responsibility as his. When Pierce asked for legislation they listened, but as often as not they rejected his suggestions. Although party loyalty was still a strong factor in congressional activity, several developments had seriously eroded the traditional two-party system. Those changes weakened the Whigs more than the Democrats, yet even the Whigs displayed unity on several important issues that did not involve the debate over slavery. Moreover, Pierce's weakness as a party leader strengthened the more assertive Democrats in Congress. Members of both parties had to deal with individuals and interest groups favoring specific laws, and always there was the matter of politics. How legislation would affect the people of the country was weighed against the impact such laws might have on the political scene. Frequently the two considerations were at odds.

Members of Congress, cherishing their power and independence, had to persuade voters to keep them in office. That necessity made them slow-moving and cautious. With an issue so controversial as slavery they tried whenever possible to avoid clear policy decisions. They hoped, unrealistically, that the 1850 settlement was final. Moreover, with new developments in all aspects of American life, Congress exasperated those seeking change by moving at a painfully slow pace. Two prominent issues of the day illustrate the point. The need for a national railroad policy had been debated for years, yet no decision was forthcoming during the Pierce presidency. Closely related was legislation to create territorial governments for the land west of Missouri and Iowa. There, too, Congress took its time in hammering out a policy that became the Kansas-Nebraska Act of 1854. Culminating more than a decade of consideration, it proved to be the only major legislative accomplishment of the Pierce administration.

Included in the complex mix of forces facing the federal government were numerous personal interests, the growing mechanization of transportation and industry, and the emergence of the United States as a potential two-ocean power requiring transcontinental railroad and telegraph lines to link its various sections. Each interest demanded a response from Congress. Western farmers and land speculators, enthusiastic boosters in various western cities, settlers demanding free land, businessmen, contractors, merchants, and workers requesting government funding for a variety of internal improvement projects, and publishers holding out their hands for government printing contracts were just a few of the many groups that devoutly believed that what was good for them was good for the nation. Each longed for a share of the $32,425,447 in treasury surplus.

Further complicating the picture was strong sectional pride, with each section containing a variety of views and interests. On some issues the division was east-west, on others, north-south. The compelling need was for a policy to unite all sections under a common objective. Henry Clay had earlier tried that with his American System, an effort that proved to be easier said than done. Also complicating the picture were the social reformers, who were turning increasingly to political action in their efforts to build a nobler, more just society. Moreover, to the majority of Americans who considered Protestantism a part of the national creed, the influx of millions of European Catholics fed suspicion of a papal plot and encouraged nativist tendencies. The resulting Know-Nothing or American party, along with the forces of Free Soil and political temperance, threatened to destroy the old party system.

Yet if the political system was expected to provide a legal structure that would care for the needs of the people it must always be remembered that its primary subject was the adult, white male. The concept of serving all the people was virtually ignored. While black Americans were no longer slaves in the northern states, they were usually disfranchised and faced daily discrimination in every area of life. Although a small minority of Garrisonian abolitionists favored a multiracial society, many Free Soilers thought removing blacks from the United States was a necessary corollary to preventing the extension of slavery. Few favored interfering with slavery where it existed. The entire debate over slavery in the territories hinged on what kind of government there should be for white settlers. It was the slave power, rather than slavery itself, that was the Free Soilers' target. Yet the fate of black Americans, who held no political power themselves, became a major issue in the Pierce years.[1]

Also largely pawns in a system that purported to protect the rights of all were Native Americans. Of course, executives and lawmakers claimed that their Indian policies protected those rights. Even Andrew Jackson, whose forced removal of the Eastern Cherokees resulted in the Trail of Tears and other horrors, apparently believed it was all done in the best interest of the Indians. Yet despite benevolent assurances, it was the land, not Indian welfare, that inspired the policy. Indeed, the ability to rationalize, even sanctify, greed for Indian lands seemed limitless. In 1839 Lewis Cass wrote in the *North American Review:* "There can be no doubt . . . that the Creator intended the earth should be reclaimed from a state of nature and cultivated." Senator Thomas Hart Benton asserted that whites had the best claim to the land because they "used it according to the intentions of the CREATOR." There was even talk of transforming Indians into Christian farmers who would gradually become part of white society, but it met resistance. Caleb Cushing would not admit as his equals "either the red man, of America, or the yellow man of Asia, nor the black man of Africa," and Stephen A. Douglas referred to the trans-Mississippi west as "filled with hostile savages." Ultimately the Indians, whose rights and interests were never really addressed, became involved in a political dispute that determined their fate and destroyed their traditional way of life.[2]

Such political turmoil characterized much of President Pierce's relationship with Congress as well as the internal workings of the legislative branch. Besides political and personnel problems that prevented a smoothly running administration, there was built-in suspicion of the executive branch. Constitutional lines defining presidential power were frequently blurred, and only such strong personalities as Jefferson and Jackson could effectively lead such a disparate body as the American Congress. Though his supporters labeled him "Young Hickory of the Granite Hills," after the election no one ever compared Pierce to Andrew Jackson. Those measures associated with the administration were as much the concern of Democrats in Congress as of the president, and the most significant piece of legislation had its origin in the halls of Congress, not the White House.

Two tragic events further eroded Pierce's influence with Congress. While writing his first presidential message, Pierce learned that New Hampshire's Senator Charles G. Atherton had died. Atherton had been chosen senator at Pierce's bidding. His election had alienated former ardent Pierce promoter Edmund Burke, who had believed a seat in the Senate would be his reward. Atherton was to have been the president's agent in the Senate. Now there was none to take that place. Then Vice-President William R. King also died. King was in Cuba during the inauguration and took the oath of office there by virtue of a special act of Congress. Ill at the time, he returned to his native Alabama where he died on 19 April. King's death was another blow to Pierce. Now David R. Atchison of Missouri, ardent defender of southern rights, became president pro tem of the Senate. Should Pierce die, Atchison would become president.

Although the Thirty-third Congress had Democratic majorities in both houses, loyalty to the party did not automatically translate into loyalty toward the administration. The New York delegation in the House, still smarting from Pierce's patronage blunders, was determined to make trouble. Personal interests and sectional views also divided the party. Democrats from the western states demanded federal money for internal improvements, despite traditional party opposition to such projects. The Whig minority favored higher tariffs, internal improvements at government expense, and more aid to business elements, thus putting them at odds with the administration. Whigs could work as a unit on matters not related to slavery, but when that issue arose, they divided along sectional lines. Furthermore, the action of individual Whigs was often unpredictable. Finally, there was a small but important Free Soil element in Congress. Some, like New York's William Seward and Ohio's Ben Wade, were Whigs. A few, like Ohio's Senator Salmon P. Chase and Congressman Joshua R. Giddings, were elected on a Free Soil ticket. The Free Soilers were always gadflies to the administration, raising the slavery issue at every opportunity. They were determined to cultivate a national policy that would give free rein to the interests of the North.

Yet other sections also had representation. Elderly and rambling Lewis Cass, Young America's idol Stephen A. Douglas, and Indiana's Jesse D. Bright all promoted the interests of the West. Bright, a strong Cass supporter in the presidential campaign, immediately took an opposition stance to the administration. Four men who boarded at a home on F Street led the southern forces in the Senate. They were David Rice Atchison of Missouri, James Murray Mason of Virginia, and Andrew Pickens Butler and Robert M. T. Hunter of South Carolina.

Together they were known as the F Street Mess. Their objective was to thwart the Free Soilers and direct Democratic policies toward southern interests. They proved to be a powerful influence on the administration. Similar divisions characterized the House, whose members, though less well-known nationally than senators, were nevertheless conscious of their own power and resisted automatic acceptance of orders from the president. Despite it all, Pierce was optimistic about his relationship with a Congress dominated by members of his own party. That optimism grew when Linn Boyd of Kentucky was reelected speaker of the house, even though Treasury Secretary James Guthrie doubted Boyd's loyalty to the administration.[3]

The four messages that Pierce sent to Congress revealed his political views and style of administration. Much of their content was a listing of proposals from various cabinet members, a litany of democratic policies, and the elaboration of his inaugural address. In the first three he followed tradition, placing matters of foreign policy first. Great Britain was the enemy, and Pierce devoted much space to chronicling United States-British relations, which included negotiating fishing rights for Americans off Canadian waters and a reciprocal trade agreement concerning Canada, protesting British recruitment in the United States during the Crimean War and constant friction over British intrusion into Central America. Blunt and uncompromising in defending the national interest, he nevertheless held out the olive branch of possible negotiated settlement.

Nor did Pierce confine his remarks to relations with Great Britain. He used the case of Martin Koszta, a Hungarian exile rescued from an Austrian warship by an American naval commander, to illustrate American determination to protect human rights, even of those who, like Koszta, had just declared their intention to become American citizens. He discussed efforts to resolve a trade disagreement with Denmark, to expand trade with various countries of Europe, Latin America, and Asia, and to settle disputes with Mexico and Peru. He spoke of the growth of American commerce, which he believed required a larger navy. Acknowledging that some countries looked upon American territorial expansion "with disquieting concern," Pierce insisted that American military forces were used solely for defense and "to preserve order among the aboriginal tribes in the Union."

While he often praised the advantages of the American system of government, Pierce shared with most of his contemporaries their racial views. In his second message to Congress he requested a larger army to deal with Indian raids on settlers traveling across the western plains. Pierce regarded the Indians as savages who killed without reason. "The recurrence of such scenes," he wrote, "can only be prevented by teaching these wild tribes the power of and their responsibility to the United States." In 1855 Pierce's message included a clear statement of his views concerning the rights of black Americans. He did not regard slavery as a moral or ethical question; slaveholders had a right to their property, and slaves had no rights at all. Only "fanaticism and partisan spirit," he said, could explain how a group of Americans so devoted themselves "to the supposed interests of the relatively few Africans in the United States as totally to abandon and disregard the interests of 25,000,000 Americans." Pierce was alluding to the new party he and his friends called the "Black Republicans." He thought them a truly subversive element, characterized by "vindictive hostility against those who are associated with them in the enjoyment of the common heritage of our national institutions." There was no middle ground for Pierce, nor any understanding of the forces leading to the emergence of a northern political party with Free Soil as part of its creed.

Pierce made a distinction between loyalty to the Union and the process of national unification, which was sweeping across the western world. His messages reiterated the importance of states' rights and the view that the federal government had taken shape "under a written compact between sovereign States, uniting for specific objects and with specific grants to their general agent." He predicted steady growth of the United States, anticipating that thousands of people then alive would live to see "more than 100,000,000 of population embraced within the majestic proportions of the American Union." It was also evident to Pierce that such a vast and varied confederation could only hold together by "strictest fidelity to the principles of the constitution as understood by those who have adhered to the most restricted construction of the powers granted by the people and the States."

Although such strict construction did not grant power to the federal government to fund local internal improvements, Pierce, in his first message, gave cautious and qualified approval to federal aid for a transcontinental railroad. By the following year, however, he used stronger language in explaining why he ordered twenty million acres of the public domain withdrawn from consideration for possible grants to railroads. The proposed railroad projects in eleven states and one territory, said Pierce, did not justify federal funding. "Is it not the better rule to leave all these works to private enterprise, regulated and, when expedient, aided by the cooperation of the State?" he asked. Commending Congress for its delay of the railroad bill, Pierce urged that the subject receive "careful reexamination and rigid scrutiny."

The presidential messages gave ample evidence of prosouthern sentiments. Pierce undoubtedly believed that the South had always been the victim of aggression from certain northern interests. His prejudice had increased in 1848 when stirrings of northern sectionalism in the form of the Free Soil party disrupted his beloved Democratic party and contributed to its defeat. He maintained in his first message that those old controversies were passing away "with the causes which produced them and the passions which they had awakened." The spirit of the Compromise of 1850 was working, thought Pierce. There would be no more agitation over slavery. That profound misjudgment set the tone for his entire administration.

Two years later, after rancorous debates in Congress over the Kansas-Nebraska Act and the consequent emergence of a new party, Pierce included in his message his own interpretation of the slave argument. The United States was the creation of sovereign states, with each state retaining the right to allow slavery within its borders. The Constitution even provided for the return of runaway slaves to their owners. He revealed his bias when he wrote: "While the people of the Southern States confine their attention to their own affairs, not presuming officiously to intermeddle with the social institutions of the Northern States, too many of the inhabitants of the latter are permanently organized in associations to inflict injury on the former by wrongful acts." Reviewing the Kansas controversy, he justified without qualification the repeal of the Missouri Compromise included in legislation creating the two new territories. To deny a state admission to the Union, said Pierce, because its institutions did not "in all respects comport with the ideas of what is wise and expedient entertained in some other State" would violate the compact and begin disruption of the Union itself. He never doubted that the slavery conflict would "inevitably dash itself in vain against the unshaken rock of the Constitution," for the Union was stronger "than all the wild and chimerical schemes of social change which are generated one after another in the unstable minds of visionary sophists and interested agitators."

That view remained firm throughout Pierce's term. In his final message, written after the 1856 election, which would bring Democrat James Buchanan to the White House, Pierce expressed relief that the voters had affirmed the constitutional equality of the states and had condemned the idea of sectional parties. Such parties he found "fraught with incalculable mischief," preying upon public excitement over "causes temporary in their character" and, he hoped, transient in their influence. Without naming the new party he accused it of pretending to stop only the spread of slavery while in fact it was determined "to change the domestic institutions of existing States." Such a revolutionary objective would cause civil strife. "Violent attacks from the North finds its inevitable consequence in the growth of a spirit of angry defiance at the South," he warned. Northern aggression "against the constitutional rights of nearly one-half of the thirty-one States," he said, included abolitionist agitation, private and legal aid to fugitive slaves, the Missouri Compromise, strong northern opposition to repeal of that compromise in the Kansas-Nebraska Act, and the troubles in Kansas, which began with northern aggression and soon created a southern reaction. He reported with satisfaction that the use of military force established peaceful conditions in Kansas. The wife of influential Senator Clement C. Clay of Alabama was jubilant about Pierce's final message, writing in her memoirs that it fell "like a bombshell on the Black Republican Party," and that "its bold pro-slaveryism startled even his friends."

The president's belief that all the sectional troubles stemmed from northern interference and aggression was a strand woven throughout the message. It was a view undoubtedly reinforced by his close friendship with Jefferson Davis and Senator Clay and by his abiding faith in the Democratic party's traditional creed. Indeed, Pierce considered Jacksonian policies of the 1830s a valid guide for the nation in the 1850s. He regarded those who believed that a republic without slavery was compatible with a vibrant, industrial society, as simply wrong. He expected free workers and farmers of the northern states to continue to coexist indefinitely with the slave labor force of the South. And as for enslaved black Americans, they were protected as their masters' property but had no personal rights. At a time when more and more citizens of the northern states were demanding that new territories and states be opened exclusively to free farmers and workers, Pierce clung stubbornly to this views.[4]

With both houses of the Thirty-third Congress safely Democratic, the Pierce administration should have had no trouble in achieving its goals. Yet many congressional Democrats did not share Pierce's devotion to Jacksonian orthodoxy or his party loyalty. As much moved by sectional and personal interests—or old grudges—as by administration policy, they followed that policy when it suited them, but they would not accept dictation. By uniting with Whigs and Free Soilers, dissident Democrats could harass the administration and sometimes frustrate its plans. The New York delegation, dominated by "Hards," was especially troublesome. An early test of administration strength was the choice of printer for the Senate and House. The prize was half a million dollars in annual government printing contracts. The president's choice was Robert Armstrong, owner of the *Washington Union*. In the House, nine "Hards" from New York and Wisconsin, along with some southern congressmen, rejected Pierce's choice, voting for the prosouthern editor, Beverly Tucker. Twenty-three Democrats rebelled, but that was not enough to defeat the administration, and Armstrong became House printer by a large majority.

It was a different story in the Senate, where Democratic ranks were more divided. In a secret ballot the senators voted 26 to 17 to make Beverly Tucker its printer. Jesse Bright and Hamilton Fish had organized the administration defeat. Nine Democrats, including the F Street group of southern rights men, had joined with Whigs and Free Soilers to elect Tucker. Although administration spokesmen called the revolt a matter of personality and power rather than a referendum on presidential leadership, others sensed trouble ahead. Kentucky Congressman Joseph Lane believed that Tucker's election would wake up the administration. It was a warning, he said, that loyal Democrats were unwilling to see their party "abolitionized," and would not support "confirmation of unsound men."[5]

Even in the House, where the administration clearly had the upper hand, Pierce faced serious opposition. Congressman Francis Cutting, leading a group of New York "Hards," tried several times to block Pierce's program. Yet Cutting's proposal to demand correspondence relating to Greene C. Bronson's removal as collector of the Port of New York for refusal to follow administration policy, and resolutions condemning the scolding letters of Secretaries Cushing and Guthrie and asking for legislation to protect state elections from federal interference, were defeated, the latter after three days of bitter debate. The House also defeated anti-Pierce legislation that originated in the Senate. One bill would have made the assistant secretary of the Treasury subject to Senate approval; another would have given control of the Senate contingent fund to the secretary of that body rather than to the secretary of the Treasury. Pierce and his friends could take satisfaction in these victories, as well as from the confirmation of Heman J. Redfield as Bronson's successor. The coalition that made up the Democratic party was seriously weakened, but in the early days of 1854 the wounds were far from mortal. These were the battles of politics. At stake was the status and power of individuals. Such activity had little to do with the country at large or with the problems faced by ordinary people.[6]

Nevertheless, there was one group of dissidents—the Free Soilers—

whose steady opposition in Congress significantly affected the national mood. The Free Soil movement was the political expression of a growing antislavery and antisouthern sentiment in the northern states. There was, in fact, a variety of northern responses to southern slavery, and the categories often overlapped. A minority of abolitionists considered slavery a sin and actively agitated for its overthrow. William Lloyd Garrison and his followers represented the more extreme of the abolitionists, emphasizing moral suasion rather than political action. A far larger group of northern citizens held more moderate antislavery views, disapproving of slavery in a vague sort of way. They did not agitate against it and many of them believed that the institution would eventually wither and die. Some of those who held antislavery views resented the demands of the South that fugitive slaves be returned and resented even more the verbal attacks on the North made by congressmen and others from the South. While they did not believe that the federal government could interfere with slavery where it existed, they opposed the creation of any new slave territory or state.

The Free Soilers in Congress were concerned with power, but they also represented a reform spirit, a crusading, sometimes religious zeal, which set them apart from their colleagues. There were just a handful—Charles Sumner, Salmon P. Chase, and Pierce's old adversary, John P. Hale—in the Senate. Hale left the Senate in 1853 but returned in 1855 as a Republican to again plague the president. Also in the Senate were Ben Wade of Ohio and William Seward of New York, longtime Whigs who were strongly Free Soil in their speaking and voting, as were several in the lower house, including Lewis Campbell and Joshua Giddings of Ohio. Those few Free Soilers and their sympathizers in Congress exerted an influence far beyond their numbers. They played a significant role in sectional polarization and in the demise of the old two-party system.

They did that by seizing every opportunity to introduce the controversial issue, though their target was not slavery itself but rather the slave power, which they saw as dominating the national political life and stifling the growing power of the North. The overriding concern of Free Soil congressmen was for the welfare of their northern, white constituents, not for the slaves. On that point they stressed their differences with abolitionists like William Lloyd Garrison. The three-fifths compromise of the constitutional convention had provided the South, through its slave population, with extra representation in Congress and in the electoral college. Southerners controlled important congressional committees, and it was difficult, if not impossible, to elect a president without southern approval. That situation caused widespread resentment in the North. When Charles Sumner spoke to the Senate in favor of repealing the hated Fugitive Slave Act, a constituent wrote him: "If all northern men had resisted the slave monarchy as you have it never would have attained the audacity and tyranny it now exhibits." An Ohio editor expressed hope that Sumner's speech would "mark the commencement of a new era in Congress—an era in which a manly Northern sentiment will make itself truly felt, and command the respect of the South." If only a few northern senators would follow Sumner's example, wrote the editor, "the power of Southern menace and bravado would be gone forever." To Ben Wade, a constituent wrote: "It is high time that the people of the whole country should know and understand, that the degraded negro is not the only class of *slaves* among us; but that the arrogance of the 'Slave Power' tramples ruthlessly upon *all* who presume to fix the limits to its dominion."

Those sentiments reflected the sharp distinction that many in the North made between slavery as an institution in the South and the political extension of that institution, which was affecting their lives. To defenders of the South and of slavery it was a distinction without a difference. They viewed an attack on slave extension as the first step toward abolition. Commenting on a Free Soil article whose author had denied he was an abolitionist, Senator Chase wrote: "It is doubtful, however, whether the writer will escape the charge of 'abolitionism.' That word is usually applied South of Mason and Dixon's line to every form of opposition to Slavery and the Slave Power from the mildest and most constitutional to the most violent and the most revolutionary."[7]

Even some defenders of the administration would not make such a distinction. Congressman Gilbert Dean of New York charged that the Free Soilers wanted Congress to interfere with slavery in the South, to which Joshua Giddings, Ohio's veteran antislavery congressman, responded with a spirited denial. Free Soilers had never wished to interfere with slavery, he said, preferring instead "to wash their hands of the contagion" and leave it to the states where it existed. The issue arose again in the next session of Congress during debate over polygamy in Utah Territory. He would not outlaw Mormon polygamy, said Giddings, as long as Congress condoned "promiscuous, unlimited concubinage in the South." He and his Free Soil colleagues confronted slavery and the slave power like evangelical preachers, and their supporters shared their sense of mission. It was a mix of political, power-centered action and religious call for reform.[8]

That zeal inevitably spilled over into other reform measures that came up in Congress. Free Soilers supported Dorothea Dix's historic bill to provide federal land grants to fund hospitals for the indigent insane.

Charles Sumner worked for cheap transatlantic postage, a move that reformer Elihu Burritt suggested as a tool to help bring about world peace. John P. Hale in the Senate and Joshua Giddings in the House listed the military and slavery among the institutions they hoped to change, if not eliminate. Hale found the navy, as it then existed, "entirely useless" and suggested that it be disbanded and all government shipyards sold. Any ships that were required should be privately built and manned by merchant seamen. He and the other Free Soilers in Congress voted against an amendment to the navy bill, which added more officers to that department. Giddings spoke and voted against a similar measure for the army, describing the peacetime military system as an "incubus resting upon the nation," no more needed than "the fifth wheel of a coach."[9]

While all Free Soilers tended to favor reform movements, one antislavery congressman was in a class by himself. New York's Gerrit Smith was first of all an advocate of basic change and only secondly a politician. Elected on the Liberty party ticket, Smith was far more radical than the Free Soilers. He insisted that Congress had the power to abolish slavery in the South should it choose to do so. He was a purist, even—thought many of his contemporaries—a fanatic. In voting he demanded that those he supported be committed to a broad reform platform that addressed the needs of "the landless robbed by bank-monopoly, and the inebriate caused by the dram-shop, as well as the slave in his chains." Besides his antislavery speeches, Smith spoke twice on land reform, insisting that no one should be permitted to own more than four or five hundred acres and that land titles should apply only to improvements, not to the land itself. Such views alienated him from his colleagues, and in 1854 Smith resigned from Congress. He liked and admired many congressmen, he said, but found that they lacked moral commitment. "Congress," he remarked, "needs to witness the achievements of the Temperance reformation, and the Tobacco reformation, and the religion of Jesus Christ."[10]

Smith's views demanded more purification than even Free Soilers could embrace. Salmon P. Chase deplored Smith's preoccupation with abstractions, urging him to join the others working to remove federal support of slavery. That dispute, though friendly, exemplified the differences among antislavery congressmen. While they all spoke against the slave power and sometimes acted in concert, they also found themselves at odds over personal views, or local and party matters. Party loyalty and personal friendship inspired William Seward's glowing eulogy of Daniel Webster, to most Free Soilers one of the most despised of all northern compromise senators. A disagreement between

Seward and Sumner over a bill to award a mail-carrying subsidy to the British Collins Steamship Line led to a serious rift. Seward thought the bill would help his reelection bid, but Sumner considered the measure unjustified and told his colleague he had not gone to the Senate to aid Seward's reelection. "Sumner, you're a damned fool," was the reply. The two did not speak for several months, though Sumner eventually voted for the bill. Henry Wilson of Massachusetts differed with Ben Wade and Seward on the tariff question, an issue that frequently divided the Free Soilers. Thus the Free Soil clique confronted the same divisive forces that plagued the older political parties.[11]

Despite their differences the Free Soil congressmen made a unique contribution to the years of the Pierce presidency. They kept alive the debate over slavery and especially slave expansion at a time when most congressmen had assumed it had been settled by the 1850 compromise. More than that, they helped make antislavery ideas respectable. The very fact that such ideas came from members of Congress and were expressed in more moderate political terms gave them legitimacy. Their printed speeches received wide circulation. They exposed every attempt of the southern faction to extend its influence and took every opportunity to point out the hypocrisy of a nation dedicated to freedom condoning slavery in a large part of its domain. They pointed out how the slaveholding minority, through political influence, legislation like the Fugitive Slave Act, and a series of judicial decisions, had made their "peculiar institution" truly national. But it was freedom, not slavery, that must be national, said Salmon Chase and the others in the Free Soil camp, and the slave power must no longer control the national government. The corollary was that there must be a party of the North to bring about such a shift in power. Paving the way for that development was the Free Soil movement's major achievement.[12]

Unfortunately for Pierce, the Free Soilers were not the only opposition forces he had to contend with. The Whig minority, joined from time to time by Democrats, managed to pass several bills that the president vetoed. The first of them clearly revealed the attitude of the Pierce administration toward government funding to meet human needs. It was a bill to set aside twelve million acres of public land to fund institutions for the indigent mentally ill. Dorothea Dix, whose efforts on behalf of the insane had brought her international fame, had lobbied for such a measure for years. In various forms the bill had been under consideration since 1848, when it was first introduced by Senator John A. Dix of New York, who was not related to the reformer. The bill had support from many Whigs and Democrats as well as from the Free Soilers, and Miss Dix even met with Pierce, hoping to win his approval. She was working for "the poor, the friendless and the wretched," said Salmon Chase. Yet it was not only reformers who supported her cause. Speculators saw in it a chance to profit from the generous land holdings that would fall into the hands of state politicians for disposition.

There was also strong public support for the bill and much favorable editorial opinion, but President Pierce would not sign it. In a lengthy veto message Pierce said he had resisted his own deep sympathies in favor of the bill's purpose because he believed it unconstitutional. If Congress could provide for the indigent insane, he warned, why not for the healthy poor as well? The Constitution did not grant authority to make the federal government "the great almoner of public charity," said Pierce. The bill would be "subversive of the whole theory upon which the Union of these States is founded," he concluded. The same Congress that had passed the Dix bill could not summon the votes to override Pierce's veto.

It was a bitter disappointment for Dorothea Dix and her many supporters. Coming in the midst of the debate over the Kansas-Nebraska Bill it further alienated great numbers of northern voters. Senator Solomon Foot of Vermont denied that the bill was unconstitutional, listing government grants that had been made to individuals and corporations for education and internal improvements. "Millions for speculation and monopoly," he exclaimed, "not one dollar for benevolence and humanity is the practical maxim which rules in the high places of power in our day." Despite Pierce's veto of the Dix bill, his constitutional scruples weakened when Congress passed legislation granting 160 acres to American war veterans and their widows and minor children. That land giveaway got the president's signature.[13]

Yet the Pierce administration was adamantly opposed to any homestead legislation that would give government land to settlers merely for establishing a farm and working the land. It was a "vote yourself a farm bill," said land speculators, whose personal interests such legislation seemed to threaten. Secretary of Interior Robert McClelland, who early in the administration had strongly favored land grants to railroads, never supported free land for settlers. While the idea was popular in the northwestern states and territories and had some support in the Southwest, slaveholders saw homestead legislation as a threat, attracting hordes of settlers who would squeeze them out. Since much of the opposition to homestead legislation came from the older, southeastern states, many in the North perceived it as a sectional issue. But when it reached the House of Representatives a number of congressmen from the Southwest voted for it, since they favored western settlement over the interests of the slaveholding minority. The bill passed the House, but Pierce was spared another unpopular veto when the Senate, under the leadership of Robert M. T. Hunter, substituted a graduation bill, which lowered the price of less desirable land. It was a weak sop to western settlers and a far cry from what they really wanted. Although northwestern congressmen reluctantly accepted the substitute measure, it added to their resentment against the administration and against the South.[14]

Another issue that took on sectional overtones was the proposed railroad to the West Coast. Widespread sentiment favored such a railroad, but opinions differed as to how it should be financed and where it should run. When the report of the topographical engineers favored an extreme southern route, one that Secretary Jefferson Davis also favored, it sparked a heated debate in Congress. Early in his term Pierce had seemed to support land grants for railroad construction. Both McClelland and Davis had openly endorsed the idea, and in his first message to Congress Pierce had implied that it would be justified by military necessity. Yet such grants opened the way for fraud, which became a reality when Congress made a railroad land grant to Minnesota Territory. The bill to provide land for a railroad originally had been promoted by officers of the newly chartered Minnesota and Northwestern Railroad Company. However, the governor of Minnesota Territory, who favored a rival company, lobbied successfully in Washington to thwart the plans of the Minnesota and Northwestern. The bill that Congress passed denied the Minnesota and Northwestern any of the land, but after Pierce had signed it some officers of the House changed a few words to remove the restriction. A congressional committee exposed the fraud, Congress repealed the law, and the Minnesota and Northwestern went to court. The entire incident embarrassed the administration. Both Pierce and McClelland felt betrayed, and Pierce ordered land reserved for railroad grants to be taken out of reserve. He was pleased that Congress was unable to agree on Pacific railroad legislation during his term in office. But the question refused to go away and was a major factor in the Kansas-Nebraska controversy that loomed ominously over Pierce and the nation.[15]

Pierce was just as inconsistent with other internal improvement issues. Although philosophically and personally he tended to reject federally funded projects, he sometimes found a basis for exception. Most of his nine vetoes involved internal improvement projects, five of them overturned by the Thirty-fourth Congress. Yet he signed a bill to improve the Cape Fear River in North Carolina and a similar measure for

Georgia's Savannah River on the grounds that the obstructions to be removed had been caused when the federal government strengthened the foundations of nearby forts. One veto hit a southern project, but most of them affected the Northwest. In 1854 Congress passed "An act making appropriations for the repair, preservation, and completion of certain public works heretofore commenced under the authority of law." It was a gigantic two-and-a-half-million-dollar general improvement bill, mostly a concession to the West, where such improvements were sorely needed. Democrats were divided over the issue and opponents added some provisions so ridiculous as to cause its defeat. That strategy failed, however, and the bill's passage caught Pierce by surprise, without a ready veto message. He simply sent a statement that he would prepare one for the next session, at which time he presented a lengthy review of traditional Democratic party policy, suggesting that such projects should be paid for by the states from tonnage duties. Northwesterners were furious. Once again they detected what they were convinced was southern influence in administration policy. The *Chicago Daily Journal* spoke for many when it editorially demanded a president who would improve "other rivers besides the political Jordan, whose waters flow only under the peculiar institution, and bear no other cargoes to market than human chattels."[16]

Internal improvement disputes illustrated how sectionalism was becoming a major force in American political life. It worked to disrupt traditional party structures, since many of the issues cut across party lines. Economic interests and considerations of power became the focal point of congressional decisions. The Kansas-Nebraska Act of 1854, the most significant legislation of the Pierce administration, exemplified the workings of sectional politics. The legislation was a response to events far removed from Washington. Involved were the demands of settlers in Missouri and Iowa for the creation of a new western territory, protection of settlers traveling across the plains to the Far West, creation of a safe right-of-way for a transcontinental railroad, the struggle between Senators Thomas Hart Benton and David Rice Atchison for control of Missouri politics, and development of a mid-continent economic and political power base, which would become the center of a growing American trade empire. The political views and ambitions of Stephen A. Douglas, the members of the F Street Mess, and of Salmon P. Chase and the other Free Soilers in Congress added further to the mix. Still another factor was the question of which part of the population should make basic decisions for a local area at a time when the industrial revolution seemed to lead toward more centralization of governmental power. Two of those population elements considered to be outside the political process—Native Americans and slaves—also played important roles in the unfolding drama.

On one level it was a clash of totally different cultures. Indians living in the eastern states had been forced to move west of the Mississippi to land often referred to as Indian Country. There were treaties, but titles were obscure, and some Indian tribes had purchased land from others. Some Indians who had intermarried with whites chose gradual assimilation into white society. The Wyandots, recognizing the inevitability of white settlement of the Nebraska country, took the lead in requesting territorial government for that area. Although some resisted the threat to their hunting grounds, eventually all the Indian tribes agreed by treaty to leave the Nebraska country. Yet at the time of the Kansas-Nebraska controversy the matter was still unresolved, and it became an issue in the debates.[17]

Slavery also contributed a unique ingredient to the emotional overtones of the Kansas-Nebraska question. Missouri slavery demonstrated both the adaptability of the institution to hemp agriculture and the tendency of slaveholders, even when in a small minority, to dominate a region's political institutions. Missouri's Senator David Rice Atchison, who took upon himself the role of Calhoun's successor as a leading defender of slavery, was as early as Stephen A. Douglas in advocating an organized western territory. One historian made the case that Atchison was the primary architect of the Kansas-Nebraska Bill. Missouri slaveholders had long resented the Compromise of 1820, which made the westward extension of their state's southern border— the 36° 30" parallel—the division between slavery and freedom in all the land acquired by the Louisiana Purchase. Many were convinced that slavery could operate profitably in the land to the west, but more than that, they feared that free territory to the west would make their own slave property insecure. They insisted, through Atchison, that legislation creating a new western territory include a provision repealing the 1820 compromise. That was the spark that set a major Free Soil fire in the North. It was clear evidence to northerners of the influence of the slave power.[18]

In 1853 the Nebraska country was considered the huge expanse of land running west of Iowa and Missouri, reaching to the Rocky Mountains to the west and Canada to the north. In the controversy over how that vast territory was to be settled and governed, Stephen A. Douglas played a key role, though he did not act alone. Douglas's presidential ambitions were obvious, and some saw that as his primary motivation. He was deeply involved in land speculation and certainly favored a Pacific railroad, which would help build up Chicago. He recognized the need to provide strong, effective leadership to a divided party. He was also a consistent expansionist and worked to make a reality of his dream of a great national destiny. In 1854 Douglas wrote to a convention at St. Joseph, Missouri, detailing his vision of the United States. Organizing Nebraska Territory was a "national necessity," he said. "How are we to develop, cherish and protect our immense interests and possessions on the Pacific," he asked, "with a vast wilderness fifteen hundred miles in breadth; and filled with hostile savages, and cutting off all direct communication? The Indian barrier must be removed. The tide of emigration and civilization must be permitted to roll onward until it rushes through the passes of the mountains, and spreads over the plains, and mingles with the waters of the Pacific." National considerations required "continuous lines of settlements," said Douglas, and those settlements must be linked by rail and telegraph lines.[19]

Douglas had promoted the idea of a western territory for nearly a decade, and a bill with such an objective was defeated by only a few southern votes during the last term of the Thirty-second Congress. As soon as the new Congress met in December 1853, Senator Augustus C. Dodge of Iowa reintroduced the same bill. Another was introduced in the House, and both were referred to committees on territories. In the Senate that committee was headed by Douglas. On 4 January 1854 Douglas introduced still another bill, creating Nebraska Territory, which would eventually be admitted to the Union as a state or states "with or without slavery, as their constitution may prescribe at the time of admission." Along with the bill was a report calling attention to a difference of opinion as to whether slavery was prohibited in the Nebraska country by any valid enactment, since there was question about the constitutionality of the Missouri Compromise. The committee would not take sides on that issue, but Atchison and other members of the F Street Mess insisted that Douglas side with the South. He then added a section to the bill that he alleged had been left out earlier through a clerical error. Among other things the new section provided that the people of the territory would decide "all questions pertaining to slavery," a restatement of the idea of popular sovereignty. Although Douglas did not spell out how the policy would be implemented, it was an important change that strengthened local self-determination and was a protection against the growing power of the federal government. It also removed Congress from direct involvement in the controversy. If the people were to decide, Congress would not have to.[20]

But Douglas was soon to learn that the political ramifications of the Nebraska Bill were even more complex than the forces that had brought it into being. Southerners rejected the idea of popular sovereignty if it could lead to a Free Soil Nebraska. While Douglas's bill implied repeal of the Missouri Compromise, some insisted that it must be made more explicit. On 16 January Kentucky's Senator Archibald Dixon introduced an amendment repealing that part of the Missouri Compromise that had established the 36° 30" line as the division of free and slave soil west of Missouri. Dixon's move put Douglas in a dilemma. Southern support was essential if the bill were to pass, yet outright repeal of the compromise would stir up what Douglas himself called a "hell of a storm." He reluctantly agreed, without consulting Cass and other party leaders or the president. On 23 January he introduced a new bill to create two territories—Nebraska to the north and Kansas to the south—declaring the Missouri Compromise "inoperative and void."[21]

The importance of dividing the Nebraska country into two territories was overshadowed by the debate over the repeal clause, but it, too, became a matter of sectional controversy. There were already some widely-separated settlements in the Platte and Kansas river valleys, and Douglas recognized that both had future importance. Moreover, each of the territories included a possible route for a transcontinental railroad. As the debate quickened the argument grew simpler: Nebraska, the northern territory, would be free, while Kansas, the land west of Missouri, would be open to slavery. That was the common assumption.[22]

When Douglas modified his bill to include repeal of the Missouri Compromise he had to persuade Pierce to support the revision. Pierce himself, along with most of his cabinet, had resisted the idea, even though he believed that the Missouri Compromise had never been constitutional. The *Washington Union* echoed Pierce's view and condemned the Dixon amendment as well as Charles Sumner's attempt to reenact the slave restriction of the Missouri Compromise. The die was cast, however, when Douglas, through the efforts of Jefferson Davis, arranged a Sunday meeting between Pierce and some leading senators, and the president agreed under great pressure to support the repeal movement. The delegation promised to discuss the matter with Secretary of State Marcy, who was the cabinet's strongest opponent of repeal, but they later let the matter drop. Against his better judgment, Marcy later agreed to support the administration stand. The *Washington Union* then reversed itself, and the bill became an administration measure.

Clearly, it was a case of administration policy formulated in congressional caucus rather than in the White House. Pierce and the cabinet had preferred an amendment that would have reaffirmed the principle of the Compromise of 1850 without openly challenging the Missouri Compromise, but such an amendment was unacceptable to the influential senators in the F Street Mess. They had never accepted the 1820 restriction as constitutional, and now they had their chance to rescind it. Pierce and Marcy and some others in the cabinet realized that open repeal would create a fire storm in the North. But with pressure, Davis and other southern senators could usually bring Pierce around to their position. Besides, he needed their support for the confirmation of Heman J. Redfield as collector of the Port of New York, and apparently a deal was made. Pierce also wanted party support on foreign policy matters pending while the Kansas-Nebraska bill was up for debate. In turn he was able to promise, cajole, and threaten those who might step out of line on the Kansas issue. For Douglas, it was a bold and decisive move. Yet experienced politician though he was, he was seriously out of touch with popular sentiment in the North on a number of issues, including Free Soil.[23]

Early opposition to the measure seemed to be mainly a protest by a handful of Free Soilers in Congress. When Douglas presented the bill to the Senate, Chase requested and won a delay on discussion because it was a new version and some had had no chance to read it. Chase then took the initiative in formulating a strategy of opposition. The objective was to rally public opinion in the North to such a degree that the bill would never become law. In late January the "Appeal of the Independent Democrats in Congress" appeared in northern newspapers. Chase had written the appeal from a draft by Giddings. Other signers were Ben Wade of Ohio, Charles Sumner of Massachusetts, who had refined the language of the document, Alexander DeWitt of Massachusetts, and Gerrit Smith of New York in the lower house. The six attacked the bill "as a gross violation of a sacred pledge; as a criminal betrayal of precious rights; as part and parcel of an atrocious plot to exclude from a vast unoccupied region immigrants from the Old World and free laborers from our own States, and convert it into a dreary region of despotism, inhabited by masters and slaves." The appeal was directed to the people, urging them to refuse to become agents "in extending legalized oppression and systematized injustice over a vast territory yet exempt from these terrible evils." The writers implored ministers and others to protest against the bill "by correspondence, through the press, by memorials, by resolutions of public meetings and legislative bodies," and pledged themselves to "resist it by speech and vote," and with all their abilities. Their appeal was based on the assumption that a slave power conspiracy had forced the repeal of the Missouri Compromise and that the two territories were suggested so that one might be slave and the other free. The Free Soilers believed that slavery could thrive in Kansas as it had in western Missouri. Many others in both sections shared that belief.[24]

There were memorials, petitions from ministers, rallies, resolutions by northern legislatures, and a flood of letters to both houses of Congress. The appearance of a prosouthern administration had rankled many northern voters, and suggested repeal of the Missouri Compromise confirmed their fears. Chase made several strong speeches against it, as did Sumner and Wade. They presented amendments designed to unmask the plot they were convinced was in back of the proposed legislation. Arguing on the assumption of a slave power conspiracy, they presented an array of reasons for defeating the measure. And they received strong support from constituents.

Years later, James G. Blaine wrote that the Kansas-Nebraska Act ''did not merely call forth opposition; it produced a frenzy of wrath on the part of thousands and tens of thousands in both old parties who had never before taken any part whatsoever in antislavery agitation.'' The Kansas proposal was the culmination of a series of acts of apparent southern aggression that included the Fugitive Slave Act and the highly publicized cases growing out of it, the Gadsden Treaty, which paved the way for a southern Pacific railroad, widespread rumors that the administration was about to force the Cuban annexation issue, and a growing suspicion that Jefferson Davis and other southern leaders were the real power behind the Pierce administration. Nothing did more than the Kansas-Nebraska Act to polarize the sections and stimulate a serious movement for a northern political party. There remained differences over the measure in the South, but there, too, a new sense of unity developed rapidly.[25]

The Democrats who opposed the bill were caught between loyalty to their party and loyalty to their section and its interests. As the debate raged, the pressure from northern constituents became almost unbearable. To counter it, Pierce and others in the administration applied pressure of their own. They were especially anxious for support from the New England Democrats led by Hannibal Hamlin of Maine. Cushing went so far as to offer him increased control over patronage. When he refused to yield, Pierce reminded him of the obligations of party members and threatened retaliation, but it had no effect on the Maine senator's position. Such tactics were more successful with others, who still hoped that enacting the legislation would remove the slave controversy from their agenda. Many, like Lewis Cass, had serious reservations, but ultimately they, too, came to support the administration.

Much of the credit for success must go to Douglas, who worked night and day for passage. He answered every criticism and spent many hours behind the scenes making promises and applying pressure. To Douglas it was a test of his and his party's power, a large step forward for the nation, and a vindication of "the great principle of self government." Later he claimed that it was wholly his product.

Early in the morning of 4 March, after a final four-hour speech by Douglas, the Senate voted 37–14 to approve the bill. Enough of the line had held to achieve victory, but the price was yet to be reckoned. Maine's Hannibal Hamlin, along with Charles T. James of Rhode Island, and Henry Dodge and Isaac P. Walker of Wisconsin were the only northern Democrats to defect. The lone southern Democratic dissenter was Sam Houston of Texas. The Whigs voted mostly on sectional lines. The vote was marked by the sound of cannon fire, a symbol of success in the political arena, but a portent of future trouble in the land.[26]

Success in the Senate by no means assured a similar result in the House, where members were far more sensitive to the wishes of their constituents. T. T. Flagler of New York was only one of many who heard the voices of his constituents "in tones deep and unbroken, like that of the mighty cataract on our border, solemnly and earnestly protesting against impairing the Missouri compromise." Northern newspapers and political gatherings, including some of the Democratic party, were crying for defeat of the measure. Salmon Chase hoped that "the Nebraska iniquity Sleeps the Sleep that knows no waking" and that the speeches in the House could be "classified as obituary notices." As early as 21 March, Francis B. Cutting, a New York "Hard," moved that the bill be sent to the committee of the whole where it would be buried under a flood of waiting bills. When that move succeeded by a vote of 110 to 95 the opponents took heart. Then Douglas marshaled every bit of power available to a strong party leader. In the House his manager was Democrat William A. Richardson of Illinois and his ally, Whig-turned-Democrat Alexander Stephens of Georgia, who did as much as anybody to achieve the final result. Douglas left his Senate seat for many days to work for the bill in the other house through caucus meetings and personal visits. After the House agreed to appoint Alfred O. P. Nicholson official printer after the sudden death of Robert Armstrong, the *Washington Union* announced that the president would no longer consider voting for Kansas-Nebraska a test of party loyalty. But administration actions soon belied that statement when the *Washington Union* announced that patronage would be used to win votes.

Pierce also asked a number of northern editors for support, and in interviews with ex-Senator Jeremiah Clemens of Alabama and Senator

Charles T. James of Rhode Island he defended the bill as a measure for freedom. All cabinet members except Marcy and McClelland helped persuade wavering Democrats to vote for the bill. Patronage entered the picture, and deals were made on unrelated matters.

Once more the administration was victorious, despite every possible delaying tactic, including a filibuster. On 8 May Richardson, by a 109–88 vote, got the House to go into a committee of the whole, won eighteen roll call votes to postpone action on bills scheduled ahead of Kansas-Nebraska. Two weeks later, due mostly to the brilliant maneuvering of Alexander Stephens, the Kansas-Nebraska Bill passed the House by a vote of 159–75. Forty-five Democrats, two of them from the South, voted "no." It was thirteen southern Whigs who ensured victory, though none of their northern counterparts voted for the bill. Whig party divisions along north-south lines signaled its death as a national party. Stephens rejoiced. "Nebraska is through the House," he wrote. "I took the reins in my hand, applied whip and spur, and brought the 'wagon' out at eleven o'clock P.M. Glory enough for one day."[27]

Glory surely, but in politics, winning can sometimes prove disastrous. The administration had prevailed, but now it had to meet the payments. Sidney Webster, Pierce's secretary, recognized the danger: "The President is and will be more than heretofore embarrassed by the inducements held out during the pendency of Nebraska," he wrote. In winning, Pierce had also lost in many ways. The resulting polarization made his expansionist dreams still more controversial. Just as he had on other issues, Pierce seemed to be catering to the desire of southern slaveholders for new territory that would be open to their peculiar institution. Although the South had tasted victory in repeal of the Missouri Compromise and the opening of new territories to slavery, the ambiguities implicit in the doctrine of popular sovereignty were bound to produce new problems in the immediate future. Whigs and others who had long worked for payments to the descendants of Americans who had suffered losses through French naval actions during the Napoleonic war were set back once again. Through agreement, a spoliations bill had been postponed until the next session, when it passed only to meet a presidential veto that Congress could not override. Echoes in Missouri of the Kansas-Nebraska fight contributed to the defeat of Thomas Hart Benton, who had led a heroic fight against the bill, in his bid for the Senate. His rival, David Atchison, also failed reelection in a three-way race, leaving Missouri with only one senator for several years. The many interests hoping to begin work on a trans-Pacific railroad suffered a setback, too. Sectional wrangling and Jefferson Davis's insistence on giving priority to a southern route temporarily stymied that important project. Ironically, the group that won the biggest prize was the Free Soil element in Congress and in the northern states. Their dedicated fight against the Kansas-Nebraska Bill, starting with the appeal of Senator Chase as soon as the bill was presented, could not have been better timed. While it did not create the fire storm that swept much of the North, it certainly helped to fan the flames. The bill played a major part in the realignment of American political parties.[28]

While Kansas became a major focal point of politics in early 1854, other forces also contributed to the demise of the Whig-Democrat party system. One of those forces, the temperance crusade, began as a movement for the moderate use of alcoholic beverages but soon acquired a political tone, demanding strict regulation and, beginning with the Maine Law of 1851, statewide prohibition. Many Americans, like their president, drank heavily. Public drunkenness was a much-noted nuisance. Congressmen and other officials faced frequent charges of speaking and voting under the influence. Drinking was a social problem contributing to widespread poverty, illness, and crime. Those who became temperance advocates were often motivated by religious convictions, and Methodists took the lead in declaring drinking liquor a sin. Often, too, temperance reformers were anti-Catholic and anti-immigrant. It was the temperance issue that brought many first-time voters to the polls and gave a major headache to politicians of both parties. When Democrats could not dodge the question they tended to oppose temperance, yet they also had to contend with reformers within their own ranks. Whigs were philosophically more attuned to the idea of government control, though they did not always side with the temperance forces, either. Whig policy on the liquor question differed from place to place.

It was the Free Soilers who almost always embraced the forces of temperance, and in a number of state and local elections a substantial number of Whigs voted Free Soil because of the temperance question. While temperance affected both parties, the Whigs suffered the greatest loss. Combining reform with political action played havoc with the older concept of party loyalty, confounding party stalwarts even in their postelection thinking. After the election of 1853 a Maine Whig wrote William Pitt Fessenden: "What a fog-bank we are in politically! Do you see any head-land or light—or can you get an observation—or soundings?" While he may have been prone to exaggerate, Maine temperance reformer Neal Dow had a point when he noted in his autobiography that the Maine Law movement was the "breaking-up plow" for the political shifts of the 1850s.[29]

A revived and intensified sense of American nativism was an even stronger force making for basic political change. Since the days of the Puritans, religious bigotry in the form of anti-Catholicism had been a powerful strain in American life. Even when there were relatively few Catholics in the United States, prejudice against them sometimes produced strident rhetoric and acts of violence. Exposure of an alleged Catholic conspiracy was part of the stock-in-trade of Protestant evangelists, whose allies in their crusade of religious hatred included such notables as Samuel F. B. Morse and Lyman Beecher. With increased Irish immigration came a stepped-up campaign against the Catholics, and when almost three million immigrants came over in the decade from 1845 to 1853—many of them Irish and German Catholics—the virus of bigotry spread rapidly. Irish Catholics were a special target, since they were often considered tools of the pope, and were held responsible for much urban crime, poverty, and drunkenness. The Vatican was accused of sending them over as part of a plot to transform a republican government into a Catholic tyranny. Several events exacerbated tensions. Early in 1854 the visit of the papal nuncio, Cardinal Bedini, convinced many Americans in the North that a plot to spread Catholicism was a more serious threat than the spread of slavery. When American Catholic bishops criticized the public schools for their Protestant bias and requested public funds for parochial schools, the tension increased. And when Pierce included James Campbell, a Catholic, in his cabinet it seemed to give credence to those who saw the Democrats as coconspirators.

Finally, when secret membership, anti-Catholic organizations began to appear throughout the country it was almost inevitable that fear of a papal conspiracy would find political expression. With both Democrats and Whigs vying for the Catholic vote, it took the form of a third party, the American or Know-Nothing party. It seemed to spring up without warning, taking many old-time politicians by surprise. The natural affinity between Know-Nothing and Free Soil ideas made it possible to combine the issues in one political party. Free Soilers saw Catholics as generally pro-Democrat, which to them meant proslavery. In 1853 and early 1854, Know-Nothing strength in a number of local and state elections hit the older parties without warning. One of Charles Sumner's constituents wrote him in March 1854: "You have seen, doubtless with some surprise, the organization of a new political body in our vicinity, styled the 'Know Nothing.' Their meetings, principles and method of organization are secret." After noting recent Know-Nothing victories in various communities he warned: "They are destined to exert no inconsiderable control in political movements." Another observer asked Sumner if he knew the extent of the Know-Nothing party in New England. "I am informed from various sources," he added, "it is rapidly embracing all other parties even the free soil party. The increasing power and influence of the Catholics, the constant collisions between the masses of Americans and Irish in the lower walks of life," along with armed Catholic military companies and alleged intimidation of judicial officers by Irish defendants had "roused the native American feeling to a much greater degree than is generally supposed." The signs clearly suggested that anti-immigrant, more especially anti-Catholic sentiment, would become the focus for any new political movement should the older parties disintegrate.[30]

Fear and hatred can exert a powerful appeal in politics, but movements stemming from such forces have limited appeal and tend to burn out quickly. That was the case with the Know-Nothing movement, for the American electorate needed a more positive platform from which to gain and wield power. Free Soil was just such a platform for thousands of northerners who were disgusted with the record of both major parties. Discontent had long been festering, and it came to a head with repeal of the Missouri Compromise and several widely-publicized fugitive slave cases. The "Appeal of the Independent Democrats" fell on well-tilled, fertile soil. Its articulate and convincing description of a slave power conspiracy attracted thousands who had paid little heed to the moral preachments of abolitionists. Protest took many forms. There were pamphlets, rallies, congressional caucuses, editorials, and political conventions in virtually every northern state. Anti-Nebraska became an umbrella for those who emphasized Free Soil as well as for antiliquor and anti-Catholic crusaders.

Astute political observers began to sense trouble. Alexander Stephens noted prophetically during the last session of the Thirty-third Congress that public sentiment was in transition. "Old parties, old names, old issues and old organizations are passing away. A day of new things is at hand." One of Sumner's constituents reported that political affairs in Massachusetts were at loose ends. "All parties seem to be approaching that happy state of solution or dissolution, for which we have sighed so long." Yet some in the old parties continued to have faith in traditional patterns. None was more wrong than Stephen A. Douglas. While the Nebraska bill was still pending in Congress he predicted that it would pass in both houses by sizable majorities and that the Democrats would then be stronger than ever, for they would be "united upon principle." Before the fall elections he was confident that his party would gain more votes than it would lose. In April he had confided to Howell Cobb that "the storm will soon spend its fury, and the people of the north will sustain the measure once they come to understand it. . . . The great principle of self government is at stake and surely the people of this country are never going to decide that the principle upon which our whole republican system rests is vicious and wrong."[31]

Douglas may have been right about the great principle of self-government, but he miscalculated the way voters would honor it. State and local elections in the summer and fall of 1854 exposed the strength of the new political forces. Locally, Know-Nothings appeared like magic and elected candidates to numerous offices formerly safe for the Democrats. In the North, fusion tickets, which included Free Soilers, temperance advocates, nativists, and some disgruntled Whigs and Democrats, met with overwhelming success at the polls under the anti-Nebraska banner. In Michigan and a few other northern states fusion efforts assumed the Republican label. Despite every effort of the Pierce administration and the Democratic machine, the fall elections proved a disaster.

"The Democratic banner," lamented an Illinois editor, "has gone down before a torrent of abolitionism, Whigism, freesoilism, religious bigotry and intolerance." Know-Nothings had helped elect 121 members to the new Congress. About a hundred and fifteen anti-Nebraska men were elected. The Democrats had lost every northern state except New Hampshire and California. The new House of Representatives had an anti-Nebraska majority, most of them also nativists. Election victories had been the result of many local coalitions, and it was still unclear where attempts at fusion and organizing a new northern party might go. Douglas was convinced that Know-Nothingism rather than Free Soil was the source of all future trouble, and the strength of nativist prejudice seemed to support his view.[32]

For the Whigs, the 1854 elections proved fatal. Less than 20 percent of the House was Whig and nearly three-fourths of them were from the South. Some had already abandoned ship. In early 1853, after his reelection to Congress, Free Soiler and former Whig Joshua Giddings had commented: "I take it to be well settled that the Whigs will never again rally under their own name." Their disbandment was inevitable, he thought, and he predicted most would fall in with the Free Soilers while the others would join the Hunker Democrats. Seward and several other national Whig leaders had still hoped to transform themselves into a northern national party no longer connected with the southern wing. But the 1854 elections showed such hopes were unrealistic. Despite a remnant that refused to accept the obvious, Whigs aspiring to positions of power would have to join either the Republicans or Know-Nothings. It was still uncertain which choice they would make.[33]

The Pierce administration was a second casualty of the elections. The contrast with the 1852 electoral victory was dramatic. Pierce's poor record with a Congress that was dominated by his own party underlined his weakness and ineptitude. Many Democrats of both sections had come to despise him, and few respected him. Douglas did all he could to improve the Democrats' prospects, but it was far beyond his power to sell the Nebraska Act to northern voters. While the party was still capable of passing some legislation, its program and philosophy were based on a vision of the past rather than the future. More and more northern voters were rebelling against what they saw as the arrogant demands of the slave power. Exactly what shape the new politics would take was murky. What was clear was a strong rejection of the old. For Franklin Pierce, the prospect of a hostile Congress was frightening. Events in Kansas, in Boston, and even on the Senate floor would soon feed the flames of sectional violence, which the Pierce administration had tried so hard to avoid.

5
★ ★ ★ ★ ★

A POLARIZED SOCIETY:
FUGITIVE SLAVES AND
BLEEDING KANSAS

For the Pierce administration and for the country at large, passage of the Kansas-Nebraska bill changed everything. Events in Kansas focused the nation's attention on a struggle for land and power that was reduced in the popular imagination to a simple formula of good and evil, a formula that could not accommodate the complexities of life in territorial Kansas. The usual frontier violence, the presence of a drifting and sometimes irresponsible population, conflicts over land claims, and boosterism in new settlements were all seen as elements in a great ideological struggle. Moreover, southern designs to make Kansas a slave state sharpened northern resentment toward the South and more especially toward demands for the return of fugitive slaves. Incidents of arrest and rescue of fugitive slaves aroused a concern for civil liberties and a determination to confine the hated "peculiar institution" to the South.

In partisan terms the Kansas controversy had a profound impact. Congress neglected such critical issues as economic development of the nation in order to debate the fate of Kansas, for although some politicians tried to do business as usual, tensions over events in the West made that impossible. And in the northern states, temperance reformers, anti-Catholic nativists, antislavery activists, and anti-Nebraska reformers combined in a coalition movement soon to call itself Republican. The conflict over Kansas was a critical factor in crystallizing the new political fusion. Finally, the new Thirty-fourth Congress, with an anti-Nebraska majority in the lower house, gave the nation a dramatic preview of things to come with a protracted and bitter struggle over speakership of the House.

For Franklin Pierce the Thirty-fourth Congress could only mean trouble. Among the newly-elected senators was his old nemesis John P. Hale; other anti-Nebraska newcomers included Lyman Trumbull, a former Democrat from Illinois, and Henry Wilson of Massachusetts. The House still had the dean of antislavery politicians, Joshua Giddings, and his Ohio colleague, Lewis Campbell. Others new to the House were antislavery Whig Justin Morrill, Whig-Republican John Sherman, and Republican Schuyler Colfax. Among the Democrats was newly elected John A. Quitman of Mississippi, an ardent expansionist. Quitman joined Preston S. Brooks and William Aiken of South Carolina, the veterans Howell Cobb and Alexander H. Stephens of Georgia, and William A. Richardson of Illinois. The anti-Nebraska block contained a faction of North Americans or Know-Nothings, as well as Whigs, Free Soilers, Democrats, and Republicans. They all opposed the Kansas-Nebraska Act but found little else on which to agree. Party lines were blurred in such a mix, and observers reached widely differing totals for the various factions.

When Congress met in December 1855 a fight for speakership of the House turned into a prolonged and bitter struggle. Republicans, Whigs, Know-Nothings, and Democrats all had their favorites, men whom they preferred and who wanted the honor and power that went with the position. Timothy Day, congressman from Ohio, commented: "As near as I can ascertain there are about thirty modest men who think the country needs their services in the Speaker's chair. To get rid of this swarm of patriots will take time."[1]

No member of the House was more determined to select an anti-Nebraska speaker than Joshua Giddings, who even hoped for a short while to fill that position himself. Before Congress convened he wrote Free Soiler Salmon P. Chase: "As to the election of a Speaker I feel a deep interest not for myself but for our cause." He was disturbed, though, to learn that half their number appeared to "linger around the old exploded idea of compromising with the South." He would let his colleagues know that he was a candidate and that as speaker he would work to abolish the slave trade on the southern coast and in the District of Columbia and, as far as possible, would "separate the federal government from the support of slavery." Although he was unacceptable as a candidate, Giddings was able to organize a faction of Republicans to vote with him on committee appointments and slavery. Northern Know-Nothings, however, would not accept Giddings's platform, and their support was essential if the Republicans were to elect a speaker.

Before the matter was resolved, seventeen anti-Nebraska candidates got at least a few votes, though the leading contenders were Ohio's longtime Whig-Free Soiler Lewis Campbell and Nathaniel Banks of Massachusetts. William A. Richardson of Illinois, a friend of Stephen A. Douglas, was the hope of the pro-Nebraska Democrats. After several days of rancorous speeches and balloting, Campbell withdrew his name from consideration, later making clear his disappointment at what he considered his betrayal. Banks then became the best hope of the anti-Nebraska forces, even though his political credentials were suspect. He had started his career as a Democrat, then became a Know-Nothing, and finally a Republican. Although Banks was much more moderate on sectional and slavery issues than Giddings, the Ohio congressman decided to support him, hoping that his nativist connections would attract the Know-Nothings into the Republican camp.[2]

It would not be that easy, however. The anti-Nebraska coalition was kept together only through heavy pressure and impressive persuasion from a Banks steering committee. Although some antislavery men did not trust Banks, steering committee members stuck with their man, using the speaker fight effectively to deepen Free Soil feelings in the North. Antislavery writers depicted the voting in Washington as a conflict between freedom and the slave power. Constituents urged their representatives to vote a no-compromise position. Indeed, outside the capital the speakership fight seemed more exciting than scenes in the House would suggest, though from time to time there were nasty exchanges and near violence on the floor. One result was to crystallize northern sentiment in favor of the new sectional Republican party.[3]

While anti-Nebraska congressmen worked for the election of Banks, most Democrats in the House were just as active in support of their candidate, William A. Richardson. Somewhere between the two factions were more moderate anti-Nebraska members who gave their support to Whig-turned-Know-Nothing Henry M. Fuller of Pennsylvania. In fact, at one point in the balloting Fuller replaced Richardson as the pro-Nebraska Know-Nothing candidate. To break the impasse there was much parliamentary maneuvering, talk of continuing the session indefinitely or of adopting a plurality rule.

Meanwhile, without a speaker the House could not organize, the Senate could not act, there could be no legislation, and the president could not deliver his annual message. The impasse was especially irritating to Pierce, who was anxious to show the world a strong nation at a time when the United States was challenging British intrusions on several fronts. Yet Pierce's request for rapid settlement of the speaker contest fell on deaf ears. The House was not about to take orders from the White House. Late in December the wife of Senator Clement C. Clay of Alabama wrote her father-in-law: "The President still holds his message, fearing to give it to the press, . . . he, poor fellow, is worn and weary, and his wife in extremely delicate health." Soon Alexander H. Stephens and Howell Cobb urged Pierce to send his message anyway. The Senate was ready, and that was sufficient.

Pierce was uneasy about breaking a precedent, but in mid-January, after consulting with his cabinet and other advisors, he decided to send his message to Congress and release it to the press and to the American minister in England. Immediately his old political enemy, Senator John P. Hale, went on the attack, severely criticizing both the message and the fact that it was delivered before the House was organized and ready to receive it. Despite such criticism Pierce followed on 24 January with a lengthy special message to Congress in which he summarized the confusing and ominous state of affairs in Kansas Territory, casting most of the blame on the free state faction and requesting legislation to begin the process of Kansas statehood.[4]

Pierce could send messages, but Congress could do nothing more until the House organized. The January session repeated earlier scenes, adding an all-night session and introducing a series of queries on the political views of each candidate. That maneuver further delayed the process, and the answers from various candidates caused realignment of support. After several unsuccessful attempts the House finally accepted a resolution to elect a speaker by plurality on the fourth successive roll call if no candidate received a majority of the votes. By then the pro-Nebraska Democratic candidate was William Aiken, a southern Pierce supporter acceptable to many of the Know-Nothings. Aiken's chances were so promising that Pierce addressed him as "Mr. Speaker" at a White House reception on 1 February. The next day the final vote proved Pierce wrong again. Banks was elected with 103 votes to Aiken's 100 and Fuller's 6, with 4 going to Campbell and one to Daniel Wells.

The decision had taken nine weeks and 133 ballots. The South perceived the outcome as a serious threat while antislavery men, overlooking Banks's moderate views and ambiguous past, saw it as a clear victory for northern principles. "There is a North," exulted one observer. Horace Greeley later commented: "It is memorable as the very first in our National history wherein Northern resistance to Slavery Extension ever won in a fair, stand-up contest, without compromise or equivocation." Joshua Giddings considered the election of Banks a vindication of his own lengthy career as a fighter for freedom. "He was elected upon the identical doctrine for the utterance of which I was driven from this body fourteen years since," he wrote his daughter. "I have reached the highest point of my ambition. *I am satisfied.*" To dedicated antislavery and prosouthern forces, the prolonged contest for the speakership represented another chapter in the eternal struggle between light and darkness.[5]

That same struggle was expressed in the renewed controversy over fugitive slaves. In the compromise package of 1850, the Fugitive Slave Act had been the South's most significant reward, and strict enforcement came to be a test of northern good faith. Many northerners who cared little about the slavery issue resented being forced to help return fugitives to the South. The complete lack of due process for accused fugitives set a dangerous precedent for civil liberties. Nevertheless, despite some dramatic, well-publicized, and sometimes successful attempted rescues, many in the North reluctantly accepted the unpopular act in the interest of preserving the Union. Passage of the Kansas-Nebraska Act in 1854 changed all that. Repealing the Missouri Compromise unleashed resentment in the northern states, seeming to give credence to the abolitionists' charge that a slave power conspiracy would not be satisfied until the whole nation groveled before its dictation. Inevitably there were also many who supported the compromise and the Pierce administration, as well as those who simply could not have cared less. One discouraged Free Soiler was convinced that the country did not care "a copper for the Missouri Compromise." Yet those who did care, cared deeply. And their ranks swelled with news of fugitive slave incidents that coincided with passage of the Nebraska legislation.[6]

From the time of its passage the Fugitive Slave Act kept the debate over slavery alive. The Fillmore administration had been determined to enforce it regardless of northern public opinion. For northern blacks it was a frightening threat, since the new legislation encouraged kidnapping of free blacks, sometimes by a new class of professional slave catchers. Abolitionists reorganized vigilance committees to protect free blacks and to thwart any attempt to return runaway slaves to the South. In a few instances runaways were returned without incident, but attempted arrests of fugitives were likely to be met with effective opposition. Several widely-publicized incidents involved successful rescues. In Boston, William and Ellen Craft, who, on their own, had escaped a thousand miles from Georgia, were hidden and taken away before an agent hired by their former master could have them apprehended. Rescuers in Boston also saved a fugitive named Fred

Wilkins, known as Shadrach, from return to the South, but attempts to rescue Thomas Sims failed. In 1851 in Christiana, Pennsylvania, a slaveholder was shot to death and his son wounded when they attempted to capture a fugitive slave. Several of those on the scene were indicted for treason, though none was convicted. Yet the so-called Christiana Riot got nationwide attention.

Such incidents tended to personalize the debate over slavery. Some former slaves became popular abolitionist speakers and brought the issue alive for many who had been indifferent. It was one thing to listen to abolitionist arguments but quite another to hear a fugitive slave tell of the impact of slavery on human beings. Those fugitives and their autobiographies had the air of authenticity, and they converted large numbers to the antislavery movement. Pursuit of fugitive slaves into the free states proved the abolitionist contention that slavery was national. Harriet Beecher Stowe's *Uncle Tom's Cabin* also created interest in fugitive slaves. Stowe's novel, written as an answer to the Fugitive Slave Act, quickly became an all-time best seller after its first appearance in 1851. As northern citizens became increasingly appalled at the process of returning escaped slaves to bondage, southern spokesmen, in and out of Congress, were demanding that the law be enforced and that all Americans submit to its harsh provisions.[7]

Southern slave owners pointed specifically at actions of northern legislatures in denouncing repeal of the Missouri Compromise and were even more incensed when several states demanded repeal of the Fugitive Slave Act itself. Seven states also enacted personal liberty laws designed to thwart the kidnapping of free blacks and to make it difficult to return a fugitive slave. All those laws were a response to the Nebraska Act. Combined with growing northern resentment against the power that rested on slavery, the result was practical nullification of the law throughout much of the North.

That outcome was intolerable for the Pierce administration. Even Secretary of Interior McClelland, who was less inclined than others in the cabinet to cater to the slave interest, assured the Pennsylvania marshal of federal aid to enforce the unpopular law. Attorney General Caleb Cushing went further. In a series of opinions he strengthened the law beyond the original intent of Congress and sent Pierce legal justification for federal payments to defense counsel in any case where a United States marshal was sued by a black for illegal imprisonment. In another opinion, Cushing said slave owners had the right to remove fugitives from all states and organized territories and even from unorganized territorial possessions of the United States. If no commissioner was available the owner could recapture his slave without legal process.

Later, Cushing declared that a United States marshal in pursuit of a fugitive slave had the authority to enlist all able-bodied men "as a *posse comitatus*" and to call for military force if necessary. He ruled as well that habeas corpus did not apply in cases involving the legal arrest of a fugitive slave. Those judicial opinions reflected the attitude of the Pierce administration and greatly expanded the power of the attorney general.[8]

Although many Americans, before 1854, had been willing to comply with provisions of the Fugitive Slave Act, the uproar over passage of the Kansas-Nebraska Act brought northern opposition to a level not seen before. Events in Boston during the spring of that year added a new dimension to the controversy. On the evening of 24 May Anthony Burns, a fugitive slave, was arrested on a false charge of breaking into a jewelry store. Several nights later the city's leading antislavery reformers held a mass meeting at Faneuil Hall, where Theodore Parker stirred his listeners by referring to them as "fellow-subjects of the State of Virginia." Soon there were calls for a raid on the courthouse where Burns was held. Wendell Phillips tried to dissuade the crowd from reckless action but failed when word came that a mob of blacks was in Court House Square trying to rescue Burns. The crowd rushed to the square just as a small group of blacks, led by vigilance committee member Thomas Wentworth Higginson, was breaking down the door. There was stiff resistance from the marshal and police, and in the scuffle a volunteer policeman was stabbed in the groin, a wound that proved fatal. Burns remained a prisoner.

The next day Marshal Watson Freeman informed President Pierce by wire of the rescue attempt and that there were two companies of U.S. troops stationed in the courthouse. "Everything is now quiet," he concluded. "The attack was repulsed by my own guard." Pierce wired back: "Your conduct is approved. The law must be executed." Three days later the U.S. attorney reported to Washington that he expected armed resistance and asked if the military expense could be paid should they be called out by the mayor. Pierce's answer was unequivocal: "Incur any expense deemed necessary by the Marshal and yourself, for city military or otherwise, to insure the execution of this law." Thus, the same Franklin Pierce who could not find constitutional grounds for providing federal funds for the indigent insane gave a blank check to the Boston courts to return a human being to slavery. Property rights and upholding the law were paramount for him. Seldom was a president so out of touch with popular opinion.[9]

In court, Anthony Burns was defended by the author-lawyer,

Richard Henry Dana, Jr., who held moderate antislavery views. Despite Dana's skilled presentation and the contrasting carelessness of the United States attorney, Commissioner Edward G. Loring ruled that Burns was the slave named in the warrant and must be delivered to his master in Virginia. All available police and federal troops were necessary to escort Burns from the courthouse to a revenue cutter, which took him south. Fifty thousand Bostonians watched as the power of the federal government was enlisted to send one man back to bondage. The city was draped in mourning, and there were shouts of "Shame!" as the battle-ready troops marched by with their prisoner. Cost estimates ranged as high as $100,000 for Burns's trial and return to slavery. The *Richmond Enquirer,* angered at public reaction in Boston, called the incident "a mockery and an insult."

In Boston there was talk of prosecuting the antislavery men who had attempted to rescue Burns and were thus involved in the death of the volunteer policeman. Although murder charges were ruled out, Higginson, Parker, and several others were indicted for riot. The trial was postponed until the spring of 1855, when the judge quashed all the indictments on technical grounds. It was just as well, for it was unlikely that any Boston jury would have convicted those defendants.[10]

Public opinion in the North, especially in Boston, had changed drastically since 1851 when Thomas Sims was sent back to slavery from that city. In the three intervening years the Pierce administration had reopened the simmering controversy over slavery, and a long period of abolitionist preaching was beginning to bear fruit. Fugitive slave incidents pointed up civil liberties issues, while increased demands from slaveholders brought heightened resistance in the North. The timing of the Burns incident had a powerfully negative impact on the slave power. Although it was a cruel blow to Burns himself and seemed to be a defeat for antislavery forces, the case crystallized Free Soil sentiment and heightened opposition to the Fugitive Slave Act. "Thank God," wrote a constituent to Charles Sumner, "the chains that have bound the people to their old organizations, have been snapped assunder." The arrest of Burns and threats to Sumner coming on the heels of the "nefarious Nebraska bill," thought another, did more than anything else "to unite the good men of all parties in a common sentiment of hostility to the encroachments of the slave power." Theodore Parker was jubilant. "More than 1900 persons signed the Petition for the Repeal of the Fugitive Slave Bill," he exulted, "most of them men who supported that wickedness before. . . . Affairs never looked more promising than now." In his journal, Richard Henry Dana confided similar sentiments. "Men who were hostile or unpleasant in 1851," he wrote, "are now cordial and complimentary, and the prevailing talk among merchants and lawyers is that of hostility to slavery and the slave power.'' The picture was clear. Yet Pierce and his cabinet officers seemed oblivious to the impact of Free Soil sentiment in the North. Even as matters were getting out of hand they failed to understand, preferring instead to view apparent victories, like Burns's rendition, as proof that their policies were working.[11]

The cornerstone of those policies was enforcement of the law, though few slaves were returned under its provisions and even fewer rescuers prosecuted. Yet there were enough incidents to spark northern opposition to making concessions to the slave power. In 1854, Sherman M. Booth and three others were arrested in Wisconsin for assisting in the rescue of Joshua Glover, a fugitive slave who had been working on a farm near Racine. The Booth case received national attention because it was one of several that created a jurisdictional dispute between state and federal authorities. After Booth's conviction in federal court his lawyer appealed to a Wisconsin court, which issued a writ of habeas corpus and declared the Fugitive Slave Act void in that state. To shouts of joy from onlookers, the Wisconsin Supreme Court affirmed the decision. Soon, however, a federal judge ordered Booth's rearrest, prompting the *Milwaukee Free Democrat* to comment: ''If President Pierce wishes to create an Anti-Slavery sentiment that nothing short of the total abolition of slavery will quiet, he cannot accomplish it in any other way as soon as by sending into each State such tools of Slave Power as this same Judge Miller.'' Legal questions in the Booth case were not settled until 1859 when Supreme Court Chief Justice Roger B. Taney wrote, in *Ableman* v. *Booth,* that the power of federal courts transcended state courts on constitutional questions. Taney's ruling also affirmed the constitutionality of the Fugitive Slave Act.[12]

Had that ruling come four years earlier it would not have stopped such fugitive slave incidents, which helped to influence a growing spirit of northern nationalism. In Philadelphia Passmore Williamson, secretary of the Pennsylvania Anti-Slavery Society, ran afoul of the law when he advised a slave woman that, since she was on free territory, she was free. A group of Philadelphia blacks then helped Jane Johnson and her two children to escape. The man who claimed her as his slave was John H. Wheeler, the United States minister to Nicaragua, who was en route to that country. Wheeler got a writ of habeas corpus from a federal court, hoping that it would force Williamson to reveal the location of the fugitives. The judge found Williamson evasive and jailed him for contempt. Williamson probably did not know where Jane Johnson and her children were, but his ordeal stirred abolitionists to publicize it as another example of the slave power running roughshod over the rights of northern citizens. While in a Philadelphia prison, Williamson received notes of support and congratulation from antislavery sympathizers throughout the North. Members of the Western Anti-Slavery Society, in session in Alliance, Ohio, sent reassurances to the abolitionist that his incarceration would teach the American people that their own power was at risk "while the slave power rules—that while it is in the ascendancy law will be prostituted to do its bidding, and in the name of justice the grossest enormities perpetrated." Herbert Gard, a citizen of Trenton, New Jersey, wrote Williamson: "I am glad slavery has laid its hateful paw on a free, white male citizen of pure blood."

Williamson himself was confident that the ordeal would have a good effect. "History teaches," he wrote, "that communities are disposed to tolerate the grossest errors and sustain existing wrongs, until some great outrage has been committed in their behalf, which has stricken their individual members with terror for their personal safety. This has never been more thoroughly illustrated than in the Anti Slavery agitation of this Country." The use of contempt procedures to force obedience to the Fugitive Slave Act proved counterproductive. While proadministration and southern editors castigated Williamson, Jane Johnson remained free, and northerners became increasingly sympathetic to the former slave and to the abolitionists. After three months in jail Williamson returned to court where he said he had not intended contempt nor to evade the legal process. Judge John K. Kane accepted the statement, ordered Williamson released, and closed the case.[13]

In Ohio, several incidents fueled the sectional fire. In April 1855 a sixteen-year-old slave, Rosetta Armstead, was taken in Columbus from her owner's agent, with whom she had been traveling, and delivered to a probate judge who appointed a guardian for her when she said she wished to be free. Her owner, armed with a writ for her arrest, had Rosetta taken to Cincinnati for trial under the Fugitive Slave Act. Then followed another conflict between state and federal authorities. Before the commissioner could try the case in federal court, a common pleas judge pronounced her free. The marshal who rearrested her was held for contempt of court until Federal Judge McLean overruled the contempt charge. Ultimately the commissioner decided against the slaveholder and freed Rosetta Armstead, but by then both sides had become thoroughly agitated. A Kentucky editor, noting that Cincinnati commerce depended heavily on southern patronage, threatened: "If she is determined . . . to submit to the government of a few over-zealous Ethiopians and fanatical abolitionists, and to broaden the already broad line of demarcation between us, the trade of the South will seek out new channels, and her business be done in some place other than the 'Queen City.' "[14]

Despite such threats, antislavery sentiment in Cincinnati grew. Early in 1856 that city witnessed a fugitive slave incident so tragically dramatic that—more than a century later—it would provide raw material for Toni Morrison's Pulitzer Prize–winning novel, *Beloved*. Eight slaves, including Margaret Garner and her three children, had escaped from Kentucky and found a hiding place in Cincinnati. A master of some of them got a warrant and tracked down the fugitives. In desperation, as officers approached her hiding place, Margaret Garner cut her daughter's throat to prevent the child's return to slavery but was stopped before she could kill her two small sons. Complicated legal maneuvers followed, with Ohio authorities seeking to hold Margaret Garner for murder. Undoubtedly, Governor Salmon P. Chase hoped that the process would free Garner, but before that could happen, United States Commissioner John L. Pendery returned the fugitives to Kentucky. There the governor was ready to extradite the woman to Ohio, but her master kept her out of reach of the authorities. It was a legal impasse, but a practical victory for slave owners. "There is no hope for the slave," declared the Western Anti-Slavery Society, "but over the ruins of this tyrannical and bloodstained Union." In contrast, the *Cincinnati Daily Enquirer* rejoiced that "the sovereignty of the United States was vindicated." Still, it was at best a Pyrrhic victory for southern interests. The story of Margaret Garner circulated widely, destroying the myth of satisfied slaves, and Republicans exploited the incident. Indeed, the editor of the proadministration *Enquirer* wrote correctly of the tragedy: "Not since Chase's election have the Black-Republicans had such a victory."[15]

In faraway Kansas Territory, too, spreading fires of sectional conflict were benefiting the new Republican party. David R. Atchison and others who represented the slaveholding interests in Missouri believed a Free Soil Kansas would threaten slavery everywhere. A free state to their west, they feared, would tempt antislavery groups to run off slaves, and soon the Free Soil virus would spread to the border states until slavery, confined to a small enclave, could not survive. Wrote a contributor to a southern magazine: "If Kansas is not secured, there will never be another slave state, and the abolitionists will then rule the nation; the Union will then become a curse rather than a blessing." Yet what Missourians saw as a problem became an opportunity for northern advocates of Free Soil, who were equally determined. William Seward summarized the Free Soil view in the Senate after passage of the Kansas-Nebraska Bill: "Come on then, Gentlemen of the Slave States, since there is no escaping your challenge, I accept it in behalf of the cause of freedom. We will engage in competition for the virgin soil of Kansas, and God give the victory to the side which is stronger in numbers as it is in the right."[16]

Under such explosive conditions it was important that procedures for settlement in Kansas be well established and that the territorial officers be fair-minded. Unfortunately, neither was the case. Kansas Territory was opened for settlement on 30 May 1854, before all Indian titles had been adjusted or the Indians removed. In fact, the opening was a breach of faith with the Indians, who had been given that land for their own use. With settlers moving to the territory before the land was legally available, everyone there was a squatter. In 1856 Governor John W. Geary reported: "One of the greatest, if not *the* greatest, obstacle to overcome in the production of peace and harmony in the Territory, is the unsettled condition of the claims to the public lands." Soon after, in November 1856, the government held its first land sale in Kansas Territory, though some settlers could not legally purchase the land they claimed for another twelve years. More than 25 percent of the land— fifteen million acres—was technically closed to settlement. The scramble for good land and confusion over titles became major factors in the Kansas upheaval, yet the partisan press reported the struggle in simplistic terms, a clash between good and evil.[17]

Franklin Pierce tended to view events just as simplistically. Only those who supported the Kansas-Nebraska Act with its repeal of the Missouri Compromise were, in his eyes, true to the Union. He appointed no one with Free Soil ideas to important positions in Kansas. The three men he appointed as territorial governors, at least at the outset, were loyal to Democratic policies. Lower-ranking officials were even more inclined to take the southern side in sectional disputes. The first of the three Kansas governors Pierce appointed was Andrew H. Reeder, a 47-year-old lawyer and party regular from Easton, Pennsylvania, who was known to sympathize with the southern view of Kansas settlement. He had no frontier experience and lacked administrative ability. Commissioned on 19 June 1854, Reeder did not reach Kansas until the fall, when he spent as much time selecting sites for his own speculative activity as he did studying the people and their interests. Pierce ordered Reeder's dismissal in July 1855.

His successor was Wilson Shannon, a Cincinnati lawyer who had served as congressman, governor of Ohio, and minister to Mexico. While Reeder had moderated his prosouthern views and became, after his removal as governor, a leader in the free state movement, Shannon was more decisively in favor of introducing slavery into Kansas as a concession to Missouri. By the summer of 1856 Shannon found himself unable to control the political turmoil in the territory and resigned, placing the extreme prosouthern territorial secretary, Daniel Woodson, in the position of acting governor. Finally, after his repudiation by the Democratic convention of 1856, Pierce appointed a strong and capable governor, John W. Geary, whose fairness and evenhanded approach brought temporary relief to that troubled territory. Unfortunately, the territorial judicial system included Samuel D. Lecompte of Maryland and Rush Elmore of Alabama, two extreme southern rights men. The Pierce appointments were clearly a part of the problem in Kansas.[18]

Attempts to polarize the territorial population over slavery was an even greater source of trouble for the administration. Even before the Kansas-Nebraska Bill became law, Eli Thayer, a flamboyant Yankee school teacher and politician, devised a plan to combine profit-making with assurances that Kansas would become a free state. In April 1854, Thayer got the Massachusetts legislature to incorporate the Massachusetts Emigrant Aid Company, which aimed to raise money, publicize Kansas, and attract settlers to the territory, where the organization would then promote mills, hotels, and other enterprises to serve public needs. Liability concerns for the stockholders prompted Thayer to acquire a new charter for what was renamed the New England Emigrant Aid Company.[19]

Rather than Garrisonian abolitionists, the Emigrant Aid Company was composed of moderate Free Soil men, including such members of the New England elite as John Lowell, Dr. Samuel Cabot, and Amos Lawrence, who served as treasurer for many years. The stockholders viewed a free Kansas as both an essential element in their industrial capitalist economy and an important step in humanitarian reform. Above all, they looked for a good return on their investments. Although the company sent relatively few settlers to Kansas Territory, it did play an important role in setting up new towns and helping to formulate and popularize an antislavery position. More important, it became a hated symbol of New England interference in the natural frontier process, especially to those Missourians who held slaves and lived near the border. When the Kansas issue was projected on the national screen, the Pierce administration attacked the company as the root of all the troubles in the territory.[20]

The Emigrant Aid Company was only half the root of those troubles, for it was one of two polarizing elements in Kansas Territory. The other originated in bordering Missouri, where slaveholders were as determined to take their institutions into the newly-opened country as the New England settlers were to keep them out. They were led and encouraged by David Atchison and other prosouthern activists like Dr. John Stringfellow. Behind the rhetoric was essentially a struggle for land and power. A new territory—ultimately a new state—offered the chance for political careers and government jobs, and especially the chance to gain wealth through land speculation. Heightened tensions followed Atchison's appeal for young men from the slave states to settle in Kansas and to come "well armed." Of several southern emigration plans, the most significant was the work of Col. Jefferson Buford of Alabama, who spent a small fortune advertising for Kansas recruits and offering to pay their expenses for a year until they could manage for themselves. In the spring of 1856, Buford, who carried a large Bible, and about three hundred followers left Montgomery, Alabama, for Kansas, convinced that God was on their side. Still, lengthy and heated discussions in other southern communities persuaded only a small number to assist the Missourians in their struggle.[21]

Instead, it was settlers from the older, midwestern states, where slavery had never been permitted, who formed the majority in Kansas. They were not activists on either side of the slavery issue but were interested rather in building a life on a newly-opened frontier. Yet even the first political test demonstrated that the slave issue could not be ignored in Kansas. When Governor Reeder scheduled an election for territorial delegate in November 1854, nearly two thousand of the voters were Missourians who came into Kansas only for that purpose. Predictably, a proslavery Tennesseean and Indian agent, John W. Whitfield, was elected. That incident set the pattern. Elections the following March were just as tainted when Missourians again flooded into Kansas Territory to elect an extreme proslavery legislature. Free state settlers labeled it a "Bogus Legislature," but the Pierce administration consistently recognized it as the legitimate authority.[22]

Realizing the extent of fraud in the election, Governor Reeder returned to Washington to report to the president. Stopping in Easton, Pennsylvania, his hometown, he characterized the recent voting process as shameful. "Kansas has been invaded," he declared, "conquered, subjugated by an armed force from beyond her borders, led on by a fanatical spirit." For several weeks Reeder had daily appointments with Pierce, who seemed to be impressed with his report but scolded the governor for not criticizing free state settlers as sharply as he criticized the southerners. In fact, Pierce was under increasing pressure to get rid of Reeder, who would not accept hints that he resign.

Instead he returned to Kansas and a series of confrontations with the new legislature. Reeder wanted it to meet at Pawnee, where he had extensive land claims, but the legislators decided to meet at Shawnee Mission, which was closer to Missouri. The governor vetoed a resolution changing the place of the territorial capital, only to have his veto quickly overridden. When legislators reassembled at Shawnee Mission they revised and adopted many of Missouri's statutes. Under those proslavery laws Kansas residents could be jailed for reading a Free Soil newspaper or for declaring slavery illegal in the territory; only slaveholders could hold office; the punishment for refusing to take an oath supporting the Fugitive Slave Law was disfranchisement; and for circulating any publication that might incite a slave revolt, the penalty was death. Reeder vetoed every such bill, and the legislature overturned every one of his vetoes. Such legislation was enacted partly to assure that Kansas would be a slave state, partly to demonstrate to the South that the line against Free Soil had been drawn. Reporting to an Alabama newspaper, John Stringfellow's brother Ben said: "They now have laws more efficient to protect slave property than any State in the Union. These laws have just taken effect, and have already silenced the Abolitionists; for, in spite of their heretofore boasting, they know they will be enforced to the very letter and with the utmost vigor. Not only is it profitable for slaveholders to go to Kansas, but politically it is all-important."[23]

Pressure mounted on the administration to get rid of Reeder, and in July 1855 Pierce fired him as governor. The president was distressed at Reeder's apparent sympathy with the free state faction, a perception that kindled the wrath of the legislature and of its friend Atchison. Moreover, Reeder was vulnerable because of his deep involvement in land schemes. In partnership with two judges, Reeder had contracted for the purchase of large tracts of land that had been reserved for mixed-blood Indians. Indian Commissioner G. W. Manypenny, himself sympathetic to the southern faction, reported to Washington that the contracts were clearly an attempt to cheat the Indians of valuable lands, and the report provided an excuse for Pierce's action. Apparently, Manypenny was genuinely trying to protect Indian rights as well as catering to the South. To appear impartial, Pierce also dismissed two southern judges, but in their place he appointed two strong, proslavery men. Col. William Montgomery, the commander at Fort Riley, was court-martialed and removed from the army for permitting Reeder and his associates to occupy part of the land within the military reservation.[24]

For the second Kansas territorial governor Pierce appointed Wilson Shannon, a lawyer and politician from Cincinnati. Shannon was proslavery, and as soon as he reached Kansas he made clear his unequivocal support for the elected legislature. It was obvious that he would not be as evenhanded as Reeder. Facing a prosouthern governor, a "bogus legislature," and a strong proslavery judiciary, the free state faction had to make counter moves if it was to have a chance at its objective. A convention met to stimulate discussion and lay the ground for a free state political party. The gathering was dominated by the colorful and extreme Jim Lane, Charles Robinson, who represented the Emigrant Aid Company, S. C. Pomeroy, and former Governor Reeder. Denying that its participants were abolitionists, the convention condemned the "miscalled legislature," which had "trampled under foot the Kansas bill, . . . defiled the power of Congress, . . . libelled the Declaration of Independence, violated the constitutional bill of rights, and brought contempt upon . . . republican institutions at home and abroad." Delegates vowed to defy the laws of the "so-called legislature" and to fight, if necessary. They made plans to hold their own election for territorial delegate and to meet as a possible constitutional convention in Topeka on 19 September.

By the end of 1855 the free state party had elected Reeder its congressional delegate and had established a free state constitution, which included a Negro exclusion clause to be voted on later. In January 1856 another election chose Robinson as governor. In effect the faction had taken the first step in a political revolution, establishing an alternative government to the one that was officially recognized. All those moves, by both parties, were reported in detail and with considerable exaggeration in the press.[25]

Such a political impasse and the explosive nature of the slavery issue made armed conflict in Kansas almost inevitable. Although open warfare did not erupt at once, the incidents around Lawrence in December 1855 became known as the "Wakarusa War." Governor Shannon considered the Topeka free state movement a conspiracy to subvert public order and evade duly constituted authority. Certainly by the end of 1855 both factions were preparing for war. An important element in that preparation was the arrival of large numbers of Sharps rifles for use by the free state group. An early breechloader that fired ten shots a minute, the Sharps was one of the most efficient weapons then available. The rifles were nicknamed "Beecher's Bibles" because Henry Ward Beecher had said that the guns would do more for the morals of the "Border Ruffians" than the Bible. His congregation donated twenty-five rifles for the Kansas troops.

The murder of Charles Dow, a free state settler, by a prosouthern settler over a land claim threatened to ignite the conflagration. Sheriff Samuel J. Jones of Douglas County ignored the murder, while free state settlers demanded it be punished. A free state vigilance committee set fire to the cabins of three witnesses who refused to testify, and when Jones arrested a member of the committee the man was rescued by friends. That convinced Governor Shannon that the free state faction must be punished and made to accept the established authority. His call for a militia brought few responses in Kansas, but hundreds came from Missouri to join the expedition. He also asked for help from the army, but Col. E. V. Sumner, who commanded the Fort Leavenworth troops, would not act without orders from the president. The militia, largely an undisciplined mob, moved toward Lawrence but hesitated at knowledge of the Sharps rifles in the free state ranks.

In the end there was no attack. Governor Shannon negotiated an agreement with the free state group, which wisely refrained from starting a skirmish. The free staters agreed not to obstruct the law, and Shannon agreed to permit them to defend themselves. The Missourians returned home, having been urged by David Atchison not to destroy Lawrence. Such action, he said, would only bring about the election of an abolitionist president. "Wait a little," he cautioned. "You cannot now destroy these people without losing more than you would gain." The Wakarusa Treaty helped the free state cause in several ways. Governor Shannon, aware during the negotiations of the viciousness of some "border ruffians," moderated his proslavery views. Moreover, Lawrence was safe, and the governor had given tacit recognition to its government. The bitter Kansas winter also contributed to a brief interlude of peace.[26]

It proved to be the calm before a storm. Even during the terrible winter—one of the worst on record—there were isolated incidents of violence. Part of the Kansas drama was played out in Washington. The fate of the territory assumed national significance on 24 January 1856 when President Pierce, perhaps under the influence of Jefferson Davis and Caleb Cushing, sent to Congress a special message on the controversy. Although he criticized former Governor Reeder's official deeds and his speculative activity, Pierce based his support for the proslavery legislature on the fact that Reeder had accepted it as a legal body. He refused to differentiate among the laws it passed, insisting that they were all valid and that he would uphold them with the use of force if necessary. He condemned the Topeka Constitution and the request of the free state party for statehood under it. He alluded only briefly to the Missouri invasion, which was the basis for the proslavery legislature, blaming the Kansas troubles on "inflammatory agitation," which for twenty years had produced "nothing save unmitigated evil, North and South." Without such agitation, he insisted, the Kansas issue would have aroused little emotion. Instead, soil, climate, hard work, and the hope of rapid advancement would have led the settlers themselves to decide the question quietly, "with good wishes, but with no interference from without." He recommended that as soon as there were enough settlers in Kansas Territory they should elect delegates to a constitutional convention to prepare for statehood "through regular and lawful means," and he asked Congress to enact the necessary legislation.[27]

The clear bias of the message in condemning the entire Free Soil movement had repercussions throughout the nation. Southern opinion-makers cheered Pierce's strong stand, while in Ohio, Governor Salmon P. Chase answered with a special message of his own to that state's legislature. Chase, with presidential ambitions, undoubtedly thought that leading an Ohio crusade for a free Kansas would improve his chances for the White House. With his own remarks he sent a letter from two Kansas leaders who told of an army gathering on the Missouri border "for the avowed purpose of invading our territory, demolishing our towns, and butchering our unoffending Free-State citizens." The legislature accepted Chase's recommendation for resolutions of sympathy and support for a free Kansas. The Ohio action prompted similar expressions in other northern states. A constituent from Alton, Illinois, wrote the newly-elected Senator Lyman Trumbull: "What is the matter with *your* president—Franklin Pierce? He seems to be *a fugitive from freedom* . . . We of the free States must call for a law to re-capture *our fugitives*—though the President is hardly worth pursuing into the back parts of South Carolina or Georgia." As events in the territory unfolded and it became clear that the administration would support the prosouthern legislature at all costs, such views were commonplace in the press and on the street.[28]

The arrival in Washington of former Governor Reeder and John W. Whitfield, each claiming to be the legally-elected territorial delegate to Congress, gave that body an opening to become involved. After a series of heated debates the House voted to accept a resolution proposed by George Dunn of Indiana to send to Kansas a three-member fact-finding team. The commission, to be chosen by the speaker, was to collect evidence of election fraud and violent acts and would have full power to demand access to all available evidence. It was an important victory for the free state faction. In the Senate the temperature was also rising rapidly. After a two-month illness, Stephen A. Douglas returned to his desk on 12 March when, as chair of the Committee on Territories, he offered a report giving his view of the Kansas troubles. Douglas believed that Pierce was correct in his policies. Disregarding widespread Free Soil sentiment in Kansas, Douglas laid all responsibility for the troubles on the struggling Emigrant Aid Company.

His report sparked more controversy. Congress soon had before it two proposals for Kansas statehood. The one, sponsored by Douglas, provided for a census that could precede a legislative provision for electing delegates to a constitutional convention. Until there was sufficient population for statehood, proslavery officials would rule the territory. The Douglas bill could never pass the Senate. Nor could the other, sponsored by William Seward, which asked for immediate admission of Kansas as a free state under the Topeka constitution. Georgia's Senator Robert Toombs then submitted a proposal based on the Douglas bill but with some significant concessions to the North. Even staunch Free Soilers Hale and Seward conceded that the measure had much to commend it, and it eventually passed the Senate. Yet in midsummer it died in the Republican-dominated House because of suspicion that Pierce and his appointees would not administer it fairly. Even Amos Lawrence believed the administration would implement the Toombs bill in good faith, but his support did not save it. Douglas saw the Republican rejection as nothing but a power move. "All these gentlemen want," he charged, "is to get up murder and bloodshed in Kansas for political effect. They do not mean that there shall be peace until after the presidential election."[29]

Indeed, a limited civil war was already raging in Kansas. As spring moved across the prairie, sporadic incidents of violence flared into open warfare. In early May a grand jury under the guidance of Judge Samuel Lecompte indicted Andrew Reeder, James Lane, and Charles Robinson for treason, two free state Lawrence newspapers, the *Herald of Freedom* and *Kansas Free State*, for their "inflammatory and seditious language," and the Free State Hotel for being "regularly parapeted and port-holed for use of small cannon and arms." Reeder and Lane evaded arrest, but Robinson was apprehended and held for trial. Those actions coincided with the work of the three-man congressional delegation that was then taking testimony from Kansas settlers. It was while meeting with the delegation that Andrew Reeder resisted attempts of a United States marshal to arrest him. A contempt charge was then added to the indictment for treason.[30]

Governor Shannon returned from Washington to find the territory drifting into serious violence. In addition to shootings, including some killings, there was a good deal of horse stealing by members of both factions, who rationalized such thefts as retribution or even as acts of war. Disturbed by what was happening, Shannon called out federal troops to help restore order. One of the more serious incidents was the shooting and serious wounding of Douglas County Sheriff Samuel J. Jones, an act that shocked responsible settlers on both sides of the conflict. In mid-May the United States marshal called for a posse to help serve the grand jury papers. A mob of border ruffians, headed by Jones, Atchison, Buford, and other proslavery leaders, responded by marching into Lawrence. Although the free state settlers of Lawrence used only nonviolent tactics, the mob fired artillery shells at the Free State Hotel and then burned it down. They also burned Robinson's home and destroyed both of the free state presses. The only death occurred when part of the burning hotel fell on a proslavery man.

With wild exaggeration, many northern newspapers depicted the vandalism as the "Sack of Lawrence," while in the South it was heralded as a "Glorious Triumph of the Law and Order Party Over Fanaticism in Kansas." In the North, the nonresistance of the free staters aroused a great deal of latent sympathy, for while the sheriff and his gang had made their point, they had lost heavily in the struggle for the hearts and minds of the northern people. In part it was a struggle among various factions to control the territorial government and reward followers with such favors as recognition of land claims. Yet those factors were totally ignored by the press. Once again it was portrayed as a struggle between the forces of light and the forces of darkness.[31]

While events were taking so violent a turn in Kansas Territory that the term "Bleeding Kansas" would soon be commonplace, another violent event in the hall of the Senate considerably escalated the tension between the sections. Since he entered the Senate in 1851, Charles Sumner of Massachusetts had proved anathema to the southern faction. He had engaged in heated exchanges over his various proposals to repeal the Fugitive Slave Act and had been the subject of frequent threats. As violence in Kansas increased, Sumner wrote Salmon Chase of his determination to make the most significant speech of his career. "My soul is wrung by this outrage," he said, "and I shall pour it forth." And pour it he did, in an eloquent, provocative oration. He not only spoke of a widespread conspiracy involving the Pierce administration to foist slavery on the settlers of Kansas, but he also leveled insulting personal attacks on Stephen A. Douglas, Virginia's James Mason, and South Carolina's Andrew Pickens Butler. Even Seward had asked Sumner to avoid personal attacks in his talk. Lewis Cass denounced the speech as "un-American and unpatriotic," suggesting that it made Sumner subject to "the highest censure and disapprobation." Douglas charged that Sumner had carefully planned the insults, had "repeated [them] from night to night in order to catch the appropriate grace," and had then risen in the Senate to "spit forth that malignity" upon men who did not share his opinions. Sumner's object, suggested Douglas, had been "to provoke some of us to kick him as we would a dog in the street, that he may get sympathy upon the just chastisement."[32]

Douglas's remarks only underscored the damage that Sumner had already inflicted on the effect of his presentation by such calculated and excessive personal attacks. Yet to Congressman Preston S. Brooks of South Carolina, a relative of the aged, well-respected Senator Butler, verbal chastisement was not enough. Two days after the speech, as Sumner sat at his Senate desk, Brooks approached with a small gutta-percha walking stick. Declaring the speech a libel on South Carolina and on Senator Butler, he began striking Sumner with the cane. Startled and in pain, Sumner wrenched the desk from its mooring and fell, bleeding profusely from scalp wounds. A doctor thought Sumner would be fit to return to full-time work within a week, but the physical and psychological damage prevented his return to the Senate until 1859. Although Sumner's wounds were serious, hostile newspapers circulated rumors that he was malingering. Republican politicians capitalized on the vacant chair of the Massachusetts senator as mute testimony to the perfidy of the slave power.[33]

Even though Sumner was unable to carry out his duties, Massachusetts voters reelected him in 1857. An investigating committee of the House recommended expulsion for Brooks, but the entire body would pass only a resolution of censure. Brooks resigned but was quickly reelected to his House seat. Essentially a bullying attack answering words with blows, the incident further polarized the sections. Although cool heads and responsible voices north and south kept opinions from being unanimous, much of the press reported the matter in simplistic terms. "Every southern man sustains me," wrote Brooks to his brother, encouraged in that view by the many messages he had received. The *Richmond Enquirer* editorialized: "We consider the act good in conception, better in execution, and best of all in consequences. The Vulgar Abolitionists in the Senate are getting above themselves. . . . They must be lashed into submission." A South Carolinian wrote Sumner: "If you infernal abolitionists don't mind your own business at home, and let ours alone, the People at the south, will take the matter in hand themselves and go in a mass to the Capital—tar and feather—horse-whip and expel every rascal of you." The long overdue punishment, thought many southerners, would cause Free Soilers to cease their attacks on the South.[34]

In reality the attack on Sumner had precisely the opposite effect, contributing substantially to the growth of a northern Free Soil political party. Many moderates, including some Democrats, viewed the attack as a clear attempt to destroy free speech in the North. It was the slave power, they said, demanding that the same restrictions on liberty that it inflicted on the southern population now be mandatory in the North as well. "It was not yourself alone for whom the blow was aimed," wrote a constituent to Sumner. "It was aimed at Massachusetts, at every antislavery man in the country, and especially at free speech." Another saw the attack as "legitimate fruit of that worst despotism—*Slavery*. It is a repetition of what is taking place, weekly, in Kansas, and daily on every plantation in the South." Sumner's caning, wrote a third, had changed him "from a decided pro-slavery man into as decided a supporter of the Republican or Northern ticket, be the names on it what they may."

Sympathy rallies in Boston, New York, and other northern cities led moderates, who previously had ignored the antislavery forces, to support a sectional cry of indignation and anger. Typical was the political transition of moderate Whig George Templeton Strong to the ranks of the Republican party. Strong had detested the idea of a one-section party, considering it a threat to the Union. Yet after hearing of Sumner's beating he recorded in his diary: "I hold the anti-slavery agitators wrong in principle and mischievous in policy. But the reckless, insolent brutality of our Southern aristocrats may drive me into abolitionism yet." Bleeding Sumner was to take its place with Bleeding Kansas as a rallying cry for pronorthern sentiment.[35]

Word of the "Sack of Lawrence" arrived at about the same time as news of the attack on Sumner. By then Kansas was moving into a period of guerrilla war, hastened by John Brown and his followers in their move to avenge the attack on Lawrence. Brown had moved to Kansas in 1855, following five of his sons, who had emigrated primarily to improve their economic situation. In Kansas, Brown's obsession with antislavery surfaced, and though he played only a minor role in the early struggle, he seemed determined to force a violent confrontation and to become a major player in that confusing scene. Judge Sterling G. Cato's proslavery court may have considered prosecuting him along with others who were under indictment for treason. At any rate, Brown decided to avenge Lawrence. On the night of 24 May, with four of his sons and two other men, he forced five proslavery settlers from their homes in the Pottawatomie country and shot or hacked them to death. Several of the bodies were horribly mutilated. Although precise motives were never established, all those killed had had some connection with Judge Cato's court. When word of the killings circulated, many free state settlers were shocked beyond belief. Some accused the Indians of the crime. Eastern promoters of Kansas emigration ignored it. Brown's act destroyed any reputation that the free state faction may have earned for responsible behavior and nonviolent resistance. While its significance grew after Brown's later, more famous action at Harpers Ferry, the Pottawatomie killings provided the proslavery group with an excuse for full-scale war.[36]

What followed was a series of attacks and threats of attack on both free state and proslavery settlements, with each skirmish reported as a battle. With the free state governor, Charles Robinson, and a number of others in jail on charges of treason, Robinson's wife referred to "the President's army of subjugation." Those elected to the legislature under the Topeka Constitution scheduled a session on 4 July to enact laws and carry on other business as though they were the government. President Pierce issued a proclamation ordering them not to meet. They defied the order, assembling in Topeka where they soon faced Col. Edwin Sumner with two hundred dragoons and a squadron of artillery of the United States Army. Obviously prepared to use force, Sumner ordered the legislature to disperse, which it did without a struggle. Several weeks later the House of Representatives adjourned without passing the Army Appropriation Bill, refusing to act upon the legislation until it included a provision that the military would not be used to put down free state men in Kansas. Meanwhile, Secretary of War Davis censured Colonel Sumner for taking such drastic action merely "in anticipation of serious difficulties." Davis's act probably helped pave the way for passage of the bill when Congress was called back to act upon it.[37]

During the time of violence and confusion in Kansas the national nominating conventions were meeting. In early June the Democrats convened in Cincinnati and rejected Pierce, who by that time was unpopular with the majority of his own party, especially with its more powerful leaders. Facing the inevitable prospect of leaving the presidency, Pierce began to give more consideration to electing a Democratic successor and became more evenhanded in his relations with Kansas Territory. In August, with events out of his control, Wilson Shannon resigned as territorial governor. Pierce finally appointed a competent governor, a man with frontier experience who was determined to keep the interests of all the settlers in mind. He was John W. Geary, who had served in the Mexican War, had lived for a time in Kentucky, and had served as the first mayor of San Francisco.

Geary rushed to Kansas as quickly as possible, but found his task complicated by the brief period of unabashed prosouthern government under Daniel Woodson, who became acting governor when Shannon resigned. After taking charge, Geary reported to Secretary of State Marcy that he found "existing difficulties of a far more complicated character" than he had anticipated. He had trouble not only from armed bands of ruffians but also from some in authority who were using "all the destructive agents around them to promote their own personal interests at the sacrifice of every just, honorable, and lawful consideration." He found most proslavery settlers themselves to be "well-disposed citizens," adding that the same was true of most free state residents, who "if uninfluenced by aspiring demagogues" would not break the law. "But many of these, too," he lamented, "have been rendered turbulent by official meddlers from abroad." A visit to Leavenworth convinced him that there was enough blame on both sides and that he must steer a constructive middle ground. Two orders hinted at his policy. The first disbanded the proslavery volunteer militia. The second requested all "free male citizens qualified to bear arms" to join the regular militia, a force that would include both free state and prosouthern settlers as well as those not formally aligned with either faction. Through the presence of federal troops he prevented an attack on Lawrence, convincing the inhabitants that they would be protected and ordering the would-be attackers to disband. In the meantime President Pierce, influenced by pleas from Amos Lawrence and by the political need to modify his Kansas policy, had ordered the release of Governor Robinson and the others charged with treason.[38]

Beyond those actions, reforming the territorial court system was essential if the new governor was to convince free state settlers that he would be truly impartial. Although he met resistance from Judges Cato and Lecompte, Geary attempted judicial reform, determined that justice must be meted out equally, without reference to politics. Geary's agent arrested Charles Hays, a known killer of a free state settler, only to see him released on Judge Lecompte's order. Geary had him rearrested. All of this occurred while more than a hundred prisoners were being held for the killing of one proslavery man. After the second arrest of Hays a grand jury, made up of proslavery men, found the evidence so clear that it indicted him for murder in the first degree. Lecompte was not ready to surrender, however, and he freed Hays on bail. Geary called the action a "judicial outrage, without precedent" and requested the removal of both Lecompte and Marshal Israel B. Donaldson. Again Pierce backed away from decisive action, failing to support Geary. Lecompte and Donaldson continued to dispense their own brand of justice in the territory.[39]

Despite such frustrations, Governor Geary succeeded in bringing an element of impartiality to his official assignment by protecting free state settlers while recognizing as legitimate the proslavery legislature. A major obstacle to peace disappeared when the free state legislature at Topeka failed to gather a quorum for its proposed session. The new governor also had to deal with an impending invasion of free state forces from Nebraska when Jim Lane and three hundred heavily-armed men crossed the border. Secretary of War Davis had ordered Geary to use troops to put down any such rebellion. Instead, Geary used the army to disarm and detain the group, but after a short time they were freed to go about their business. Geary was confident that the time of civil disorder had passed, and a trip throughout the territory strengthened that belief. To Secretary Marcy he reported: "The general peace of the Territory remains unimpaired. Confidence is gradually and surely being restored; business is resuming its ordinary channels; citizens are preparing for the winter; and there is a readiness among the good people of all parties to sustain my administration." To Amos Lawrence, Geary described himself as "perfectly enthusiastic" about his mission, and he declared 20 November—about two weeks after the election of the new president—a day of general thanksgiving. While "Bleeding Kansas" was still part of Republican heavy artillery, its impact had been lessened considerably by the modified policies of the Pierce administration and by the effect of John Geary's actions as governor.[40]

The troubles in Kansas, however, were not over. Nor were Geary's. Rumors persisted that Geary had made a deal with Robinson to bring Kansas into the Union as a free state, and in turn he would become its first governor. In his report to Washington Geary hinted that Robinson had suggested such an arrangement but that he had turned it down. He also refused an offer from the Law and Order party, changed in name to the National Democratic party of Kansas, to join them in return for becoming the new state's first senator. Geary said he despised their promises of reward as much as their earlier "infamous threats of injury."

Early in January 1857 the official territorial legislature met in Lecompton, where much of its time was spent castigating the governor and his evenhanded policies. Before convening, the extreme proslavery legislators had secretly agreed to override all of Geary's vetoes. That attitude marked the session, which, among other things, saw the governor threatened at gunpoint by William Sherrard, a rash and violent young man whom he had refused to commission as sheriff. Geary's most notable veto was of a census bill to prepare for a summer election of delegates to a constitutional convention. All the census-takers and judges of election were to be proslavery men. Geary vetoed the bill on the grounds that there was no provision for a referendum. The measure passed over his veto. Although there was the appearance of peace in the territory, the governor was increasingly frustrated with what he referred to as "almost a thankless work." On 4 March, the day James Buchanan took the oath of office, Geary sent his resignation to Washington.[41]

In time it would be clear that the great majority of those who went to Kansas Territory, including many who were not part of the free state movement, wanted statehood without slavery and without the presence of free blacks. But their principal goals were to legalize their land claims, improve their property holdings, and better themselves economically. To view the Kansas story as simply a struggle between the forces of freedom and slavery was to distort the record. Yet increasingly, that is the way it was viewed both north and south. To some extent, Franklin Pierce's policy of supporting only the proslavery element and castigating the free state faction lent credence to such a distorted view. That policy was also shortsighted and politically disastrous.

Nearing the end of his term, the lame-duck president took a more evenhanded approach that helped calm the storm, but it was too late to rehabilitate Pierce's personal reputation. "Bleeding Kansas" came to symbolize the failures of the administration. A majority of Americans saw the president as, at best, incompetent. Some, including old friends, judged him more harshly. B. B. French, his former secretary, commented in July 1856 that Pierce was "in rather bad odor, and will stink worse yet before the 4th of next March." At that point the president could no longer please anybody. Even a wise and highly skilled leader would have had great difficulty. Pierce was neither. He failed to understand the forces at work in the country, and he tried to perpetuate policies of the past rather than confronting the problems of his own time. Jacksonian democracy had run its course. The fundamental changes at work in all aspects of American life required a degree of political adjustment that the president from New Hampshire could neither understand nor implement.[42]

6

FOREIGN POLICY:
LAND, TRADE,
AND INFLUENCE

American foreign policy has always been influenced both by domestic developments and by internal politics in the countries with which the United States wished to do business. During the years of the Pierce administration, the expansionist views of the Young Americans overshadowed all else. Their principal objectives were to add new territory, to expand American trade opportunities, and to protect American traders. They spoke of extending democratic principles while some of them sought new land for slavery, often combining arrogant nationalism with racist arguments. In addition there was a bid for power on the international scene, where most of the world's leaders still viewed the young republic as an upstart.

Business interests also influenced the Pierce foreign policy. Owners of whaling vessels needed safe ports for restocking supplies and a place in the islands of the South Pacific for sailors to rest. Farmers who understood the importance of fertilizers demanded a cheap source of guano from Pacific islands. Fishermen wanted the right to take their catch unmolested from the shores of Newfoundland. Merchants claimed the right to trade anywhere and with all parties. Land speculators sought wealth and power in other lands and demanded the opening of new markets in Asia, while slave owners sought new lands for settlement. A cluster of economic interest groups applied pressure on Washington to further their scramble for profits, at times supporting a largely unauthorized foreign policy. Adventurers, sometimes called filibusters, who tried to further those policies often had close ties to business and government. Their name came from the Spanish word for freebooter, and their method was to infiltrate and settle a region, then to invade it, often in alliance with local revolutionaries looking to amalgamate with the United States.

Moreover, the deepening sectional crisis profoundly affected United States foreign policy. While most defenders of slavery opposed moves to acquire Canada, many northerners opposed expansion to the south, which they feared would open new land to slavery and increase the power of slaveholding interests. Sectional polarization of foreign policy issues was especially true of American relations with Spain, which pitted prosouthern forces against Free Soilers in a struggle to acquire Cuba. While one group had an obsessive fear of "Africanization" of the island and hoped to annex it for slavery, the other hoped for abolition in Cuba and saw in plans to acquire it another example of the slave power conspiracy. That a majority of Pierce's diplomats and special agents were southern expansionists only deepened the suspicions of Free Soilers.

Although Secretary of State William Marcy was not a southern apologist, he strongly supported asserting American power wherever possible. Yet he tempered his expansionist views with political pragmatism, often acting as a check on the more adventuresome Caleb Cushing and Jefferson Davis in the cabinet, and Dan Sickles, George Sanders, and especially Pierre Soulé in the diplomatic ranks. Marcy's well-publicized "dress circular," suggesting that American diplomats reject the ceremonial dress of the day, illustrated his contempt for the old order in Europe and his faith in a republican form of government. Even the usually critical *New York Herald* commended the secretary's display of American spunk. "All the country from Cape Cod to California, will cry amen."[1]

Marcy's handling of the Martin Koszta affair was equally popular. Indeed, some thought it reflected the secretary's presidential ambitions. Koszta, a Hungarian refugee whom the Austrians sought for participating in the 1848 uprising, fled to the United States and declared his intention to become an American citizen. In 1853, while on a business trip to Turkey, Koszta was seized by the Austrians and placed in chains on a ship bound for Trieste. At the order of the American chargé d'affaires, Capt. Duncan N. Ingraham of the American corvette *St. Louis* demanded Koszta's release, threatening to fire on the Austrian vessel. The Austrians agreed to turn Koszta over to the French consulate in Smyrna until the matter could be settled. In Washington, the Austrian chargé delivered a strong protest against Ingraham's "act of hostility," demanding that the United States return Koszta to Austrian custody, disavow the action, and give "a satisfaction proportionate to the outrage."[2]

Marcy's reply—a seventy-three page document—helped establish his reputation as a major player in the Pierce administration. Although intent to become a citizen did not automatically entitle a traveler to the protections of a citizen, argued Marcy, the letter of protection from the American consul that Koszta carried was much the same as a passport. Marcy's note caused a stir both at home and abroad. Ten thousand copies were distributed in New York, where Horace Greeley reprinted it in the *Whig Almanac for 1854*. Editors of all political persuasions saw in the document a ringing example of how the United States defended even those who had merely declared their intent to become citizens. Foreign offices also took notice. Great Britain's Lord Palmerston called it a "very clever paper, very clever paper." And from London, where he was correspondent for the *New York Tribune*, Karl Marx commented: "It is a remarkable fact that the first mark of interest taken by the United States in European affairs concerns the Eastern question. . . . One should not forget that America is the youngest and most vigorous exponent of Western civilization." Then, by a fortunate coincidence, three days after publication of Marcy's note the Austrian chargé reported that his government relinquished any claim to Koszta on the condition that he return to the United States and stay there.[3]

While Marcy's success was gratifying, it was differences with Mexico that produced the first, and one of the most important, treaties of the Pierce administration. In 1848, through the Treaty of Guadalupe Hidalgo, which ended the Mexican War, the United States had acquired approximately half of Mexico. Failure to grant access to the Gulf of California, however, irritated the burgeoning population of California. Mexico had also refused to guarantee access to the increasingly important route through the Isthmus of Tehuantepec, though it had granted that privilege to two private companies. Worst of all, the most practical southern route for a future transcontinental railroad was still in Mexican hands, and both countries claimed territory in the Southwest, where the treaty had not clearly defined the boundary. A series of Indian raids into Mexican border towns and rumors of filibustering increased the tension, for the United States was obligated by treaty either to prevent such raids or to compensate all Mexican victims.

Many expansionists, including Pierce, favored acquiring more Mexican land, without war if possible. At the suggestion of Jefferson Davis, James Gadsden was appointed minister to Mexico with instructions to negotiate a new treaty. Gadsden, a South Carolina railroad promoter, seemed a good choice, although he had contempt for the Mexican government and people. Working in his favor was the desperate economic situation of Antonio López de Santa Anna, once again ruler of that land. Gadsden was joined by Christopher L. Ward, Pierce's special messenger, who carried secret instructions. Ward was an unfortunate choice, since he also acted as agent for speculators who had claims on Mexico. Based on a repudiated 1842 grant to José de Garay, a private Mexican contractor, those claims were for the right to operate and control a railroad across the Isthmus of Tehuantepec. Garay had sold the right to a British firm, which then sold it in 1849 to New York businessman P. A. Hargous. After Mexico annulled its first grant it awarded the same privilege in 1852 to a third group headed by Col. Albert G. Sloo of New Orleans.

To further complicate matters, the minister to Mexico, Alfred Conkling, in 1852 negotiated a treaty committing the United States and Mexico to protecting the Sloo interests. The president and Congress never accepted the so-called Conkling Convention because Conkling had acted without authorization. The intense rivalry between the speculating groups became a major factor in the fate of the Gadsden Treaty. While claimants applied pressure on the administration, the issue of an all-important transportation route connecting the two oceans tended to slip into the background. Such a route was vital if the United States were to capitalize on its new access to Asian markets. Over the objections of Pierce and Marcy, Ward took it upon himself to include the Garay claims in the Gadsden negotiations.[4]

Pierce's objective was to add another large slice of northern Mexico to the United States while rescinding the agreement making the United States responsible for Indian raids on Mexico. Marcy's instructions to Gadsden suggested four possible borders, with a different payment for each. Neither Gadsden nor Santa Anna was a diplomat by personality, and it was only the Mexican leader's desperate need for money that provided any hope of a settlement. Matters were further complicated by the first filibustering venture of William Walker, a Tennessee-born doctor and journalist. Late in 1853 Walker and about two hundred followers invaded Mexico's Lower California peninsula, proclaimed the area's independence and set up a republic. In January he announced that Lower California had annexed the neighboring state of Sonora. Walker's venture into Mexican politics lasted only six months before he was run out, yet it fed Santa Anna's suspicions that the United States wished to devour his country. In January 1854, Pierce issued a proclamation against unlawful expeditions into Mexico. Walker was later tried for violating neutrality laws, but the jury acquitted him.

Motivated by a thirst for fame and power, such adventurers played a significant role in U.S. diplomacy. Although they lacked official recognition and sometimes faced prosecution for their deeds, they got unofficial encouragement from some in Congress and, at times, from members of the administration. Walker's expedition into Mexico revealed that nation's vulnerability to invasion from the north, hardened Santa Anna's resolve against any large cession, and led Mexico to seek British support for its cause. In truth, Walker created a major problem for the negotiators. Years later Gadsden told a Charleston editor that, but for ''the insane expedition of Walker,'' Lower California and a part of Sonora would likely have been added to the United States.[5]

Instead, the Pierce administration had to settle for much less. Negotiations ended in late 1853 with the signing of the Gadsden Purchase Treaty, whose terms included payment of fifteen million dollars to Mexico for thirty-nine million acres of land. In addition the United States would assume all U.S. claims against Mexico, with specific mention of the Garay-Hargous claims, while Mexico granted Americans the right of transit across the Isthmus of Tehuantepec for mail, merchandise, and troops. The terms also readjusted the boundary of 1848 and abrogated a section of the earlier treaty that bound the United States to end Indian raids on Mexican settlements. It was such a disappointment that Pierce was inclined to turn it down without submitting it to the Senate, but several months of heated cabinet debate dissuaded him from that course. Pierce feared that without a treaty, war with Mexico was a real possibility. Moreover, the agreement had some positive features. The arguments of Marcy, Cushing, Davis, and Dobbin, who favored ratification, prevailed over those of McClelland and Campbell, who wanted to reject it. Pierce sent the treaty to the Senate on 10 February 1854, suggesting it be ratified with some changes, including removal of the clause honoring the Garay-Hargous claims.[6]

As soon as the treaty terms were made public, editors and politicians took sides. Many northern editors accepted the Free Soil view that the treaty was part of the slave power's conspiracy to dominate the nation. Most of their southern counterparts supported it in the hope that a southern transcontinental railroad would permit the South to share the profits of the Asian trade. Investors in the Garay-Hargous and the Sloo speculations, including a number of congressmen, saw the treaty as their best chance to salvage those investments. In the Senate it was the Garay-Sloo controversy that dominated debate. Supporters of the treaty got a serious setback when Robert Ward's secret mission was discovered and Pierce honored a request for the agent's correspondence with Gadsden. The Ward papers supported the charge of Senator John Clayton of Delaware—a former secretary of state—that fraud and corruption marked the treaty. Pierce insisted he had never given Ward permission to negotiate private interests and defended him against charges of misrepresentation. When the treaty came to a vote on 18 April it met defeat, 17 to 18. Much as he disliked the treaty, Pierce was deeply offended by its rejection. It was the first such treaty of his administration, and he believed that it was essential for peace.[7]

Rejection was an even greater setback to southern railroad interests. Three southern senators who had been absent from the voting began a movement to reconsider when they returned to Washington. Teamed with supporters of the Sloo claim, they succeeded in winning ratification by a 33 to 12 vote on 25 April. But there was a price: to win support of the Sloo interests they inserted a clause that promised United States protection of the Sloo project. The new treaty also reduced the land grant and cut the payment to ten million dollars. The land purchase would provide a railroad route to the West but included no natural boundary or port on the Gulf of California. The treaty was a greater disappointment to Pierce than the one Gadsden had originally negotiated, but it was the best he could get. Once again, Secretary Marcy was able to convince him to accept it. Coming as it did in the midst of the Kansas-Nebraska debate, it was remarkable that the Senate could agree on any version. Hope that the treaty would divert attention from an increasingly dangerous sectional rift proved futile.[8]

Word of Mexico's acceptance of the treaty reached Pierce on 20 June. The next day he notified the House and requested an appropriation for the agreed-upon payment. Again there was stiff opposition from Whigs, Free Soilers, and discontented Democrats. No congressman was more opposed than Missouri's Thomas Benton, who recognized in the treaty a threat to his interest in a northern railroad route. He objected, he said, to paying ten million dollars for territory "so utterly desolate" that "a wolf could not make a living there." Ohio's Joshua Giddings thought that the proposed road would benefit Mexico as much as the United States and that the treaty would provide "rocks, volcanic mountains, [and] precipitous bluffs," but very little arable land. He and fifty others voted "no," but the bill passed with 103 in favor. The next day it passed in the Senate with only 6 Free Soilers opposed. By the end of June 1854, Pierce was able to announce that the treaty was in effect.

Despite its shortcomings in leaving many disputes unresolved, the Gadsden Treaty was a success in ending a serious threat of war.[9]

One reason that war with Mexico had not broken out was a perceived threat from north of the Canadian border. An 1818 agreement had granted U.S. fishermen limited privileges off the shores of Canada, but in the early 1850s those privileges were tightly restricted, and Canadian officials began seizing American fishing boats. By the time Pierce took office American fishermen were arming their boats. Marcy requested and Pierce agreed to send a naval force to cruise the disputed waters. Jingoists on both sides talked openly of war. Canada was then in serious economic difficulties caused in part by British repeal of the corn laws, which had protected their grain from foreign competition, and in part by U.S. tariff policy. Matters were so desperate in Canada that a small but highly vocal element began discussing the advantages of attaching their country to its neighbor to the south. More realistic politicians began working for a treaty of reciprocity to improve the Canadian economy. After eight years of continual agitation, their proposal bore fruit.[10]

While the Americans were primarily interested in gaining access to fishing areas, the Pierce administration also supported a policy of expanding opportunities for manufacturers and merchants. Earlier attempts to legislate a program of reciprocity with Canada had achieved nothing, so Pierce turned to diplomacy. Marcy and John Crampton, the British minister to the United States, hammered out the basis for an agreement, but in order for it to take effect the Canadian provincial legislatures would have to pass compatible legislation. To facilitate this, Marcy hired Israel D. Andrews, a private lobbyist, who secretly spent more than ninety thousand dollars for editorials, elaborate dinners, and outright bribery. For their part the British sent to Washington a special mission, headed by the popular and debonair Lord Elgin, for their own wining, dining, and lobbying. The resulting treaty of 5 June 1854 gave the United States expanded fishing privileges and included a lengthy list of raw materials, which would be admitted duty free to both countries. The treaty, which did not include manufactured items, was popular on both sides of the border and was a triumph for Marcy. Pierce himself thought the treaty had larger implications. Sidney Webster, his personal secretary, wrote years later that Pierce had expected the agreement to lead to a peaceful merger of the two countries that was ''sooner or later, inevitable.''[11]

The treaty with Canada was a small step toward removing trade restrictions and opening commercial opportunities to U.S. interests. Such a program of free trade was a basic ingredient of Marcy's foreign policy. American military and commercial agencies encouraged new trade routes and markets in South America and Asia. A naval expedition that explored and studied the Amazon valley in the hope of new trade relations failed to open that waterway to U.S. commerce. Local political upheaval also frustrated efforts to open the Río de la Plata to American navigation. Efforts to share the riches of the China trade were more successful after 1844, when Caleb Cushing, then the first United States minister to China, signed a treaty of commerce and extraterritoriality with that Asian nation. In China, British and French merchants shared the profits, since the country was large enough to provide commercial opportunities for all.[12]

Although Marcy opposed the possible dismemberment of China by any power, Dr. Peter Parker, U.S. commissioner to China, suggested American occupation of Formosa. The proposal came near the end of Marcy's tenure as secretary of state, and he never replied. Annexation of Formosa was also one of the objectives of Commodore Matthew C. Perry, whose expedition to open Japan to the United States and the West began under the Millard Fillmore administration. Perry's expedition demonstrated the important role naval commanders played in furthering the cause of American imperialism. Although his mission was clearly diplomatic, as a naval commander he was solely accountable to the secretary of the navy, not the secretary of state. Perry was the embodiment of a military man whose strong nationalism led him to favor aggressive annexation and colonization of Pacific islands. He believed that U.S. commerce and the need for future coaling stations required control of a chain of islands: Okinawa, Formosa, and the Bonins—along with colonization by Americans, which would inevitably lead to annexation. Perry also suggested that Washington extend its "national friendship and protection" to Siam, Cambodia, and Cochin China, as well as to parts of Borneo and Sumatra. To Perry such views were a matter of national pride, economic necessity, and racist belief.[13]

None of Perry's suggestions was acceptable to Secretary of the Navy Dobbin. Officially, the expedition was instructed solely to open Japan to western trade. When rumors of the Perry expedition began to circulate, the New York Express editorialized: "Japan has no right to bury her treasures behind her walls." Moreover, continued the writer: "It is the duty of those who know her, even better than she knows herself, to force upon her the dawning of a better day." The New York Times disagreed, asserting that such action would amount to a declaration of war. "To do evil that good may come," asked the Times, "is it not rather the maxim of an extinguished Jesuitism, than of the religion of primitive or present times?''[14]

In truth, Perry's tactics were more aggressive than Marcy would have approved. Secretary Dobbin was just as cautious. While Perry's instructions were to avoid the use of force unless attacked, he was granted "large discretionary powers," which he meant to interpret broadly. The Japanese viewed his July 1853 appearance in Yedo Bay with four warships as a serious threat, and his statement to the authorities implied the use of force should his message from the president to the emperor not be delivered. With its acceptance he left, suggesting he would return in the spring with an expanded naval force.

In February 1854, Perry returned with seven black warships. Again he met with officials and distributed such gifts as a miniature, scale model steam locomotive that worked, a volume of Audubon's *Birds of North America*, as well as muskets, swords, and pistols. The Japanese presented President Pierce with two hundred sacks of rice but with the grains carefully sifted so that not one kernel contained the germinal vessel intact, making it impossible to use the rice for horticultural experimentation. After the formalities and a festive banquet where American liquor flowed generously, Perry addressed the real purpose of his expedition, obtaining a trade agreement with Japan. Japanese officials, though reluctant to change a two-century-old policy of isolation, were divided over the best response to make to increasing pressure from the outside world.

Eventually, choosing the lesser evil, they drove a hard bargain: they would open only Shimoda and Hakodate, two relatively inaccessible ports. American ships could bring on provisions, wood, water, and coal at Shimoda, and within a year Hakodate would also open. Shipwrecked sailors would be turned over to American consuls at the two ports. Should there be future concessions to other powers, the United States would be granted the status of most-favored nation. Although the treaty fell short of Perry's hopes, it was a good beginning. Marcy's choice of Townsend Harris as consul general at Shimoda was especially fortunate, for his skill as a diplomat produced new concessions in 1857 and a model trade treaty the following year. Although Perry's treaty with Japan received little press notice and only a brief mention in the president's annual message, its importance grew with the passage of time.[15]

In his determination to free world trade from traditional restrictions, Marcy also looked to European commerce, where such restrictions were common. One such area was the Danish Sound, where

Denmark levied heavy dues on all ships using that waterway. It was a practice going back to a time when the Danes used the funds to protect other nations' shipping from pirates, but by midnineteenth century the dues had become a major irritant to the United States and other mercantile nations.

On 1 July 1853, Marcy took action, sending a note to Henry Bedinger, American minister at Copenhagen, in which he evaluated the damage to American shipping from the tolls. Bedinger broached the matter with the Danish foreign affairs minister, who argued that the dues had been collected from "time immemorial," that nations accepted them as based on international law, and that if the United States did not have to pay them other nations would soon follow and Danish revenues would suffer. When the American press published that reply there was even talk of war with Denmark. In February 1855, Pierce got permission from the Senate to give Denmark notice of termination of the commercial convention of 1826. In March Bedinger notified the Danish government of Pierce's intention but promised that dues would be paid until a new agreement could be reached. In October the Danish government announced plans for an international congress to resolve the dues issue and invited the United States to attend. Marcy replied that the president would not cooperate, since the meeting itself would constitute admission that the tolls were legitimate. He made one concession: the United States was willing to pay a fair amount for the cost of erecting lighthouses and buoys for safe passage through the sound.

The congress convened on 4 January 1856 at Copenhagen with both Great Britain and Russia attending, despite the fact they were then adversaries in the Crimean War. There was no settlement until shortly after Pierce left office, when the signatories agreed to pay Denmark compensation based on the amount of Baltic trade they enjoyed. Marcy had worked out much the same policy independently through a treaty that he drew up and his successor signed. The American assault against the Danish Sound payments ultimately succeeded, and Marcy could take most of the credit.[16]

Dealing with the struggle for power among the great nations of Europe, however, was quite another matter. The Crimean War—which pitted Great Britain and the France of Napoleon III against Russia for control of the European holdings of Turkey—once again involved the United States unwillingly in European politics. Although the United States declared its official neutrality, the Pierce administration was sympathetic to Russia, and on at least one occasion was willing to aid the Russian cause overtly. Russia hoped to use that bias to get the United States directly involved, first by attempting to provoke an incident and then by planning, without success, to outfit privateers in U.S. ports. While there was some pro-British sentiment, most Americans shared their government's position. One rumor spawned by the war predicted the imminent sale of Alaska to the United States. While that was unlikely, Marcy did find ominous a statement by British Foreign Secretary Lord Clarendon that good relations between France and England had been extended "beyond Eastern policy" to the rest of the world and that foreign policies of the two countries were "in entire harmony." To Marcy that meant more meddling in Central America. To Richard Rush, former minister to Great Britain, he confided that the British had shown "too much of a disposition to be guardians of the whole world." In turn, the British charged U.S. violations of "the spirit of neutrality." Clearly, both the United States and the European belligerents considered U.S. policy to be an important element in the war then raging.[17]

For some in the Pierce administration, the war offered unique opportunities. Young Americans in European diplomatic positions, for instance, saw in it a chance to further the republican cause. One of them was George Sanders, the U.S. consul in London, who was active with others in helping various revolutionary groups. The war, they thought, might also help their plans to annex Cuba. Still others saw the Crimean War as a golden opportunity for the United States to take the lead in peacemaking. Peace activist Elihu Burritt, working with the American and London peace societies, tried to convince Pierce that the United States should use its influence to bring the war to an end through international arbitration. The United States, wrote Burritt, was "the only power in Christendom whose status and position would inspire confidence in the justice and impartiality of its arbitrament." Burritt and Charles Sumner even visited Pierce, who expressed sympathy but said the United States was unable "to deal competently with the merits of the question, and might embarrass the powers, without preventing a collision."[18]

Marcy, it appeared, was much more interested in asserting American power than in bringing the war to an end. Nothing furthered that goal more effectively than a scandal resulting from a British policy of military recruiting in foreign lands when grim reports from the battlefields dried up the supply of English recruits. In late 1853 Parliament passed legislation permitting such recruiting, and no country seemed a richer source of enlistees than the United States. The popular and urbane British minister, John Crampton, was ordered to obtain American recruits without violating stringent American neutrality laws, not an easy assignment. By June 1855, the British Home Office had ordered

Crampton to cease all recruiting in the United States, but at about the same time British consuls in Cincinnati, Philadelphia, and New York were indicted for violation of the neutrality law. Attorney General Cushing was so relentless in the recruiting controversy that administration opponents accused him of creating a war scare to divert attention from Kansas and to help Pierce get another nomination.

Marcy, for a change, agreed with Cushing's strong action, while from London Buchanan urged moderation. When the British government refused to honor Marcy's request that Crampton and the three consuls be removed, Pierce, on 27 May 1856, dismissed Crampton and revoked the exequaturs of the consuls. Meanwhile, Buchanan had left his London post as planned, and George M. Dallas became the new American minister to the Court of St. James. With American war talk increasing and British opinion turning against the government, word came from the Foreign Office that, although there had been no conspiracy, the British government considered the matter closed. Although Dallas was not recalled, no other British minister was sent to Washington while Pierce remained in office.[19]

A parallel concern for Marcy, as representative of a neutral nation during wartime, was possible interference with seagoing commerce. Russia was no problem, since it was not a major naval power and in any case was not inclined to irritate the United States. Much to Marcy's relief, both France and England accepted the American argument that, for the duration of the war, free ships meant free goods and that, excepting contraband of war, neutral goods on enemy ships should be permitted free passage. Marcy thought the policy should be incorporated in treaties and made a part of international law. The powers would not consider this proposal until the Paris Conference of 1856, which followed the Crimean War. In the Declaration of Paris the participating countries agreed on permanent abolition of privateering, that a neutral flag protected enemy goods except for contraband of war, that neutral goods could not be seized from enemy ships, and that blockades would be binding only if they were maintained by force.

When the United States was invited to sign the declaration, Pierce and Marcy balked at ruling out privateering, which was important to the United States with its limited naval fleet and large merchant marine. However, the United States would agree to give up privateering if the declaration were amended to exempt the private property of belligerents, except for contraband, from seizure by enemy craft, a provision the other nations would not accept. The declaration took effect without American participation, though the United States never again used privateers. Europeans thought the United States was playing the role of gadfly. Yet Marcy's stand on privateering was extremely popular in the United States, whose people looked upon it as justified assertion of American rights in dealing with Old World powers.[20]

While developments growing out of the Crimean War intensified Anglo-American tensions, the major cause of those tensions was rivalry for commercial and political influence in Central America. With acquisition of Oregon and California and the ensuing gold rush came schemes for gaining wealth by providing easier transportation to the West Coast. A canal or railroad could provide the needed service, and Mexico's Isthmus of Tehuantepec, the southern tip of Nicaragua, or New Granada's Isthmus of Panama were the most likely routes. British trade in Central America was well established, however, and any move to build a U.S. canal appeared as a threat to that nation's interests. For its part the United States wished to prevent any further European colonization in any of the Americas.

The Clayton-Bulwer Treaty of 1850 had been designed to resolve both issues. By its terms Great Britain and the United States agreed that any canal would be jointly constructed and neither fortified nor under the exclusive control of either country. Article I ruled out occupation, colonization, or exercise of dominion over ''any part of Central America'' by either nation. The agreement, which seemed to provide for major improvements in British-American relations, was unpopular in the United States, where many saw it as truckling to the superior military power of the British. Furthermore, the treaty's language was ambiguous enough to permit varying interpretations, which soon led to arguments. Americans had hoped the treaty would end British influence in Central America, but the British Foreign Office claimed that its terms were applicable only in the future and that Great Britain would continue to exercise full rights on her own lawful territories in Central America.[21]

Friction over the treaty began in the Fillmore administration and was exacerbated by the bullying attitude and diplomatic appointments of the Pierce administration. James Buchanan had opposed the treaty from the start and, as minister to Great Britain, was determined that its shortcomings be corrected and the British deterred from continuing their expansion in any of the Americas. Solon Borland, Pierce's minister to Nicaragua, was frank about his hope to inject more U.S. business operations into that country, even, eventually, to annex it to the United States. The U.S. commercial agent to Central America, Joseph W. Fabens, was almost the stereotype of an unprincipled businessman-adventurer. The ambitions and economic interests of several private citizens added to the problem. Among them were Cornelius Vanderbilt, whose Accessory Transit Company carried goods and people across Nicaragua; Texas promoter and operator, Henry L. Kinney, whose schemes of wealth through exploitation of Nicaragua's natural resources had the support of several men high in the Pierce administration; and William Walker, the doctor and politician-adventurer who succeeded in becoming dictator of Nicaragua for a few years. The British saw all of them as parts of a U.S. conspiracy to dominate Central America, an outcome they could not permit to happen.

Belize, or British Honduras, provided the British with their best excuse for maintaining a colony in Central America. Their claims to the region stemmed from an eighteenth-century Spanish grant to cut tropical trees, which was renewed in 1826 when the area was part of Guatemala. The British valued Belize as a depot for smuggling goods into Central America, and U.S. demands that they pull out only hardened their determination to stay. In 1852 they converted the Bay Islands to the south into a crown colony, and, using the excuse that they were protecting the Mosquito Indians from Nicaragua, they made several hundred miles of the coast into what amounted to a British protectorate. In his instructions to Buchanan, Marcy was adamant that the 1850 Clayton-Bulwer Treaty had assumed an end to British presence in Central America. He was willing, however, to make some commercial exceptions for Belize, and he did not mean to push the issue to the point of confrontation.[22]

During much of the time that the British and Americans were exchanging notes and charges, the British were preoccupied with European events and, after March 1854, with the Crimean War. The British foreign secretary, Lord Clarendon, offered major concessions to the U.S. position, including withdrawing protection from the Mosquito Indians and giving up all claims except to the Belize settlement under the limited terms granted by Spain in 1783 and 1786. However, the conciliatory memorandum was never delivered because of the rash action of a naval commander at Greytown.[23]

The settlement on the Atlantic terminus of the San Juan River, originally called San Juan del Norte, was seized by the British in 1848 to serve as a base for protecting their Mosquito Indian wards. Renamed Greytown, it eventually acquired the dubious status of an independent, free city under British protection. The population of four to five hundred included merchants, adventurers, and speculators, few of whom were interested in stability or orderly process. Americans began a settlement at Punta Arenas across the river from Greytown, which was headquarters for the Accessory Transit Company, by then managed by two unscrupulous operators who had squeezed out its founder, Cornelius Vanderbilt. Joseph Fabens, in league with the U.S. commercial agent at Greytown, believed the unsettled conditions justified assertive action to introduce stability. The excuse came in the summer of 1854, after the murder of a black pilot by a Transit Company ship captain. The captain, who was clearly guilty, was protected by Solon Borland, who had resigned as minister over differences with Marcy and who happened to be in Greytown at the time of the crime. In a disturbance following the incident someone threw a bottle at Borland, injuring him slightly.[24]

The Pierce administration responded by sending the warship U.S.S. *Cyane*, under the command of Capt. George N. Hollins. Marcy advised Fabens to take up the matter with the leading citizens of Greytown, at the time the only group there that resembled a government, hoping they could reach agreement before the sloop of war arrived. Marcy considered the attack on Borland—who, his resignation not yet accepted, was still an official of the United States—an insult to the nation. Only an apology, he said, would avert "the infliction that such an act justly merits." Secretary Dobbin sent similar instructions to Hollins. A letter to Fabens purporting to be from a Vanderbilt associate was not even subtle. The letter, which appeared in the press, expressed hope that the United States would take control of Greytown and, hinted the writer, "you know the rest."[25]

When Captain Hollins arrived he immediately demanded an apology and $24,000 in damages. Receiving no response he warned that the town would be bombarded. The inhabitants fled, and the *Cyane* fired on the town for two hours. A contingent of marines then went ashore, burning the remaining structures and leveling the town. There were no casualties, but damage estimates ran as high as three million dollars. It was clearly an act of aggression, which the *New York Tribune* called "a needless, unjustifiable, inhuman exercise of warlike force." Lord Clarendon characterized the action as an outrage without parallel in modern times.

Marcy was on the spot. He had hoped Hollins would settle the matter without such action, and he advised Pierce not to uphold it. Although Hollins had clearly acted within his instructions, Buchanan assured the British that the commander had not had Washington's approval. In discussions with Crampton, Marcy tried to shift the blame to a British naval officer who, he said, had encouraged the citizens to reject the U.S. request. While Fabens and others associated with him persisted in this story, evidence proved it a fabrication. The British temporarily set aside Clarendon's conciliatory memorandum, but they did not threaten war. In his annual message of 1854, Pierce tried to justify the destruction of Greytown. It was a "pretended community," he said, "a heterogeneous assemblage gathered from various countries, and composed for the most part of blacks and persons of mixed blood, who previously [had] given other indications of mischievous and dangerous propensities." Furthermore, by remaining silent the residents seemed ready "to provoke chastisement rather than escape it," he wrote. Stung by protests from other governments, Pierce fell back on an old excuse: others had done worse when "communities far less offending and more defenseless than Greytown" had received more severe punishment and when not only property but human life had been "recklessly sacrificed and the blood of the innocent made profusely to mingle with that of the guilty."[26]

The Greytown incident produced a temporary setback in Anglo-American relations, but it was the activities of two filibusters that proved most unsettling. They were Texas speculator-promoter Henry L. Kinney and the "grey-eyed man of destiny," William Walker. Both dreamed of acquiring power and wealth in Central America, and their actions fueled British suspicion that the United States was using such adventurers to expand its own hegemony. Kinney purchased a large tract of land in Nicaragua from an elderly trader who claimed to have bought it from the "king" of the Mosquito Indians, a man whose title was questionable. A master salesman, Kinney organized a corporation to colonize and develop his holdings, even selling stock to some who should have known better, including men high in the Pierce administration. Rumor suggested that Pierce himself was involved.

Kinney also joined forces with Fabens, promoting the project as one of construction, agriculture, mining, and the exploitation of valuable gold fields. But José de Marcoleta, the Nicaraguan minister to Washington, suspected a plan to take over his country. Receiving no satisfaction from complaints to Marcy, he released his evidence to the press. Although Kinney publicly denied the charge, he acknowledged it privately in a letter to a Texas friend; "It required but a few hundred Americans, and particularly Texans, to take control of all that country. I have grants of land, and enough to make a start soon safely and legally. I intend to make a suitable government, and the rest will follow." He would start at Greytown, he said, where the people were "anxiously waiting" for him.[27]

Kinney's plan also alarmed the Accessory Transit Company, whose monopoly in Greytown faced a threat from Kinney's company. Growing suspicion of Kinney and Fabens resulted in their arrest in New York on 27 April 1855 on charges of conspiring to attack Nicaragua. Fabens lost his job as official commercial agent for the government, while Kinney failed to appear in court, turning up next in Greytown. Bankrupt, still facing strong opposition from the Accessory Transit Company, he managed to persuade citizens of the ruined town to appoint him civil and military governor of a fictitious provisional government. In the meantime Fabens, having been permitted to leave the United States, joined William Walker, who had established a puppet government in Nicaragua. That regime pronounced Kinney's claims in Nicaragua null and void, but the persistent adventurer would not give up until Walker ordered his arrest and expulsion.[28]

Henry L. Kinney proved a nuisance to the Pierce administration, but William Walker, because he succeeded in taking over Nicaragua, became a major distraction. Walker, with an army of unemployed laborers, some high-spirited adventurers, and a number of Mexican War veterans seeking excitement, gained support in Nicaragua by taking sides in a civil war. He instituted a provisional government with Patricio Rivas as president and himself as commander-in-chief of the army. The Accessory Transit Company helped by sending additional U.S. colonists. At last Nicaragua was to be governed by an administration that would end civil conflict and maintain order. John H. Wheeler, who had succeeded Solon Borland as United States minister to Nicaragua, proclaimed the new republic independent and sovereign, and assured Walker that his proclamation echoed the "kind regards and good wishes entertained towards it by the Chief Magistrate of the United States." Wheeler saw Walker's regime as a bulwark against British expansion in the region. The British saw Wheeler's support of Walker as proof of official U.S. complicity. The Accessory Transit Company, then run by Vanderbilt's opponents, saw in the Walker regime relief from large payments it owed to the Nicaraguan government. And while Walker still enjoyed considerable northern support, it was southern expansionists who saw in his program a chance for slave extension southward.[29]

Secretary Marcy viewed the matter in a different light, considering Walker and his men "a band of foreign adventurers" who probably lacked the support of the Nicaraguan people. He ordered Wheeler to stop dealing with the Walker government, and when that government sent Parker H. French as its representative to Washington, Pierce, at Marcy's suggestion, refused to recognize him. In the United States, French recruited settlers and fighting men for Nicaragua. On 8 December Pierce issued a proclamation against such activity, and Cushing ordered federal attorneys in port cities to stop any ships bound for Nicaragua with recruits aboard. In the meantime Walker betrayed the Accessory Transit Company, again under the control of Vanderbilt, thereby transforming a powerful ally into a dangerous adversary. In the spring of 1856, new problems arose for the Rivas-Walker regime when Costa Rica invaded Nicaragua. American minister John Wheeler sent to Marcy an intercepted letter that revealed a British agreement to send a warship to Punta Arenas and an offer to sell two thousand muskets to aid the Costa Rican cause. The letter, noted Wheeler, exposed the "jesuitical policy of Great Britain."[30]

To the Pierce administration, however, Nicaragua was only one piece in an international puzzle that turned on Anglo-American relations. British opposition to the Walker regime was only part of a plan to expand its power and influence in the Western Hemisphere, and every American setback was seen as another victory for British diplomacy. In addition, foreign policy issues always faced domestic political considerations. By April 1856, Buchanan had returned to the United States and, observed Pierce's supporters, was making an obvious bid for the presidential nomination. Recognizing the Walker regime, thought Pierce, would strengthen his much-needed southern support. Despite Marcy's disapproval, Pierce granted recognition to the new Nicaraguan representative, Augustine Vijil, a Catholic priest.

Marcy's judgment proved sound, however. After about a month, Vijil returned home, and Walker sent Appleton Oaksmith, an American whose Nicaraguan citizenship was just two weeks old, as his successor. Learning that Wheeler, on his own authority, had resumed diplomatic relations with Nicaragua, the enraged Pierce and Marcy recalled him and refused to receive Oaksmith. By then Walker had assumed the presidency through a fraudulent election and was ruling Nicaragua directly. He decreed the return of legal slavery, hoping to reopen the international slave trade. He envisioned an independent country with slavery as its cornerstone to which southerners could look for support and sanctuary should they leave the Union or take up arms against the North. But civil war and invasion in Nicaragua, along with the determined opposition of the Transit Company, made Walker's status precarious. A coalition of Central American states, encouraged and supported by Vanderbilt's agents, led to his downfall. The U.S. warship sent by the Pierce administration to rescue Walker completed its mission a few months after Pierce left office.[31]

By then, relations between the United States and Great Britain had moved beyond confrontation to rapprochement. The possibility of war with the United States frightened British merchants and caused criticism of the government's behavior. Speaking in Commons on 16 June 1856, Tory leader Benjamin Disraeli suggested that Britain recognize "that the United States, like all the great countries of Europe, have a policy, and that they have a right to have a policy." On the same day, Lord Palmerston told the House of Lords that, despite the recall of Crampton, Buchanan's successor, George M. Dallas, would be permitted to remain in his post and that friendly relations between the two countries would continue. Dallas assured Marcy that talks on Central America were going well. In August he sent to Washington a proposed treaty that dealt mainly with Nicaragua. Its terms would grant the Mosquito Indians a reservation either with independent status under the protection of Nicaragua, or as a part of Nicaragua. Greytown was to be a free city with self-government under the authority of Nicaragua. Costa Rica would have rights of navigation on the San Juan River. A separate article referred to a new agreement between Great Britain and Honduras under which both nations would recognize the Bay Islands as a free territory and would respect its independence and rights. The United States was to recognize Belize as a British holding exempt from provisions of the 1850 treaty.

The Pierce administration submitted the treaty for Senate ratification, which Marcy predicted would fail. Although Pierce had persuaded the British to leave Nicaragua and Honduras, he had backed down on his demand for total British withdrawal from the Americas. Marcy was right again: after lengthy debate the Senate added so many modifications to the Dallas-Clarendon agreement that the British turned it down. Yet despite that setback, relations between the two powers remained substantially improved.[32]

Those relations had always required accommodation to growing U.S. influence in Central America where, in 1855, the United States Mail Steamship Company constructed the first railroad connecting the Atlantic and Pacific. Its purpose to foster trade and realize profit, the line was built across the Isthmus of Panama in what was then New Granada (present-day Colombia). The line required three years to build and was forty-eight miles long. Cutting through the tropical jungle and facing the ordeal of heat and disease took its toll on workers. It was a marvel of the age, a triumph of American skill and science, which reduced to five hours the time it took to cross the isthmus and brought immediate profit to its owners. Marcy's enthusiasm for the project was dampened by a controversy over New Granada's attempt to tax users of the line, an issue finally settled in favor of the United States.

A far more serious conflict arose because of a riot in which twenty Americans, many of them passengers from the Panama railroad, were killed, and twenty-nine Americans and Panamanians injured. Erupting out of a minor disagreement, the melee quickly brought to the surface resentment against Americans. Demands for compensation and apology were complicated by the arrogance and insensitivity of Consul Thomas Ward, a veteran of the Mexican War who conducted his investigation in such a manner as to constantly irritate the officials at Bogotá. When the presence of two U.S. warships and the temporary occupation of the railroad station failed to move officials, Pierce sent a special envoy with instructions to negotiate a settlement, to get recognition of both railroad terminals as free ports, and to purchase or otherwise gain control of the island of Tobago and other small islands in Panama Harbor. Such a settlement was not to occur, however, until 1857 under the Buchanan administration, when Lewis Cass, then secretary of state, signed a convention with New Granada settling the matter to the satisfaction of the United States.[33]

Pierce also turned to threats and diplomacy in a futile attempt to acquire control of Samaná Bay in the Dominican Republic, which had recently broken away from Haiti and was plagued by a series of revolutionary governments. Persistent rumors warned of French and Spanish efforts to gain control of that important harbor, and in the fall of 1853 Marcy sent to the island William L. Cazneau, a Texas land speculator, to investigate conditions and arrange for diplomatic recognition. Without such support, Marcy reasoned, the Dominicans would turn to one of the European powers for assistance. Cazneau described in glowing terms the great resources waiting to be developed. The United States, he said, should recognize independence and move to take control of Samaná Bay. But when Stephen A. Douglas introduced a Senate resolution asking the Foreign Relations Committee to consider the question of diplomatic recognition he met with immediate opposition from northern interests.

The most formidable roadblock to a treaty with the United States were the British and French diplomats who followed every move and warned Dominican politicians of the worst possible outcome. When Marcy and Cazneau proposed a treaty of recognition and amity, the Dominican Congress demanded an amendment providing that "the same rights and privileges which American citizens would enjoy on their arrival throughout the Dominican Republic, should equally be conferred upon Dominican citizens without distinction of race or colour throughout the United States composing the Union." Without that modification the Dominicans would not accept the treaty, yet with it the treaty was unacceptable to the United States. Even with a U.S. sloop of war in the harbor and with Cazneau making threats that another Greytown might be in the offing, the Dominican legislature would not give ground. British and French diplomats called for an increase in their own naval presence, but the British Home Office was more cautious.

Lord Clarendon scolded the British consul, ordering him to confine his actions to offering himself as mediator and protesting any injury done to British or French subjects. In December 1854, Marcy ordered Cazneau to return. His mission had failed, only strengthening the fears of Dominicans and their Latin American neighbors.[34]

The plans of some Young Americans to annex the Sandwich Islands (Hawaii) had much the same fate. By the 1850s the native island population had declined while Europeans and Americans were arriving in large numbers. Missionaries had converted many of the native people to Christianity, and Americans had developed a growing sugar plantation economy. Hundreds of U.S. whaling ships stopped at the islands where their crews spent many thousands of dollars. Hawaii was an economic and strategic plum, ruled by a Hawaiian king with a western-style government. Each of the three western powers operating there—the United States, Great Britain, and France—was suspicious of the intent of the others.

Marcy believed that United States acquisition of Hawaii was inevitable, but while annexation would have been in line with Pierce's announced policy, it would meet British and French opposition. A Hawaiian faction preferred annexation to the United States, and the king, Kamehameha III, agreed to a treaty of annexation, but only if Hawaii were admitted as a state with all its multiracial population recognized as citizens with full rights. Pierce knew that such a treaty would alienate much of his southern support, and he never submitted it to the Senate. Negotiations ended when the reigning monarch died, since his successor, Kamehameha IV, would have nothing to do with the annexation move. British and French intrigue among anti-American Hawaiians had again helped to frustrate a U.S. policy goal.[35]

Just as Hawaiian leaders had originally proposed annexation, they suggested a two-part reciprocity treaty. One part would grant commercial reciprocity so that Hawaiian sugar would be duty free; the other would guarantee Hawaiian independence from the United States, Great Britain, and France. To negotiate such an arrangement they sent an American, Judge William Lee, who was then chief justice of Hawaii. On 20 July 1856 Lee and Marcy signed a reciprocity treaty, but the matter of territorial guarantees was more difficult. Rejecting Lee's suggestion of a jointly-announced policy, Marcy finally agreed to a unilateral declaration that opposed interference from any source with the security of the Hawaiian government and that promised to move against filibustering and to station a naval force near the islands. Although Davis argued strongly against the antifilibustering clause, the cabinet adopted the declaration. Nevertheless the reciprocity treaty met stiff oppostion from U.S. sugar interests and died in 1857 in the Senate, where it never reached a vote. Thus one more of Pierce's Young America objectives was defeated, partly by British and French intrigue, partly by local opposition, and partly by American economic interests.[36]

Despite disagreements over specific projects, some individuals saw opportunity for new riches in each move to expand United States power. In the case of the guano islands it was southern farmers, demanding a richer and less expensive source of the natural fertilizer, and merchants wishing to sell it, who supported acquisition. Even though many U.S. farmers were wasteful of the soil, ready to look for new land rather than replenish the acres they were then working, some were turning to the use of fertilizers. By the 1830s and 1840s, advertising for guano—the accumulated droppings of seabirds—began to appear in the U.S. press. Guano had collected for centuries and, by aging, had become rich in natural nitrogen. Some Pacific islands, with mountains of guano, suddenly became the object of commercial ventures that led to serious international complications. The highest grade guano was found in the Lobos and Chincha islands off the Peruvian coast. Peru, which claimed the islands, looked upon guano as a limited resource. By the early 1850s the Peruvian monopoly had driven up the price to more than fifty dollars a ton. Entrepreneurs, determined to break the Peruvian stranglehold and share in the profits, looked for new supplies. One group pursued a rumor of rich guano deposits in the Galapagos, which Ecuador claimed. Before it became known that the rumor was baseless, Philo White, the U.S. minister at Quito, had negotiated a pact making the islands and even the coast of Ecuador a kind of U.S. protectorate. White had gone far beyond Marcy's instructions, and the agreement never received serious consideration in Washington. Nevertheless, it fueled European resistance and led a number of South American countries to sign a treaty of mutual defense in which U.S. filibusters were called "pirates." The treaty, intended as a first step in forming a confederation, was clearly an anti-American alliance to which the Pierce administration never officially responded.[37]

Amidst these diplomatic maneuvers came the first official move by the United States toward creation of an overseas empire. In the fall of 1855, Michael Barker, a New England sea captain, revealed that years earlier he had discovered rich guano deposits on a barren island several hundred miles south of Hawaii. He then joined with some Boston and

New York merchants to form the American Guano Company and requested Pierce to send a warship to survey and claim Barker Island for the United States. Secretary of the Navy Dobbin ordered such a survey, and a company representative asked the Senate to proclaim the island a U.S. possession. The law, passed on 18 August 1856, provided that any U.S. citizen who discovered an unoccupied and unclaimed island containing guano deposits could claim it for the United States. Thus the droppings of birds played an important role in the history of U.S. imperialism. In the next thirty years the law led to claims for some seventy islands, including Midway and the Christmas Islands, as "appertaining" to the United States.[38]

While guano diplomacy provided one of the few successes of the Pierce foreign policy, Cuba provided its most significant failure. The Emerald Isle in the Caribbean was a prize that administrations as far back as that of Thomas Jefferson had coveted. Its strategic position strengthened the U.S. assumption that Cuba was destined to leave the Spanish empire and join the United States. By the 1850s, advocates of southern expansion hoped that Cuba might become one or even two new slave states. That, of course, brought opposition from northern Free Soilers and made the Cuban question part of the growing sectional struggle. In 1848, President Polk's plan to purchase Cuba came to nothing, and three attempts of the filibuster Narciso Lopez to invade the island ended with his arrest and execution and so alarmed the French and British governments that they jointly sent a fleet to the Caribbean to defend Cuba against possible invasion. The United States turned down their proposal for a three-nation treaty guaranteeing Spanish possession of the island.[39]

The Young America faction of the Pierce administration put Cuba high on its list of priorities. Ending Spanish rule there, they thought, would strike another blow against monarchical power in the New World and would contribute to the abolition of monarchy in the Old. Pierce came to office with a program of anticipated expansion, and when he spoke of the "acquisition of certain possessions not within our jurisdiction eminently important for our protection," observers assumed he meant Cuba. Within the administration there was little disagreement on acquiring Cuba. The differences—which turned out to be profound and divisive—were over means, not ends. Banker-politician August Belmont had a plan for persuading international Spanish bondholders to pressure Spain to sell Cuba in order to retire its enormous debt. Pierce named Belmont as minister to the Hague, in part to implement that idea, which James Buchanan, minister to the Court of St. James, also supported. Secretary of War Jefferson Davis favored the direct approach through war or filibustering expeditions. Always the politician and pragmatist, Secretary of State Marcy, without making a firm commitment, seemed to favor any of several approaches so long as they would not embarrass or harm the administration. Pierre Soulé, Pierce's minister to Spain, was willing to try anything that promised to make Cuba a part of the United States, for that was his only reason for accepting the assignment.[40]

Indeed, it is difficult to imagine a more inappropriate choice for the diplomatic post than Pierre Soulé, who was in exile from his native France for participating in revolutionary activity there. A wealthy lawyer and an important figure in Louisiana politics, Soulé was personally charming, but lacked all sense of propriety. When in the Senate he spoke of the inevitability of U.S. acquisition of Cuba. After his appointment to the Spanish post he met in New York with Cuban dissidents and proexpansionist Young Americans, and in Spain he was arrogant and tactless. His misguided sense of personal honor led him to fight a duel with the Marquis de Turgot, the French minister to Spain, whom he wounded seriously. He openly conspired with Spanish republicans involved in plots to overthrow the monarchy. He made pathetic and fruitless attempts at flattery in order to persuade the queen to sell Cuba. He disregarded most of Marcy's instructions and failed to keep him informed of his actions. His own secretary, Horatio Perry, was so appalled at Soulé's activity that he wrote Marcy secretly, confirming Marcy's original opposition to Soulé's appointment.[41]

Marcy's first instruction to Soulé was to forgo any attempt to purchase Cuba. Since Marcy himself wished to acquire Cuba, he probably expected a filibustering venture or revolution to remove Spanish control. In 1854, former Mississippi governor and Mexican War veteran John Quitman planned a takeover of the island to prevent its "Africanization." A writer in DeBow's Review argued persuasively for the Quitman expedition. By helping the revolutionaries in Cuba, the writer asserted, Quitman would aid U.S. commerce and give new strength to the southern states. "The safety of the South," said the author, "is to be found only in the extension of its peculiar institutions, and the security of the Union in the safety of the South—towards the equator." Northern profit from trade would in turn help cement the bonds of the Union. "What wealth will float upon our waters," he exulted. "What a bright gem will she, 'the Queen of the Antilles,' be in the coronet of the South, and how proudly will she wear it!"[42]

On 7 March 1854 a threat of war with Spain arose when Cuban

officials seized a U.S. vessel, the *Black Warrior*, and arrested its captain for a technical violation of harbor regulations. It was the most serious of several incidents that seemed designed to harass U.S. shipping interests in retaliation for threats and filibustering activity from the United States. In cabinet meetings Cushing and Davis pushed for war. To House requests for information about the incident Pierce also sent a special message in which he seemed to prepare the way for war. Because of Cuba's proximity to the U.S. coast and its importance to commercial interests, he said, it was "vain to expect that a series of unfriendly acts . . . can long be consistent with peaceful relations." Should an amicable adjustment of the trouble with Spain fail, he continued, he would "not hesitate to use the authority and means which Congress may grant to insure the observance of our just rights, to obtain redress for injuries received, and to vindicate the honor of our flag."

As usual, Pierce was trying to have it both ways. While he threatened war he also expressed hope for an adjustment of difficulties with Spain. Pierce's ambiguity was probably a recognition of growing opposition to his Cuba policy from Free Soilers and other northern interests in Congress. The day after the president's message, Ohio's Congressman Joshua Giddings delivered a lengthy attack on its threat of war, which he saw as a step toward acquiring Cuba. "We are to have war with Cuba," he said, "not on account of the seizure of the cotton on the *Black Warrior*, but to forestall emancipation, to stay the progress of liberty there." Many in the North shared that view. On 15 March, the day Pierce sent his message to Congress, Marcy sent instructions to Soulé to request indemnity and an early reply from the Spanish. War would have been justified for so serious an outrage, he said, but the president was "anxious to preserve peaceful relations." Soulé, however, castigated the Spanish Foreign Office and made two demands beyond Marcy's instructions: a reply in forty-eight hours, despite the fact that a religious holiday was in progress, and dismissal of responsible Cuban officials. It was one of the worst blunders that Soulé made while minister to Spain. The Spanish foreign secretary, sensing that Soulé had exceeded his instructions, stalled. When nothing happened, Soulé lost face. The Spanish dealt with the *Black Warrior's* owners, released the ship and paid $53,000 in damages. There were other incidents during the Pierce years but none brought the powers so close to war.[43]

Although the desire to annex Cuba remained strong in the Pierce administration, Cuban military preparations, including the arming of free blacks, made a filibustering attempt far more risky. When Soulé reported that Spain's financial crisis was crippling her and Buchanan sent word that there would be no Anglo-French military defense of Cuba, Pierce decided it was a good time to try again to buy the island. On 3 April 1854 Marcy instructed Soulé to try to open negotiations to purchase Cuba for as much as $130 million. He admonished Soulé to be discreet, since it would be "a delicate and difficult negotiation." If purchase was not possible Soulé should direct his efforts "to the next most desirable object, . . . to detach that Island from the Spanish dominion and from all dependence on any European power." Spain might balk at selling Cuba, he said, yet be willing to grant it independence. In that eventuality the United States was willing to help the Cubans. Pierce was under pressure from radical Young Americans to move quickly to support the Quitman filibuster. There were even rumors that he had sent instructions to Soulé that conflicted with those from Marcy. Yet Pierce also faced a growing revolt in the North, where Free Soil sentiment was quickly gaining ground. A delegation from the Senate Foreign Relations Committee told the president it supported a Senate resolution to suspend the neutrality laws, prompting him to recommend sending a three-man commission to Spain with the message that the only options for Spanish Cuba were session to the United States or an invasion by filibusters.

The next day, 31 May 1854, Pierce issued a proclamation calling for all Americans to observe the neutrality laws. Soon Cushing ordered Quitman arrested and placed under bond. The commission plan never went to Congress because of the impact of the Nebraska question, which, Marcy confided to John Y. Mason, ambassador to France, had "sadly shattered our party in all the free states and deprived it of that strength which was needed & could have been much more profitably used for the acquisition of Cuba."[44]

The enthusiasm and lack of political realism of the Young Americans played an important role in the drama over Cuba. Early in August 1854, one of their number, Daniel Sickles, secretary of the London legation, arrived in Washington for conferences with Pierce. He told of a small republican faction in Spain that would grant Cuba independence if it won power and of Soulé's request for funding for that rebellious group. He also told of other republican movements on the continent that he and others were supporting. Only later Marcy learned that V. Fronde, a representative of the republican committee in London, had acquired an illegal U.S. diplomatic passport, which he had used to carry messages to revolutionary groups in Portugal and Spain. Fronde also intended to go to France to encourage a revolution and arrange for the assassination of Napoleon III. Not knowing of Fronde's activities, Pierce was pleased to hear about simmering revolts in various European countries. As was Pierce's custom, in his conversations with Sickles he seemed to accept his overall view, giving the impression that he would act decisively should there be a revolt in Cuba.[45]

In July 1854, Soulé wrote Marcy that he thought the time had come to send a commission to Spain to deal with the Cuban question. Marcy replied that he still favored purchase and suggested inviting other countries with interests in Spanish and Cuban issues to become involved. He wished Buchanan, Mason, and Soulé to meet as soon as possible "to consult together . . . and to adopt measures for perfect concert of action in aid of your negotiations at Madrid." He suggested Paris for a meeting place and instructed Soulé to make the arrangements. Marcy still hoped that the old August Belmont plan might work to detach the island from Spain. He also expected Buchanan to restrain any extreme actions Soulé might suggest. Although Buchanan opposed the meeting, he kept his counsel and obeyed Marcy's order to join the others in Ostend, which he hoped would provide more privacy than Paris. To a relative Buchanan confided that the conference would probably make "noise enough in the world." It was worse than that. In Paris some of the most extreme Young Americans who represented their country abroad had caught the attention of the press and various foreign offices. Wherever they met or whatever they discussed, the three ministers would be closely watched.[46]

In fact, Ostend was so full of reporters and so rife with rumors that after three days the Americans moved to the less accessible Aix-la-Chapelle to conclude their deliberations. Their final recommendation was Buchanan's edited version of a rough draft, which Soulé had written. Mason's principal contribution was his signature. The document, which came to be known as the Ostend Manifesto, was supposedly a secret communiqué to the State Department. With slight modification it was a repetition of Marcy's instructions to Soulé, listing all the reasons for Spain to sell Cuba to the United States. The diplomats could not imagine the failure of their mission except "through the malign influence of foreign powers." Cuba was as necessary to the United States, they concluded, as any of its present states, and even the Cubans would benefit from the transfer. Yet if Spain refused the offer, the United States should consider whether continued Spanish control of Cuba posed a threat to its own peace and security. If so, said the ministers, "then, by every law, human and divine, we shall be justified in wresting it from Spain if we possess the power; and this upon the very same principle that would justify an individual in tearing down the burning house of his neighbor if there were no other means of preventing the flames from destroying his home." All the arguments were a brief for annexation, by whatever means. To avoid misunderstanding, Soulé sent a letter with the communiqué in which he proposed immediate war if Spain would not agree to a sale.[47]

The communiqué from the three ministers arrived the very day of midterm congressional and state elections, which were largely a referendum on the Kansas question. Republicans, Whigs, and Know-Nothings swept the field in an election that was a disaster for the administration and the Democrats, who suffered losses in all but two states. In the new House the Democrats would be a minority of seventy-five. Thus, practical politics required a repudiation of the manifesto. Indeed, the document shocked the Pierce administration, as Sidney Webster recalled years later. "Nobody," wrote the president's former secretary, "could understand the motives of Buchanan in signing it." Yet a careful reading of Marcy's instructions could well explain their connection to that document, especially since Marcy understood Soulé's single-minded determination to acquire Cuba and his inclination to interpret communications loosely.

However, new factors, including the election returns, caused Marcy to back away. Instead of approval he sent a harsh critique to Soulé. He agreed with the president, said Marcy, that seizing the island had never been their intention. Should Spain refuse their offer to buy Cuba it would not mean "imminent peril" to U.S. security unless there was also "material change in the island's condition." Ordering Soulé to put aside efforts at purchase and concentrate on negotiation, Marcy also chided him for his high-handed tactics in the *Black Warrior* incident. Clearly, the administration was abandoning its earlier Cuba policy and needed a scapegoat. Soulé had set himself up for that role, and he would have to accept it. But the letter from Marcy stunned Soulé, who could not believe that Pierce had approved it. His response was to resign in indignation.[48]

If any response to the manifesto could help the ailing Democratic party and Marcy the politician, it was the one he himself provided. Certainly, the episode would taint Buchanan and lessen his chances for the presidency. Yet Marcy continued to hedge the issue, never completely rejecting the idea of Cuba's becoming part of the United States. Writing confidentially to a New York friend he said: "I am entirely opposed to getting up a war for the purpose of seizing Cuba; but if the conduct of Spain should be such as to justify a war, I should not hesitate to meet that state of things. . . . Cuba would be a very desirable possession, if it came to us in the right way, but we cannot afford to get it by robbery or theft." Marcy's new position, however, did not lessen public suspicion. The administration resisted demands for the papers relating to the manifesto until 5 March 1855, when it released a highly edited version. The most serious omission was Marcy's recommendation that Soulé take measures to "detach" Cuba from Spain should offers to buy it be rejected. Yet even with omissions, publication of the papers provoked a strong reaction. Slidell, noting the omitted documents, believed that Marcy's response was part of his bid for the White House, and Edward Everett thought Marcy's chance at the nomination was good. Newspapers at home and abroad attacked the Ostend plan. Greeley's *Tribune* branded it a "Manifesto of Brigands," and the *Philadelphia North American* criticized Marcy's "wretched fickleness," "duplicity," or "vacillation." It was obvious that the Cuban issue had seriously damaged the administration.[49]

But this was not the end of the matter. In early 1855 Quitman was still trying desperately to collect money, men, and materiel, and to arouse public support for an invasion of Cuba. Cuban authorities proclaimed a state of seige and, with the help of English naval vessels, ruthlessly crushed Quitman's Cuban collaborators. Yet Quitman would not give up his dream, even when the weakness of the expedition became apparent. In mid-march Quitman—either on his own or in response to a summons—went to a conference with the president, Marcy, and the Spanish ambassador. The result was to terminate the project. On 30 April 1855 Quitman announced he was abandoning the expedition, the last serious attempt during the Pierce administration to end Spanish rule in Cuba. At about the same time a brief war scare over a Spanish warship stopping a U.S. vessel in Havana harbor came to nothing. The United States and Spain were both determined to avoid hostilities. Marcy instructed Henry Dodge, Soulé's successor, to encourage the Spanish to grant independence to Cuba and to negotiate a commercial treaty. Although Dodge did not succeed, the international situation had calmed, and with the passage of time war between Spain and the United States became virtually unthinkable. It was a disappointment for an administration whose southern supporters had been assured it would add Cuba to the nation. Sectional rivalry had defeated imperialistic ventures that might otherwise have had national support.[50]

In only two instances was Pierce able to expand U.S. holdings. They were the Gadsden Purchase, which was considerably smaller than the administration had wanted, and acquisition of the guano islands, which produced legislation justifying the addition of new land to the United States. Nevertheless, U.S. commercial, agricultural, and military interests continued to operate in areas that the United States had tried and failed to obtain, as well as in many other, faraway places. The Pierce administration negotiated half a dozen commercial treaties and ten extradition agreements during Marcy's tenure at the State Department. The United States was assuming a more powerful role on the international stage, and its influence expanded during the Pierce years. That trend had begun much earlier and would continue into the future. Pierce had added little territory to a potential empire. Yet sparring with Great Britain, Spain, and France, forcibly opening Japan to the West, bringing to a head the Danish Sound dues issue, and establishing an increased U.S. presence in Hawaii, Central America, and the Pacific islands demonstrated the importance of foreign policy during the years of the Pierce administration.[51]

7

★ ★ ★ ★ ★

THE FINAL ACT:
THE ELECTION OF 1856

Considering the records of his recent predecessors, Franklin Pierce's prospects of a second term were dim. Five of the first seven presidents each served two full terms. From Martin Van Buren's inauguration in 1837 until Lincoln's presidency, no one held the office for more than one term. Some did not even win nomination a second time. Although aspirants for high office shared basic values and ideals, the party system so exaggerated differences in program and personality that national elections became more emotionally charged than substantive differences justified. In his time, Andrew Jackson *was* the issue, and the fervor of those who supported him matched the hatred of those who did not. In the 1850s, Democrats were still living in Jackson's shadow, though none of them could hope to equal him in dynamism and popularity.

Besides attacking personalities, out-of-power parties could always capitalize on unpopular policies, economic depressions, or usurpations of power, real or imagined, which they could tie to the current administration. Politicians drew not only on ideals and aspirations of the voters, but also on their fears, anger, and disgust. The system worked far better in times of relative stability and order, when slow change caused less disruption. The growth of industry in the northern states and massive population movement westward brought profound changes, which in turn disrupted the political order. Chronic tension between the sections combined with industrial and demographic conditions to pit northern and northwestern states against the South, which was dominated politically by the small minority whose wealth and power rested on chattel slavery.

Many American politicians tried desperately to avoid the slavery issue. Yet by the time Pierce assumed the presidency there was little hope that slavery would die out, as some writers of the Constitution had believed would happen. Instead, there was a "slave power" that dominated a section, and southern representatives in Congress defended their institution against even mild criticism. They insisted that the states had the authority to endorse and protect local institutions. For southern blacks, federalism became the curse that bound them in servitude. Most northern politicians tried not to offend their southern colleagues, since both parties needed support in the South when they nominated candidates for the presidency. Yet the North was becoming more restive under the old agreement, which favored the South through the three-fifths compromise of the Constitution. Division over such matters as federal funds for railroad construction, free homesteads for farmers, and tariff policy became increasingly bitter. The so-called Compromise of 1850 was meant to end the debate over slavery, but the Fugitive Slave Act, part of that compromise, only made it worse. Pierce won election on a platform that supported all the compromise measures, and he believed those measures had put the slave question to rest.

He was wrong, of course. In part, the slave issue would not rest because vocal and determined minorities in both sections kept it alive. Beyond that, the causes of the division were real: the sections had vital and conflicting interests. By 1856 Americans had to confront the issue. Southern extremists were sounding the alarm in answer to what they perceived as an abolitionist attack. Before 1850 the slave states had controlled half the Senate and two-fifths of the House, and most early presidents had been southern slaveholders. Yet it was clear, by any index of progress, that the North was gaining. Southern congressmen detected abolitionism in each proposal from northern representatives.

Moreover, many in the South believed and preached that slavery, in order to survive, had to expand. The Free Soil idea of containing slavery in the states where it already existed would surround the South with an expanding population antagonistic to slavery. Slaveholders needed new land to work after they had depleted the soil of their original farms, and they resented any restrictions on their "property" rights. Many Americans believed that slavery had already reached its natural limits, but slaveholders did not think so, and their assumptions and beliefs influenced their actions. Slavery should expand to the west, they believed, but southern expansion would also be made possible by the acquisition of new territory: Cuba, Santo Domingo, and perhaps the lands of Central America. Thus, the nationalist impulse toward expansion beyond the continental United States became entangled in sectionalism. To support their viewpoint, southern spokesmen used invective and an appeal to prejudice: "Free society! We sicken at the name! What is it but a conglomeration of greasy mechanics, filthy operatives, smallfisted farmers, and moonstruck theorists?" ranted the editor of an Alabama newspaper during the campaign of 1856.[1]

Sectional polarization produced similar attitudes in the North, where any bill of particulars against the South always included slavery. Having abandoned slavery themselves, many northerners disapproved of the institution, though they did not become abolitionists in large numbers, either. For the most part, their opposition to slavery was mild, since it seemed remote from their interests. In 1854, Horace Greeley, who was himself opposed to slavery, told Theodore Parker that he had never found a "strong, pervading, over-ruling Anti-Slavery sentiment in the Free States." Indeed, he said, were any voters in the North to inherit a few slaves from southern relatives, "a decided majority would hold on to their chattels and make as much as possible out of them." A purely antislavery party could not succeed, he believed, because most voters were motivated by self-interest, and a political movement that appealed "wholly to the mind, ignoring material considerations," was doomed.

Greeley was correct. In large part, northern antislavery sentiment was a response to a perceived threat from the South: first, slavery would take hold in the territories and exclude free farmers; then it would enter the northern states. Some, fearing the whole country might fall under the slave power, became as obsessed as southern extremists. For example, in 1856 a Michigan resident reported popular excitement over a circular from the commissioner of the General Land Office requiring an oath that land purchased under the Graduation Act—legislation that reduced the price of government land not purchased within a stipulated time period—was settled and cultivated, a provision the law itself had not included. The Michigan settler saw in the circular proof of a conspiracy "by the same Power that passed the Fugitive Slave Law, repealed the Missouri compromise and that now disgraces itself by tyrannizing over the brave men of Kansas. 320 acres of land are not enough for a Slave Plantation; but makes a splendid farm for a freeman and increases the vote of the free states." A constituent wrote to Senator John P. Hale: "If the legal voters of the north only knew how they were degraded by slave representation, and their own influence lessened thereby," and that their taxes paid for representatives who were in Congress because of a "certain species of property," they would soon refuse to elect anyone who favored that system. The emphasis, always, was on what the South and its slaveholding minority was doing to the North rather than on slavery and what it was doing to the slaves. Only the small abolition movement concerned itself with the plight of the slaves.[2]

Facing the growing tensions between North and South, many Americans still hoped that the Pierce administration would usher in an era of sectional harmony based on acquiescence to the principles of the 1850 compromise. It was a futile hope. Each event widened the split between sections, and the Kansas-Nebraska Act reopened the debate with new fury. Stephen A. Douglas and the administration won the battle but lost the war when they declared the old Missouri Compromise no longer in effect. Even in his home state Douglas faced hostile crowds, and some Illinois communities burned him in effigy. Violence in Kansas, the shocking attack on Senator Charles Sumner, the much-publicized fugitive slave incidents, and an expansionist foreign policy all helped convince many northerners that the slave power controlled the national government. "The *government* has fallen into the hands of the slave power completely," wrote Wendell Phillips. "So far as *national* politics are concerned, we are beaten—there's no hope."[3]

How that could have happened was a puzzle to many antislavery workers. Poet and abolitionist John G. Whittier believed he had the answer. "The North is not united for Freedom as the South is for Slavery," he told a meeting called to protest the attack on Sumner. "We are split into factions; we get up paltry side issues and quarrel with and abuse each other; and the Slave Power, as a matter of course, takes advantage of our folly." Increasingly, however, northern sentiment demanded a check on the slave power and an end to southern control of the national government, though there was no agreement on tactics. Abolitionists, emphasizing the sin of slavery, still had limited appeal, since many northerners were as negative about blacks as they were about southerners. Opposed to slavery, they also opposed the idea of a free, multiracial society.

Indeed, racism was a strong force in all sections, and political parties catered to it. Northern politicians, no longer able to avoid the issue of slavery, took as moderate a position as possible. Excluding slavery from the territories might check the slave power without threatening the institution at home, reasoned many in the North. To slaveholders that position was only a first step toward abolition, yet thoughtful people made a distinction. Many of them, like a constituent of Illinois Senator Lyman Trumbull, saw the great purpose of the Free Soil movement as "the restoration of the old policy of our national government, and relieving it of the character of slavery propagandism." Despite widespread apathy and administration hopes of avoiding the slave question in the next presidential election, another of Trumbull's correspondents correctly observed that the subject of slavery was absorbing the minds of the people and would be "*the* issue in the coming elections." To the millions who saw in such a campaign a serious threat to the Union, that was a frightening prospect.[4]

Franklin Pierce was one of them. His devotion to the Union led him to view the antislavery and Free Soil movements as threats to the American system by forcing some states to react with extreme measures to protect their interests. Pierce saw slavery largely in terms of property interests rather than as a moral issue. Always his concern was for the white majority and the American political system. Moreover, he believed there were many other, more important issues to deal with: the prospect of railroads crossing the country, the growth of American business and trade, the expansion of the United States' republican ideals to Europe, Asia, and Latin America, the need to assert American rights while avoiding war, the need to destroy Indian resistance to their removal from areas of white settlement, and the development of a burgeoning American landscape of cities, towns, and farms. Yet by the end of 1855 the Pierce administration was clearly in deep trouble. In December Pierce asked his cabinet members for advice about running for another term. It was hardly an objective body. "All his cabinet agreed to it," reported one of Buchanan's supporters. Many northerners thought the decision proved that the slave power controlled the Democratic party, for Pierce was clearly the preferred candidate in the South. And the fall elections had demonstrated that the party, though wounded, was by no means dead.[5]

Yet any realistic observer might have questioned a second Pierce nomination. All the political signposts after the passage of the Kansas-Nebraska Bill pointed to trouble for the Democrats. The combination of anti-Nebraska sentiment in the North and a sudden upsurge of support for the anti-Catholic, anti-immigrant Know-Nothing movement had produced nationwide setbacks for the Democrats in the 1854 elections. Douglas and other proadministration Democrats minimized Free Soil sentiment, insisting that the Know-Nothings had led to their defeat. Certainly the nativists were a strong factor in the Northeast and, in combination with various anti-Nebraska elements, in the Northwest. But anti-Nebraska sentiment, when added to resentment over neglect of western interests, was far more influential than Democratic leaders dared admit. Increasingly, they could count only on the southern wing of the party, where Know-Nothing appeal was limited and Free Soil sentiment virtually nonexistent. If 1854 was traumatic, the first half of 1855 provided little reason for optimism. Early in that year the Illinois legislature defeated Douglas's candidate for the Senate, electing Lyman Trumbull instead. It was a double blow to Douglas since Trumbull, a former Democrat who became an ardent Free Soiler, was from his own state. In Missouri, Douglas's friend David Atchison also failed in his bid to return to the Senate. James Shields, the man Trumbull defeated, knew before the contest was settled that anti-Nebraska feeling was "deep—more deep than [he] thought it was."[6]

Election after election demonstrated growing antagonism to the administration's Kansas-Nebraska policies and to Pierce himself. No pro-Nebraska senatorial candidate won in any of the spring, 1855 elections. The New Hampshire contest was especially galling. Pierce believed that enough organized effort would save his home state for the Democrats. There was certainly enough effort. Speakers spread the message, and contributions of two thousand dollars from the friends of New Hampshire in Washington and a thousand dollars from New York officeholders added to Democratic coffers. Yet the results were disastrous: administration candidates lost at every level. Even worse, Pierce's old nemesis, John P. Hale, joined the antiadministration faction in the Senate, along with Trumbull of Illinois, Henry Wilson of Massachusetts, and William Seward, who was reelected from New York. A coalition effort had produced enough new voters to defeat the Democrats. Soon word arrived of Know-Nothing victories in Connecticut and Rhode Island.[7]

Amidst the bad news, Pierce took comfort in learning that Virginia's Henry A. Wise had won the governorship, a victory he viewed as a welcome trend. The Virginia election, he wrote Douglas, had "put a new face upon the prospects of the Democratic Party." Other Democrats shared the president's forlorn hope, refusing to recognize that the Free Soil movement had become a powerful political force in virtually all of the North. The real problem, they said, was the Know-Nothing movement. Marcy considered it unfair to blame administration unpopularity "in any considerable degree to the Nebraska measure" and doubted that the Know-Nothings would "assume the character of a permanent party."

Pierce himself was especially sensitive to anti-Catholic pressure. He had been accused of truckling to the Catholic hierarchy when he appointed James Campbell to the cabinet, and articles in a Maryland journal described his sympathy for Catholics. To deal with such opposition, he gave orders to remove anyone with Know-Nothing sympathies from government offices. That move caught Pierce's friend, Benjamin B. French, who had supported a Know-Nothing candidate in a local election, and John Wilson, the longtime commissioner of the land office, who complained to Chase of his removal because he preferred his own countrymen "to Foreigners, and Civil and religious liberty to Jesuit misrule." Nevertheless, Marcy was correct in perceiving Know-Nothingism as a temporary threat, for its adherents never succeeded in putting together an effective national organization. Free Soil was to become the movement of the future. Yet the twisted rhetoric of nativism had succeeded in stirring up old hatreds and contributed to several years of deadly election-day violence in many American cities until Know-Nothingism, too, fell victim to the growing dispute between the sections.[8]

State elections in the summer and fall of 1855 provided the administration with a slim hope that the tide had turned in its favor. The Know-Nothings could not repeat their earlier triumphs, though they won some—mostly local—offices in several states. The Democrats made gains in several northern states as well as in North Carolina, Tennessee, and Alabama. Pierce considered the elections a referendum on the Kansas issue, and the results strengthened those Democrats who favored his candidacy for another term. On the surface, at least, he was in better shape politically than he had been since the start of his term.[9]

The new Republican party suffered a setback in the fall elections of 1855 with one important exception: the election of Salmon P. Chase as governor of Ohio. The Ohio contest was significant because, as Chase himself said, it was "a trial of strength between the Anti Nebraska Principle & the Know Nothing idea." The antiforeign, anti-Catholic movement threatened Free Soilers as well as Democrats. If there was to be a vital Republican party it would have to include some from the Know-Nothing camp, but at what price? Know-Nothings were not unanimous on the Free Soil issue, and many who opposed the Nebraska Act still feared a Catholic conspiracy more than a slave power conspiracy. And if they joined the Free Soilers they intended to do so on their own terms, which in Ohio meant having their own candidate for governor in 1855. Chase, who worked strenuously for the nomination, was not a member of the secret order and would not agree to run unless the campaign emphasized the slavery issue. Before the Republican nominating convention, two events weakened the Know-Nothings. A Cincinnati riot on election day in April, sparked by violent attacks on the city's Catholics, helped elect a Democratic mayor. Soon afterwards the national Know-Nothing convention, meeting in Philadelphia, broke up over the slave issue. The Ohio Republican convention, meeting in Columbus, nominated Chase for governor on a Free Soil platform that did not mention the foreign or Catholic issues. To get Know-Nothing support all the others on the ticket were members of the order.[10]

That was not enough, however. Angry Know-Nothings nominated the elderly Allen Trimble for governor. Some Whigs and Free Soilers also refused to support Chase. The Democrats avoided the Kansas issue, concentrating instead on Chase's alleged radical abolitionist views and the antiforeign influence in the Republican party. In all his fifty-seven speeches, Chase emphasized the Kansas issue. His victory was paper thin, all the other Republicans winning with larger margins. Yet Chase's election demonstrated the potential power for the Republicans of a clear antislavery emphasis. It also revealed the Ohio Know-Nothing party as a paper tiger when operating alone, but an important element when absorbed by the Republicans. Chase's slim margin of victory gave hope to the new party and threatened future trouble for the Democrats.[11]

Chase and the Republicans were not the only ones to consider the Know-Nothing movement politically useful. The more conservative northern Whigs—the Silver Greys—could not stomach the thought of combining forces with a party based on sectional appeal. Their natural choice for a leader was former President Millard Fillmore, who in early 1855 had joined the secret society, a move he hoped would return him to the White House. While Fillmore and his Whig followers accepted some of the Know-Nothing ideas, their main concern was for the future of the Union. They hoped to transform the Know-Nothing party into a new version of the old Whig party, which was already ineffective as a national force. By 1856 the Know-Nothing party had become the American party, and it was the first to hold a national nominating convention, meeting on 22 February in Philadelphia. Soon, however, delegates were quarreling over the slave issue. Northern members presented a resolution that only candidates favoring the prohibition of slavery above the Missouri Compromise line should receive support, but it was tabled. Immediately a sizable group of northern members left the convention, later to reorganize as the North American party. A mostly southern convention went on to nominate Fillmore for president and Andrew J. Donelson for the ticket's second place. After that nomination a few more bolted from the group. It was a lackluster ticket headed by an unpopular former president with a program that upheld the southern position on slavery and slave extension. It had no appeal in the North and little enough in the South.[12]

Much of the same was true for Franklin Pierce, though apparently he was not aware of it. One of his strongest opponents was Stephen A. Douglas, whose outstanding service to the administration, under ordinary conditions, might have made him a strong candidate. But conditions were not ordinary, and Douglas was just as tainted by the Kansas imbroglio as Pierce. The other was the party's sixty-five-year-old elder statesman, James Buchanan, who could claim a long and distinguished career in government. Most important, he had been out of the country as minister to the Court of St. James when the Kansas issue exploded.

The Democrats, recognizing the growing political power of the West, chose Cincinnati for their convention that opened on 2 June. Their timing could hardly have been worse. Coming on the heels of the sack of Lawrence and the attack on Sumner, the convention drew attention to the administration's inept handling of the Kansas question and stirred Free Soil sentiment to a fever pitch. Besides his loyal followers, Pierce had some support among southerners grateful for his attack on free state Kansans and assistance to the proslavery legislature. Although he fully expected to receive the nomination and to serve another term, few others shared his optimism. Nevertheless, they intended to push hard. Several weeks before the convention, Harry Hibbard and Charles H. Peaslee, two longtime friends from New Hampshire, and other Pierce delegates set up headquarters above a Cincinnati restaurant. Their plan was to build support for Pierce, to make certain that the New York pro-Pierce "Softs" would be that state's official delegation, and, should the worst happen, to cooperate with the Douglas forces to prevent the nomination of Buchanan.

The latter strategy was a major worry for the Buchanan managers, who believed there had been Pierce-Douglas collusion from the start. Louisiana's Senator John Slidell, Buchanan's principal supporter, was characterized by the *New Orleans Bee* as the "Warwick" of that movement. He had not intended to be in Cincinnati, but when word came of heavy lobbying for Pierce and Douglas, Slidell, Judah P. Benjamin of Louisiana, Indiana's Jesse Bright, and James Bayard of Delaware hurried to Ohio to stave off the suspected coalition against their candidate. Based on early talks with Douglas followers, they thought they had an understanding that he would not pursue the nomination beyond the first few ballots and would then throw his support to Buchanan. Douglas, however, was a shrewd and ambitious adversary, and the Douglas-Pierce strategy came close to success. It was the ability of the Buchanan forces to take control of the convention machinery that determined the outcome.[13]

If party unity was essential for victory, the opening of the convention on 2 June demonstrated how difficult that unity would be. First, an unauthorized Benton delegation rushed into the hall demanding recognition. The credentials committee turned them down. Then there was the usual battle between the New York "Hards" and "Softs," a dispute the committee settled by admitting both factions without judging either claim. That was a second setback for Pierce, who favored the "Softs," because Jesse Bright, in a Friday night caucus, had already moved the Indiana delegation from Douglas to Buchanan.

In a break with earlier procedure, the convention debated and adopted a platform before the nominating began. Much of it provoked little debate, for it was standard Democratic fare: a federal government of limited power, rigid economy in public affairs, and no constitutional basis for a national bank. There was unanimous approval for a vague plank endorsing the Kansas-Nebraska Act but leaving unresolved the question of whether slavery could be kept out of a territory before it was ready for statehood. As one Democrat had earlier predicted, it was "an elastic platform susceptible of double reading." Most sections dealing with domestic policy passed unanimously, though opposition from the eastern states defeated a plank supporting construction of a public road across the continent, a proposal with strong support from the upper Mississippi valley and much of the Southwest. The delegates finally agreed upon simply recognizing the political and commercial importance of transcontinental roads and calling upon the federal government to use its constitutional powers to promote them, "thereby binding the Union of these States in indissoluble bonds, and opening to the rich commerce of Asia an overland transit from the Pacific to the Mississippi River, and the great lakes of the North."

Foreign policy planks had a distinctly Young America flavor and aroused some opposition. One, calling for "free seas and progressive free trade throughout the world," passed with a vote of 211 to 49. Another asserted United States supremacy in Central America and implied abrogation of the Clayton-Bulwer Treaty, while a third demanded that the principles of the Monroe Doctrine be applied with "unbending rigidity." Both met opposition before passage. A plank that hinted at annexation of Cuba—"that every proper effort be made to insure our ascendancy in the gulf of Mexico"—passed only after a heated exchange. The *Charleston Mercury* lashed out at those "extreme proposals," saying that "the Monroe Doctrine, as now interpreted, is a pure figment of political demagogues and filibusters." On the whole the platform reiterated the politics of the Pierce administration. Ironically, it was only after the nomination that the convention passed a resolution in praise of the Pierce record.[14]

The convention opened on Monday morning, but it was not until Thursday afternoon that the balloting began. Except for the courtesy nomination of Lewis Cass, the contest was between Pierce, Douglas, and Buchanan, with the latter receiving the largest number of votes on every ballot. From the start it was clear that a majority of the delegates believed Franklin Pierce could not be reelected. He had too many enemies and his policies had stirred up too much opposition. Above all, their candidate must not be handicapped by association with the conflict in Kansas.

After fourteen ballots the first day, no candidate was near the two-thirds majority needed for the nomination. Strategy meetings that night led to an agreement between some Pierce and Douglas supporters, and when the meeting opened Friday morning Hibbard withdrew Pierce's name. Most of the Pierce delegates then went to Douglas in a last ditch effort to stop Buchanan. The strategy nearly worked, but after the second ballot William Richardson announced that he was withdrawing Douglas's name, reading a letter from him expressing fear that "an embittered state of feeling" might endanger party harmony and approving withdrawal of his name. Should Pierce or Buchanan, "or any other eminent statesman," receive a majority of votes, said Douglas, he urged his supporters to unite in giving him the needed two-thirds. That paved the way for Buchanan's victory by unanimous acclamation. It also gave Douglas a sound basis for the nomination in 1860. Delegate after delegate praised his unselfishness, often expressing relief in private that the convention had chosen, not necessarily the best candidate, but the one most likely to be elected. As a further gesture of reconciliation, Buchanan chose Douglas's friend, John C. Breckinridge, for the second spot on the ticket.[15]

For those Democrats who had hoped for some recognition of growing Free Soil sentiment in the North and of the threat from the slave power, the only choice was to leave their party. Although Buchanan had avoided direct involvement in the Kansas controversy, he had endorsed all the Douglas-Pierce policies and in doing so abandoned his earlier position of support for the Missouri Compromise. Buchanan's nomination was one more bitter pill for Free Soil Democrats, who saw him as the quintessential "Doughface," a northerner with southern sympathies. The resolution endorsing the departing administration, a sop the delegates threw to the defeated president in the last hours of the convention, heaped lavish praise on Pierce. "[The administration] has asserted with eminent impartiality the just claims of every section," said the convention, "and has at all times been faithful to the Constitution. We therefore proclaim our unqualified approbation of its measures and its policy."

A Maine congressman thought the platform "an insult to the North" and abandoned the party, as did his colleague Senator Hannibal Hamlin, who said: "The old Dem. party is now the party of slavery. It has no other issue in fact and this is the standard on which it measures every thing and every man." Northern voters followed by deserting the Democrats in droves. Even southern voters were dissatisfied. Many of them distrusted Buchanan, preferring Pierce, or better yet, a southern dark horse candidate, and they were angry that John Quitman did not win second place on the ticket. But they, unlike discontented northern delegates, had nowhere else to go. The note of apparent unity at the convention's end merely hid the tensions developing within party ranks.[16]

Despite tensions in Democratic ranks, Buchanan's nomination posed serious problems for the new Republican party, which now faced a skilled and experienced opponent whose mission to England had protected him from Pierce's unpopular moves in Kansas. National political parties in the United States have always comprised many disparate elements and power-seeking individuals, resulting in coalition parties rather than coalition government. If any individual was responsible for forming a national anti-Nebraska party it was Salmon P. Chase, who participated in a caucus in December 1855 in Silver Spring, Maryland. That caucus led directly to the first national Republican gathering in February where Free Soilers, antislavery Whigs, anti-Nebraska Democrats, and some with Know-Nothing sympathies organized a national party and produced a platform. Politicians from all the free states attended, as well as a few from border slave states; those attending ranged from radical abolitionists to conservative Whigs. Moderates were in control, with Maryland's Francis P. Blair, a slaveholder and old Jacksonian, in the chair. The resulting conservative platform criticized the Pierce presidency, urged that Kansas be admitted as a free state, and that slavery in the territory be prevented by constitutional means. Those who expected a more heady brew—attacks on the Fugitive Slave Law or on slavery in the District of Columbia—were disappointed. It was a reserved beginning to what would become a highly emotional campaign. The official platform would be hammered out in June at the national convention in Philadelphia. Its actions would show the country how far the northern rights party would go in challenging the right of a prosouthern Democracy to enjoy power for four more years. All Republicans hoped to prevent that. They differed on how it might be done, and under whose banner.[17]

The Republican convention opened in Philadelphia on 17 June, attracting more than two thousand participants. The North was fighting back, ready to challenge continued obeisance to the slave states. The enthusiasm of participants gave the convention more the flavor of a religious camp meeting than a traditional political gathering. Among old Liberty party members, former Democrats, former Whigs, and Know-Nothings there were a hundred New York Free Soil Democrats who took their seats but were not official delegates. The first significant item of business was writing a strong antislavery platform. That document endorsed the principles of the Declaration of Independence as well as Chase's view that the founding fathers had been antislavery men who wished to keep slavery out of the territories. Linking prejudice against Mormonism to hostility toward slave expansion, the platform insisted that Congress had the right and duty to prohibit in the territories "those twin relics of barbarism—Polygamy and Slavery." The Republicans indicted the Pierce administration not only for wrongs inflicted on the people of Kansas but for "high crime against the Constitution, the Union, and humanity," warning they would "bring the actual per-petrators of these atrocious outrages and their accomplices to a sure and condign punishment thereafter." They followed that threat with a call for the immediate admission of Kansas as a free state.

The Pierce foreign policy fared no better. The Ostend Manifesto was "unworthy of American diplomacy" and would dishonor the govern-ment. Almost as an afterthought the platform supported the construc-tion, with federal aid, of a transcontinental railroad and federal improvement of rivers and harbors "of a national character, required for the accommodation and security of our existing commerce." Only the final plank was somewhat controversial. After an invitation to all who supported the platform to affiliate with the party, it declared that because the Constitution guaranteed "liberty of conscience and equality of rights among citizens," Republicans would oppose "all legislation impairing their security." They hoped the intentionally ambiguous allusion to equality of rights would attract votes of recent immigrants, especially the Germans, without antagonizing nativists who talked of "liberty of conscience" as protection against the Catholic "conspiracy." Still the important planks dealt with antislavery issues. Even such veteran activists as Joshua Giddings and George Julian were pleased with the platform, though it said nothing about the Fugitive Slave Act, possible admission of new slave states, or of slavery in the District of Columbia. Yet they thought it a vast improvement over the earlier, more conservative Pittsburgh platform. "I think it is ahead of all other platforms ever adopted," commented Giddings.[18]

The platform in place, selecting their standard-bearer became the next order of business. The antislavery political ranks provided a number of prospective presidential candidates, along with some late arrivals to the Free Soil position. From the beginning of his political career Chase had dreamed of becoming president. He corresponded with various political figures and took the initiative in organizing a national movement to use the power of the federal government to restrict slavery. If devoted service was a requirement, Chase was well qualified. Among his other accomplishments, he had helped initiate the popular outcry against the Kansas-Nebraska Act. When he left the Senate his Ohio election demonstrated the strength of a party that emphasized antislavery rather than nativism. Unfortunately, besides loyal supporters Chase also had determined enemies. His antislavery views were too strong, and his personal ambition too obvious. Political reality forced him to remove his name as a candidate in 1856.

New York's William Seward probably would have been the strongest candidate for the office he, too, coveted. However, his old friend Thurlow Weed convinced him that the Republicans could not capture the White House in 1856 and that he should wait four years to make his bid. Moreover, some of his antislavery statements could paint the party as extremist. Supreme Court Justice John McLean appealed to many Republicans. He also had had a long public career and was moderate on slavery, too moderate for some. Many former Know-Nothings and Whigs, including Abraham Lincoln, favored McLean, who had strong support in Pennsylvania, Ohio, Delaware, and New Jersey. But he, too, had serious handicaps. He was more than seventy years old, with little personal appeal, and many antislavery advocates distrusted him.[19]

For months before the convention the nomination of John C. Frémont had seemed most likely. Although his supporters pointed to spontaneous popular movements in all sections of the country, his nomination was, in fact, a case study in behind-the-scenes political organizing. Republicans, like all third parties under the American political system, had to decide whether to nominate a strong candidate and stand on principle, or to make a serious bid for control of the White House. While there was no unanimity in the ranks, the more seasoned operators hoped to make a serious run for victory. For that they needed a national hero. Frémont had gained national attention for his explorations of the Oregon Trail and a great part of the trans-Mississippi West, as well as for his capture of Los Angeles during the Mexican War. These well-publicized exploits, as well as a court martial resulting from his loyalty to the naval commander rather than the army general in

California, gave him a reputation as a romantic adventurer and rugged individualist, characteristics that made him a logical prospect.

Although he considered himself a Democrat, Frémont's only political experience was a term of a few months as senator from California. He was the son-in-law of Thomas Hart Benton, having married Jesse Benton when she was seventeen. The marriage angered Senator Benton, but he eventually became reconciled to it and supported some of Frémont's western expeditions. He would not accept him as a candidate, however, throwing his support to Buchanan. It was House Speaker Nathaniel Banks who first promoted Frémont in 1855. As the world-famous "Pathfinder," Frémont could be depicted as a second Andrew Jackson who had built his political career on military exploits and bravery on the frontier. Even some Democrats recognized Frémont's potential and offered to promote him for their ticket. On the advice of his politically astute wife, Frémont turned them down. He had serious presidential aspirations and contemplated running for the anti-Nebraska Democrats or the Know-Nothings, since he felt comfortable with their restrictions on immigrants. Years later he said that his opposition to repeal of the Missouri Compromise, along with the possibility that he might get the nod from the Republicans, had contributed to his decision.[20]

Frémont's prospects improved when the old Jacksonian, Francis Preston Blair, joined with Banks to support the western explorer. Blair promoted Frémont during the Free Soil meeting at his Silver Spring home on Christmas of 1855. He persuaded editors to come out for Frémont and got positive responses from antislavery Whigs Ben Wade and Thurlow Weed, nativists Schuyler Colfax and Henry Wilson, some eastern Free Soilers, and a few conservative Whigs. The growing support was remarkable, considering how little anyone knew of Frémont's political views. He had never taken a strong antislavery stand except for a letter of support for the Kansas free state leader, Charles Robinson. His primary appeal for Republicans, said Ben Wade, was that he had "no past political sins to answer for." Republican leaders hoped voters would support the dashing young adventurer, assuming his opinions coincided with the platform on which he ran.

The one stumbling block at a Frémont nomination in Philadelphia was the relationship of the Republicans to the antislavery Know-Nothings—the Know-Somethings or North Americans—who had split from their parent party and called a nominating convention to meet just before the Republican gathering. Republicans needed North American support, but they did not want them to nominate Frémont first, nor did they want the anti-Catholic, antiforeign issue to dominate the campaign. When the North Americans met in New York, Thurlow Weed and other Republican managers met with them to propose that they nominate Nathaniel Banks, with a conservative Whig as his running mate. Once the Republicans had made their choice, Banks would withdraw in favor of the Republican nominee, taking the Know-Nothing vote with him. The plan worked—possibly lubricated by large amounts of money—and the convention nominated Banks and William F. Johnston. When the Republicans gathered in Philadelphia, Frémont's supporters believed they had cleared the way for his nomination.[21]

But it would not be that easy. Many delegates were suspicious of Frémont's antislavery credentials. They were part of a crusade, and they wanted a leader with a record and deep convictions. Some talked of a McLean-Frémont ticket, and there was still substantial support for Seward. Yet Frémont's support was formidable. To assure success, the Frémont faction released his letter to Robinson in which he expressed opposition to any extension of slavery. When Seward, Chase, and McLean removed their names from consideration it appeared that the issue was settled, until a small, powerful group of McLean delegates, led by the Pennsylvania faction, refused to give up. An informal ballot, taken before the regular voting began, showed the futility of their effort: 359 for Frémont, 190 for McLean. The official ballot then settled the matter with 520 for Frémont, 37 for McLean. The convention made it unanimous and assigned second place on the ticket to William Dayton, a conservative Whig from New Jersey. As planned, Banks stood aside, but the North Americans were embittered by the Republican's vice-presidential choice. They had hoped that their man, Johnston, would get the honor, or at least that one of their number would receive it. Yet they had no other place to go and several months before the election the tickets were combined.

After the nomination, many Republicans who had not favored Frémont began to consider him their best choice after all. William Herndon reported that young men in Illinois felt ''a hot zeal for him,'' and older men ''a firm, ardent, but logical determination'' to elect him. Herndon said Buchanan was a ''devoted, obedient, unresisting Slave to the Slave power; . . . *He must be beat.*''[22]

Yet all attempts to portray Frémont as an antislavery version of Young America, even a latter-day Jackson, failed to convince some of the old-line abolitionists. Garrisonians had long opposed political action, believing that only strong language and agitation would shake the southern slave system, and they certainly did not trust politicians who had to swear to uphold a Constitution that protected slavery. Yet even they saw the emergence of the Republican party as a hopeful sign, at least a thorn in the side of what Sumner called the "Slave Oligarchy." Garrison himself conceded that much but would not budge from his absolutist, nonvoting position.

Others were more flexible, viewing the Republican platform as a statement of much that they had preached for years. Salmon Chase said of the platform writers: "I cannot but suspect that the convention 'builded wiser than they knew.'" Samuel J. May, a friend of Garrison, even campaigned for the Republicans and urged his fellow abolitionists to join the crusade. "If you will have free soil, a free press, free speech, and be yourselves free men," he said, "then go to the polls and vote for Frémont." Gerrit Smith's individualism put him between the two positions. He and a handful of others supported the radical abolitionist Liberty League, which ran Smith himself for president. To him, slavery was such an outrage that neither the constitution nor any law could uphold it. The Constitution, he said, was not a proslavery document, because "the Constitution that offered shelter to Slavery would have no validity." He was convinced that Congress could abolish slavery if it wished, and he deplored the Republicans' unwillingness to go beyond opposition to slave extension. Although a minuscule effort, their work performed one of the valuable functions of minor parties by pushing the others into a stronger stand. Indeed, Smith saw enough value in the Republican cause to contribute five hundred dollars to the Frémont campaign. One of his leading followers, Frederick Douglass, also switched to the Republicans. In fact, most black Americans who had the franchise voted Republican.[23]

As the new party began its first national campaign, Republicans had formulated an ideology for the North that included deep resentment of the South's power, attachment to the American Union, both pragmatic antislavery and a moral revulsion against the institution, and a strong commitment to the economic and social order of the North. Never before had a major political organization openly pitted one section against the other. Viewing slavery as a serious threat to their own freedom and way of life, Republicans played upon that fear to attract voters. The day for compromise had passed, they said, and a newly-aroused North must take command of the federal government and end the era of the slave power. "We are not one people," said the *New York Tribune*. "We are two peoples. We are a people for Freedom and a people for Slavery. Between the two, conflict is inevitable." Facing that challenge, the South responded in kind. The Republicans, said a southern newspaper, were "the mortal enemies of every man, woman and child in the Southern States." A northern victory would repeal the

Fugitive Slave Act, warned the editor, and "would put the torch to our dwellings and the knife to our throats." Increasingly, southern editors and politicians talked openly of secession, and constant repetition of that idea made it more and more acceptable. The campaign of 1856 was a turning point in building sectional loyalty, both north and south.[24]

Despite their being a one-section party, many Republicans believed that with Frémont they could win the presidency. "Free Soil, Free Speech, Free Men, Frémont," was their cry. "Bleeding Kansas" and "Bleeding Sumner" became verbal weapons against the Pierce administration. Part of the campaign was conducted in the halls of Congress, where Republicans one after another attacked Pierce and his Kansas policy. Henry Wilson, for instance, charged that Pierce had "the blood of the murdered people of Kansas dripping from his hands—with the lurid light of the sacked and burning dwellings of Kansas flashing upon his brazen brow." If Republicans could capture Pennsylvania and two or three other northern states, along with the half dozen safe ones, they could elect Frémont. With Know-Nothing support they tapped the strong anti-Catholic strain in American society, and using a number of well known American political leaders they attacked both popery and slavery. Promises of federal aid for a railroad to the Pacific and other internal improvements strengthened the party in the West. They also counted on support from former Whigs, even though a rump Whig convention in September threw its influence to Fillmore. They portrayed Buchanan as a has-been, totally under the sway of the South. Although neither Frémont nor Buchanan participated personally in the campaign, the Democrat was vulnerable to attack because of his age. "There is a wrong impression about one of the candidates," said Thaddeus Stevens in October. "There is just no such a person running as James Buchanan. He is dead of lockjaw."[25]

While Republicans used fear of slavery and Catholics, the Democrats tried to arouse the populace to the danger of disunion should Frémont win. In the last months of his administration Pierce had defused the Kansas issue somewhat by a more balanced approach and by his appointment of John W. Geary as territorial governor. Before November, Geary was able to report that Kansas was, at least temporarily, quiet. Democrats spoke of "Black Republicans," charging that the new party was out of the mainstream, with a program more in the interest of black Americans than of the white majority. Democratic barbs were often personal rather than ideological, making much of the circumstances of Frémont's birth, since his parents had not been married. They attacked him, falsely, as a drunkard, a slaveholder, foreign born, and a criminal. To undermine his Know-Nothing support,

Democrats charged that Frémont was a secret Catholic, producing a series of pamphlets to prove it. In fact, he was Episcopalian, but his father had been a French Catholic, and his niece attended a Catholic school. He and Jesse had been married secretly to avoid her father's wrath, and a Catholic priest was the most available prelate at the time. The attack frightened Frémont's managers, who urged him to publish a denial. But the issue was a double-edged sword, and Frémont decided the wiser course was to ignore a clearly fabricated charge. Democrats ridiculed Frémont as "a man whose only merit, so far as history records it, is in the fact that he was born in South Carolina, crossed the Rocky Mountains, subsisted on frogs, lizards, snakes and grasshoppers, and captured a wooly horse."

While they willingly stooped to such irrelevancies, Democrats continued to emphasize the danger of electing a one-section candidate. "The race," said Buchanan, "ought to be run on the question of Union or disunion." Republican statements from the past—Giddings's call for a "servile insurrection in the South," Seward's higher law proclamation, and Horace Greeley's suggestion that the free states leave the Union—all received frequent coverage in Democratic newspapers. "Tell me," said Virginia's Governor Henry A. Wise, "if the hoisting of the black flag over you by a Frenchman's bastard, while the arms of civil war are already clashing, is not to be deemed an overt act and declaration of war?" Frémont's election, said Wise, would cause a revolution.[26]

Unlike Buchanan and Frémont, Millard Fillmore had less to lose by participating in the campaign. As candidate of the Whig-Know-Nothing party, he minimized the nativist program of the Know-Nothings, hoping that the new coalition would eventually lead to a genuine Whig revival. He and his Silver Grey Whig followers could not accept an American political scene that lacked the Whig emphasis on Union and Constitution. Promising "a faithful and impartial administration of the laws of the country," Fillmore said: "I know only my country, my whole country, and nothing but my country." His campaign could only draw northern votes away from the Republicans. It was a rational, dull, and listless contribution to a campaign that otherwise rivaled the 1840 contest for the excitement of large parades and colorful rallies. It soon became clear that the Know-Nothings could not win but had a serious hope of getting enough votes to throw the election to the House, where anything might happen. Fillmore continued to believe that he might once again become president. Toward the end of the campaign he toyed briefly with the idea of uniting with the Republicans, but it came to nothing, probably because he hated Frémont more than he hated Buchanan. Indeed, many in his party accepted the Democrats' prediction of national disaster should the Republicans win, and former Whigs, especially, moved over into Buchanan's camp.[27]

All parties looked to the state elections in the fall as a portent of the presidential contest ahead. The administration had tried to settle the Kansas issue with the compromise Toombs bill, which probably would have led to statehood without slavery and thus deprived the Republicans of their strongest issue. Although the bill passed the Senate, the companion House bill provided for immediate statehood under the Topeka constitution, and as a result neither measure had enough support to become law. The Republicans then took the offensive, winning many converts in the northern states. Yet there were also significant local factors in the state elections. In Maine they were held 8 September and resulted in a sensational victory for the Republicans. Hannibal Hamlin, a recent convert, became governor. Republicans also carried the legislature and six congressional seats. A Maine Democrat called it "a most unexpected Waterloo defeat." In Iowa and Vermont, Republicans won as expected, and state elections that followed got close attention. Ohio went Republican, to no one's surprise, but Indiana voted for the Democrats. Republicans criticized the apostasy of many former Whigs and charged fraud. Pennsylvania, with its twenty-seven electoral votes, was considered a bellwether state. There a coalition Union party composed of Whigs, Know-Nothings, and Republicans made a concerted effort but lost statewide by a narrow margin. Again there were charges of fraud. Part of the problem, however, had been the coalition's inept organization, a serious shortage of funds, and Democratic propaganda portraying Frémont as a Catholic. Although the Democrats had only squeaked through, they hoped to repeat their success in November and save the nation from Frémont. He himself never acknowledged the possibility of defeat, always confident that he would move into the White House.[28]

Despite a cold and dreary November throughout much of the North, the election turnout in 1856 set a record. Although Buchanan's popular vote was small, not even a majority, he won easily in the electoral college with 174 votes to Frémont's 114. Yet he was, in fact, a minority president. The popular vote totals were 1,832,955 for Buchanan, 1,340,537 for Frémont, and 871,731 for Fillmore, who carried only Maryland in the electoral count. If about eight thousand voters in Kentucky, Tennessee, and Louisiana had cast their ballots for Frémont instead of Buchanan it would have thrown the election into the House. Democrats didn't care. They were jubilant and arrogant, and believed that they had saved the nation. Pierce sent congratulations to Buchanan, predicting that if the people supported him and the platform on which he had been elected they could "safely count upon a triumph over sectional fanaticism for many years." Once again Pierce had utterly misunderstood the national mood. So had Buchanan. The president-elect thought the principal goal of his administration would be "to arrest, if possible, the agitation of the Slavery question at the North & to destroy sectional parties." Even before his inauguration he learned of the coming Dred Scott decision and took heart that the Supreme Court would finally settle the issue of slavery in the territories.

Such optimism overlooked the remarkable growth of Republican power in so short a time. And Republicans were not discouraged but confident, said one, that the new administration could not be worse "than the one just expiring." "We are beaten," said Maine Senator William Pitt Fessenden, "but we have frightened the rascals awfully." One of his friends, believing that slavery was stronger at the polls than freedom, declared: "The only way to arrest the extension of slavery and ruffianism in this country is by *force*." His was still a minority view, however. One of Sumner's correspondents was confident that "Kansas will be free and that it has been saved by the vote for Frémont." W. H. Furness, Philadelphia Unitarian minister and antislavery advocate, said that the Republicans "have not yet got a President but they have what is better, a North."[29]

As in all elections, party leaders interpreted the results to fit their views. And why not? No one really knew why people voted as they did. Certainly the election was not a clear mandate on administration policy in Kansas. How many voted on issues and how many on personalities was, as always, an open question. The Democratic candidate, despite his many flaws and shortcomings, appeared to be the safer candidate. Even many Whigs, who detested Democratic policy, voted against Frémont and the threat of disunion rather than for Buchanan and the Democrats. Religious and ethnic considerations were prominent, and the ambiguity of the Pierce administration regarding popular sovereignty in the territories made that a weak issue. Certainly Governor Geary and the administration's last-minute fair treatment of the free state element in Kansas helped to lower temperatures. Yet Geary himself was so discouraged that he resigned on Inauguration Day, 4 March 1857. All attempts to resolve the statehood issue through compromise had failed before Buchanan came to office. Finally, the victorious party, rather than trying to reconcile with their opponents in a move toward national consensus, declared war against the Republicans. Instead of an olive branch, Pierce offered a bitter and angry final message to Congress, restating his position on abolitionism and blaming the Republicans for a deepening division between the sections. Unwarranted and foolish, it served only to call attention to the departing president's lack of political common sense and his simplistic view of sectional differences. All signs were ominous. Many in the South, once Buchanan was elected, deplored having had to choose between him and Pierce. There was renewed talk of reopening the slave trade and of secession should Republican power continue to grow.[30]

Buchanan's election was a relief to Pierce, who believed it vindicated his policies. His final year in office had been plagued by events and forces far beyond his capacity to resolve. The year had opened with the prolonged fight over the speakership of the House, which ended in victory for Nathaniel Banks and the Republicans. Impatient with the delay, Pierce had sent his message to Congress before the session was under way, thus giving his opponents another issue to use against him. Those attacks—including some by his old enemy, Senator John P. Hale—increased as the year's events unfolded. From time to time there were rumors of war with Great Britain, renewed resistance from the western Indians, problems with the filibusters in Central America, and, most troublesome of all, bloody violence in Kansas and the beating of Sumner in Washington. In August the House adjourned without acting on a money bill for the army, and Pierce had to recall Congress to get the legislation passed. The outlook improved in the fall with temporary quiet in Kansas and a tentative settlement of differences with Great Britain. Yet the final session of Congress adjourned in March leaving most administration proposals of the past four years unfulfilled. During its final days Congress did legislate support for the Atlantic cable project, increases in pay for army officers, money for five new sloops-of-war, and reductions in the tariff.

Surely Pierce must have felt great personal relief at leaving office after such a turbulent four years for himself and the country. Leaving his friends in the cabinet was quite another matter. "I can scarcely bear the parting from you," he wrote Jefferson Davis, "who have been strength and solace to me for four anxious years and never failed me." They were not empty phrases. As another national crisis loomed in 1860, Pierce proposed Davis as the best Democratic candidate for president. In answering a farewell letter from the cabinet, Pierce shared his view of his own presidency. They could be proud, he said, of "the condition of the Country during the four years now about to close." There was general prosperity, virtually no "defalcations on the part of federal officers," and the more than twenty million dollars in the Treasury was "free from the touch of fraud or speculation." Foreign questions had been "amicably and advantageously adjusted," additions made to an "already vast domain," and peace maintained "without compromise of right or a stain upon the national honor." By interpreting in his own way some highly selective evidence, Pierce could give his administration a high grade. Posterity would not be so kind.[31]

After leaving the White House Pierce devoted much of his time during the next few years to travel and to caring for his wife. As much as possible the Pierces avoided harsh northern winters. There was a visit to Madeira, a prolonged tour of Europe, and a winter in the West Indies. But Jane Pierce still mourned the death of her son, and her health continued to deteriorate. She died in Andover, Massachusetts, in December 1863. Although Pierce was out of office he was not out of politics. He followed events closely and corresponded with his few remaining political friends. When, as infrequently happened, he spoke in public, it was to denounce political abolitionists and to support the Constitution as he interpreted it. Josiah Minot, his loyal friend, tried to persuade him in 1860 and again in 1864 to accept the presidential nomination should it be offered him. Pierce refused, though he was always ready to suggest others for that honor.

Lincoln's election plunged Pierce into despair, and when war came he blamed the North and the Lincoln administration. Although Pierce had never approved of secession, he believed that northern agitation and threats to the southern way of life had impelled the South to take drastic action. His attitude toward the war made him even more unpopular, and the circle of his friends grew smaller. For most northern Democrats rebellion had changed everything. Even Cushing joined the Republicans. But Pierce would not change, he would not "bow to the storm," and he wrote his wife that he could never justify or support the "cruel, heartless, aimless, unnecessary war." In light of wartime opinion it was almost inevitable that he would fall under suspicion in the North as an enemy sympathizer. An anonymous letter accusing him of belonging to the Knights of the Golden Circle—a mostly legendary, secret, pro-Confederate organization—came to Pierce from Secretary of State Seward, who asked for an explanation. The insulting accusation cut Pierce deeply, but his denial held little weight with those who found Copperheads behind every Union setback on the battlefield or at the ballot box. It mattered little that the Knights existed only on paper and in the mind of its supposed organizer, George W. L. Bickley. The Emancipation Proclamation especially embittered Pierce, who thought it an invitation to bloody slave rebellion, a twisted policy that sacrificed property rights in the interest of people who could not adjust to freedom anyway.[32]

Increasingly, the former president was out of step with his time, even with the citizens of his hometown. Gossip mongers and the press attacked him. In 1864 a Republican campaign document revived the discredited accusation of membership in the Knights of the Golden Circle. His contribution to a fund for the sick and wounded in the Union Army did not stem the criticism. Pierce shared the nation's shock and grief at Lincoln's assassination, yet a crowd gathered outside his home to ask why he had not displayed a draped flag in mourning for the dead president. He replied that he did not need to display a flag to demonstrate his loyalty, for his whole public life did that. It was only after the war that Pierce decided to be baptized in the Episcopal Church, which steered clear of politics, and therefore to avoid embarrassing sermons. He also drank steadily during his last years. In the spring of 1869 he attended the triennial convention in Baltimore of the Order of Cincinnati, and there he delivered his last speech. His health was poor at the time of the gathering, and he lived only a few months after returning to Concord, where he died on 8 October 1869. New Hampshire honored the former president by having him lie in state at the Capitol. President Grant proclaimed a day of national mourning. After his burial Franklin Pierce's name was seldom recalled in New Hampshire or beyond.[33]

Those who play the presidential ratings game have always assigned to Franklin Pierce a below-average score. Thomas A. Bailey rated Pierce "less than a success, not wholly a failure." That is about the best one can say about his presidency. He had the bad fortune to come to office at a time when the political system of the founding fathers, with the addition of two parties, was starting to unravel. The president was meant to represent all the people, but when internal divisions became so magnified as to destroy the very basis for national consensus, how was that possible? All political systems have distinctive mythologies, and part of the American belief system is that the executive speaks to the interests of all the citizens, projecting to the world a positive and optimistic image. The system works well when the various sections complement each other in a common endeavor. To create a political program for such an operation was the dream of Henry Clay with his American System, in which each section would make its own unique contribution to help form a whole nation. By the mid-1850s that concept no longer meshed with reality. Two distinct sections had emerged, one increasingly under the influence of industrialism, the other dominated by a minority of plantation owners whose wealth, power, and way of life rested on chattel slavery. Viewing the conflict as one of slavery versus freedom was an oversimplification, yet more and more Americans were doing that. Moreover, the debate became emotionally charged, a development the founding fathers had not anticipated, though some of them feared it might happen.[34]

Writers of the Constitution concluded that dividing power between the states and what came to be called the general government would provide the best chance for success. Federalism answered the demand for local self-determination, in which each state was considered sovereign, but it also made the federal government sovereign. It was to state governments that people looked for protection of their interests. The general government might provide additional support to agriculture or commerce, or to various other interest groups, but it was never supposed to interfere with local control. Southerners believed it quite proper for the federal government to help return their fugitive slaves, but they denied as usurpation of power any attempt to keep slavery out of the territories. The government in Washington was there to protect them, not to interfere with or try to change them. Should that happen, the general government had to be resisted.

Indeed, that belief was common in all the states, north as well as south. To Franklin Pierce the Union was sacred, and he revered the Constitution as the founding fathers had written it. Those who agitated against slavery, he thought, were a threat not only to the concept of private property but to the Union itself. Like many earlier Americans he believed that slavery would eventually disappear, but that until it did the interests of the slaveholder had to be protected. The more moderate Free Soilers were just as dangerous as abolitionists for they, too, were infringing on what Pierce believed to be the just rights of the South under the Constitution. Those who disagreed—and their numbers were increasing—thought the president himself was the threat. No doubt a majority of Pierce's fellow citizens shared his view that black Americans were unfit for freedom or to participate in a democratic system. Yet even then, some argued against slavery, a few even supporting a multiracial society. They spoke, but most Americans did not listen. "All the people" really meant "all the white, male people."

Just as there was ambiguity in the political relationship between the states and the federal government, so was there ambiguity in the relationship of government to business. Clearly, the general government was to be limited in domestic matters, though it had exclusive jurisdiction in foreign policy, especially in the matter of war and peace. Just as the government should leave the states alone in domestic matters, it should permit business to operate with little or no interference. There was never a fairer trial of Adam Smith's philosophy of the free market. For the most part commercial, industrial, and agricultural interests were satisfied until they faced overwhelming obstacles or liabilities. Then they looked for government aid. Merchants wanted rivers dredged and harbors improved; western settlers demanded and speculators opposed free land; printers sought lucrative government contracts; manufacturers wanted a protective tariff and stiff patent right laws; railroad promoters sought federal aid, while myriads of would-be profiteers tried to tap the public till. The record of the Pierce administration for saving money and preventing fraud was good, but that became a major cause for complaint from those with outstretched hands. Pierce vetoed a number of internal improvement measures as well as Dorothea Dix's bill to help the indigent insane. A generation of northern reformers considered that action unconscionable. Pierce was more liberal about veterans' benefits or any project related to military needs. With government-owned and operated arsenals and shipyards competing with private enterprise, it was impossible to fully implement the laissez-faire ideals that Pierce and his cabinet subscribed to. As a result he took criticism from all sides.

The veto power often blurs the lines between the executive and legislative branches of government, as does suggesting new legislation in messages to Congress. The president can also attempt to influence legislation by using his office as a speaker's platform. In Pierce's time that meant releasing speeches or articles to the press. During the Pierce years Congress contained a number of highly vocal members hostile to the administration. Many of the president's suggestions died in committee, while others, with the administration's full support, were enacted into law. The most significant of those was the Kansas-Nebraska Act, which also became the most potent weapon of administration enemies. Between the president and Congress, during the Pierce years, there was no question where the balance of power lay. It was Congress, under Senator Douglas's leadership, which took the initiative in the Kansas legislation. Pierce, though originally reluctant, eventually gave it full support, but he had not led the fight.

Every Congress has to deal with partisanship, but under Pierce there were more than the usual divisions even within his own party. Despite his personal appeal, Pierce had little influence on Congress. In that respect he was a weak president. His strongest actions were presenting the third annual message before the House was organized, his vetoes, and his recall of Congress to enact an army bill.

Congress even became involved in foreign policy, demanding to see diplomatic correspondence from time to time and often lambasting the administration for its expansionist policy. Under Pierce the entire cabinet often hammered out foreign policy. Pierce chaired cabinet meetings, but he did not lead them. Often in those meetings the cautious and diplomatic William Marcy was pitted against Jefferson Davis and Caleb Cushing. The men Pierce appointed to overseas diplomatic posts also played important roles in foreign policy decisions. Aggressive Young Americans like George Sanders, Daniel E. Sickles, Pierre Soulé, John O'Sullivan, August Belmont, and John Y. Mason gave the United States a well-deserved reputation as a troublemaker. In a time of revolutionary upheaval they supported and encouraged anti-monarchical forces and favored American expansion. A blundering attempt to acquire Cuba only increased criticism of the Pierce administration. Except for the Gadsden Purchase and a few guano islands, the United States acquired no new territory under Pierce. Anti-British sentiment was strong, and Pierce tended to see the influence of the British, perhaps in collusion with the French, in every foreign policy frustration. Yet despite those frustrations, American trade and influence during the Pierce administration expanded in Central America and Asia.

Foreign and domestic issues play a role in establishing a president's reputation, but the personality of the chief executive is always primary. Pierce became the Democratic candidate in 1852 because he was available and showed a good chance of winning the election. He had a military record, he had played the game according to the rules, and he had served in numerous state offices as well as in the House and Senate. Although his record in office was not outstanding, even his enemies conceded that he was personally charming. "Nature sometimes endows men and women with this quality in lieu of all other advantages," remarked one of them. "There was a winning, irresistible magnetism in the presence of this man," recalled Nathaniel Hawthorne's son, Julian. Indeed, he looked like a president, and that was supremely important. During the campaign of 1852 the *New York Times* ridiculed Democratic attempts to portray Pierce as a warrior, a statesman, and a handsome man. Only with the latter, said the *Times*, would they succeed. His personal charm, however, was sometimes a liability because it accompanied a deep sense of insecurity, making it difficult for him to refuse anyone, especially a strong personality. The result was government by cabinet, a cabinet that included—with the exception of Marcy, Davis, and Cushing—men of limited experience and ability. In light of subsequent events, the Pierce administration can be seen only as a disaster for the nation. Its failure was as much a failure of the system as a failure of Pierce himself, whom Roy Franklin Nichols has skillfully portrayed as a complex and tragic figure. During the final months of the Pierce administration, Charles Francis Adams wrote Sumner: "It may be fortunate that we have been afflicted with just such a President, if the experience of him furnish a lesson which shall save us from ever having just such another." It was a brave but forlorn hope. Adams could not know that the Buchanan administration would lean even more heavily on its southern wing, that it would repeat Pierce's mistakes, and that secession and civil war were but a few years in the future. In 1856, no one could know that.[35]

NOTES

PREFACE

1. Telephone conversation with Allan Peskin, 17 Oct. 1989.

2. *Dayton* (Ohio) *Daily News*, 22 Aug. 1976; *New York Times*, 26 Apr. 1970; *Washington Post*, 7 Jan. 1972, 11 Aug. 1977.

3. Joseph Kastner, *A World of Birdwatchers* (New York: Alfred A. Knopf, 1986), p. 40.

CHAPTER 1
THE AMERICAN LANDSCAPE: 1852

1. Thomas Prince, quoted in Winthrop S. Hudson, *Religion in America* (New York: Charles Scribner's Sons, 1965), p. 101; Joseph Schafer, *A History of Agriculture in Wisconsin* (Madison: State Historical Society of Wisconsin, 1922), p. 22.

2. Larry Gara, ed., "A Correspondent's View of Cincinnati in 1839," *Bulletin of the Historical and Philosophical Society of Ohio* 9 (1951): 135.

3. For an excellent discussion of the role of the land speculator in the 1850s, see Paul W. Gates, *The Farmer's Age: Agriculture, 1815–1860* (New York: Holt, Rinehart and Winston, 1960), pp. 80–89; Larry Gara, *Westernized Yankee: The Story of Cyrus Woodman* (Madison: State Historical Society of Wisconsin, 1956), p. 88; Schafer, *Agriculture in Wisconsin*, p. 30.

4. Gates, *Farmer's Age*, pp. 192–93.

5. Larry Gara, "The Fugitive Slave Law: A Double Paradox," *Civil War History* 10 (1964): 233.

6. Allan Nevins, *Ordeal of the Union*, 2 vols. (New York: Charles Scribner's Sons, 1947), 2:243.

7. Ibid., 2:299.

8. Robert H. Bremner, *From the Depths: The Discovery of Poverty in the United States* (New York: New York University Press, 1956), pp. 3-7.

9. Nevins, *Ordeal*, 2:289.

10. Daniel J. Boorstin, *The Americans: The National Experience* (New York: Random House, 1965), p. 24.

11. Gilbert C. Fite and Jim E. Reese, *An Economic History of the United States* (Boston: Houghton Mifflin Co., 1959), pp. 231-32; Nevins, *Ordeal*, 2:270.

12. George Rogers Taylor, *The Transportation Revolution, 1815-1860* (New York: Rinehart and Co., 1958), pp. 15-22.

13. For a criticism of "railroad determinism" and an argument for the canal as a possibly unifying element in the nineteenth century see Robert W. Fogel, *Railroads and Economic Growth: Essays in Econometric History* (Baltimore: Johns Hopkins University Press, 1964); Taylor, *Transportation Revolution*, pp. 32-55.

14. Fite and Reese, *Economic History*, pp. 183-91; Nevins, *Ordeal*, 2:240.

15. Merle Curti et al., eds., *American Issues: The Social Record* (Philadelphia: J. B. Lippincott Co., 1971), p. 330.

16. Timothy L. Smith, *Revivalism and Social Reform in Mid-Nineteenth Century America* (New York: Abingdon Press, 1957), p. 35; R. Carlyle Buley, *The Old Northwest Pioneer Period*, 2 vols. (Bloomington: Indiana University Press, 1951), 2:488.

17. Smith, *Revivalism*, pp. 80-94; Hudson, *Religion*, p. 152. For an overall view of the Protestant movement for social control see Clifford S. Griffin, *Their Brothers' Keepers: Moral Stewardship in the United States, 1800-1865* (New Brunswick, N.J.: Rutgers University Press, 1960).

18. For the importance of proslavery ministers from the northern states see Larry E. Tise, *Proslavery: A History of the Defense of Slavery in America, 1701-1840* (Athens: University of Georgia Press, 1987); Hudson, *Religion*, p. 201.

CHAPTER 2
DARK HORSE FROM THE GRANITE STATE:
THE ELECTION OF 1852

1. Alice Felt Tyler, *Freedom's Ferment: Phases of American Social History from the Colonial Period to the Outbreak of the Civil War* (New York: Harper and Row, 1962), p. 454; Roy Franklin Nichols, *The Democratic Machine, 1850-1854* (New York: Columbia University Press, 1923), pp. 55, 76.

2. Ralph Ketcham, *Presidents above Party: The First American Presidency, 1789-1829* (Chapel Hill: University of North Carolina Press, 1984), pp. 214-35.

3. Richard P. McCormick, *The Presidential Game: The Origins of American Presidential Politics* (New York: Oxford University Press, 1982), pp. 164-206;

Matthew A. Crenson, *The Federal Machine: Beginnings of Bureaucracy in Jacksonian America* (Baltimore: Johns Hopkins University Press, 1975), pp. 158–74.

4. Clinton Rossiter, *The American Presidency,* rev. ed. (New York: New American Library, 1962), pp. 13–40.

5. Edward Pessen, *The Log Cabin Myth: The Social Backgrounds of the Presidents* (New Haven, Conn.: Yale University Press, 1984), pp. 170–83.

6. Roy and Jeannette Nichols, "Election of 1852," in Arthur M. Schlesinger, Jr., et al., eds., *History of Presidential Elections, 1789–1968,* 4 vols. (New York: McGraw Hill, 1971), 2:922.

7. Avery O. Craven, *The Growth of Southern Nationalism, 1848–1861* (Baton Rouge: Louisiana State University Press, 1953), pp. 1–35; Joseph G. Rayback, *Free Soil: The Election of 1848* (Lexington: University Press of Kentucky, 1970), pp. 277–87.

8. Nichols, *Democratic Machine,* pp. 35–40.

9. Allan Nevins, *Ordeal of the Union,* 2 vols. (New York: Charles Scribner's Sons, 1947), 1:209; Nichols, *Democratic Machine,* pp. 42–52; *New York Times,* 1 June 1852.

10. Philip Shriver Klein, *President James Buchanan: A Biography* (University Park: Pennsylvania State University Press, 1962), p. 215.

11. Nichols, *Democratic Machine,* pp. 53–78.

12. Nevins, *Ordeal,* 2:15; Nichols, *Democratic Machine,* pp. 92–106. Nichols characterized Marcy as "the Statesman of the Democracy."

13. Reginald Horsman, *Race and Manifest Destiny: The Origins of American Racial Anglo-Saxonism* (Cambridge, Mass.: Harvard University Press, 1981), p. 86; Thomas R. Hietala, *Manifest Design: Anxious Aggrandizement in Late Jacksonian America* (Ithaca, N.Y.: Cornell University Press, 1985), p. 57; Salmon P. Chase to James H. Smith, 8 May 1849, *Annual Report of the American Historical Association for the Year 1902,* 2 vols. (Washington, D.C.: Government Printing Office, 1903), 2:173; Glyndon G. Van Deusen, *William Henry Seward* (New York: Oxford University Press, 1967), p. 147.

14. Merle E. Curti, "Young America," *American Historical Review* 32 (1926): 43; Robert W. Johannsen, ed., *The Letters of Stephen A. Douglas* (Urbana: University of Illinois Press, 1961), p. 324.

15. Nichols, *Democratic Machine,* p. 114; Curti, "Young America," p. 41; Merle E. Curti, "George N. Sanders—American Patriot of the Fifties," *South Atlantic Quarterly* 27 (1928): 80–85.

16. Nichols, *Democratic Machine,* pp. 113–18.

17. Ibid., pp. 80–82.

18. Nichols and Nichols, "Election of 1852," 2:938–39.

19. Roy Franklin Nichols, "Franklin Pierce," *Dictionary of American Biography*; Roy Franklin Nichols, *Franklin Pierce: Young Hickory of the Granite Hills,* rev. ed. (Philadelphia: University of Pennsylvania Press, 1958), pp. 84–86, 133–37.

20. Nichols, *Pierce,* pp. 147–68.

21. Nichols, *Democratic Machine,* p. 222; Nichols, "Pierce."

22. Paul F. Boller, Jr., *Presidential Wives: An Anecdotal History* (New York: Oxford University Press, 1988), pp. 103–8; Nevins, *Ordeal,* 2:534–36.

23. Nichols, *Democratic Machine*, pp. 121-28.

24. *New York Times*, 13 Mar. 1852; Edwin M. Stanton to Benjamin Tappan, 9 Feb. 1852, Benjamin Tappan Papers, Library of Congress.

25. Nichols, *Democratic Machine*, pp. 129-45.

26. Nevins, *Ordeal*, 2:20-21; Nichols, *Democratic Machine*, pp. 227-31. The Appendix includes the 1852 Democratic platform.

27. Johannsen, ed., *Letters of Douglas*, p. 252; Robert L. Scribner, "The Diplomacy of William L. Marcy: Secretary of State, 1853-1857," Ph.D. dissertation, University of Virginia, 1949, p. 37; Hudson Strode, *Jefferson Davis: American Patriot, 1808-1861* (New York: Harcourt, Brace and Co., 1955), p. 242; Nevins, *Ordeal*, 2:39.

28. Scribner, "Diplomacy of Marcy," p. 38. There are several versions of this story, all recounted years later. Nichols, *Pierce*, pp. 209, 217; Nathaniel Hawthorne, *Life of Franklin Pierce* (Boston: Ticknor, Reed and Fields, 1852), pp. 370-71, 432; *New York Times*, 25 Sept. 1852.

29. Claude Moore Fuess, *Daniel Webster*, 2 vols., reprint ed. (Hamden, Conn.: Archon Books, 1963), 2:268.

30. Robert J. Rayback, *Millard Fillmore: Biography of a President* (Buffalo, N.Y.: Henry Stewart, Inc., for the Buffalo Historical Society 1959), pp. 334, 337, 350-51.

31. Ibid., pp. 354-63; Benson Lee Grayson, *The Unknown President: The Administration of President Millard Fillmore* (Washington, D.C.: University Press of America, 1981), pp. 137-45.

32. Nichols and Nichols, "Election of 1852," 2:956-58. The Appendix reprints the 1852 Whig platform.

33. Ibid., 2:946-48; Paul F. Boller, Jr., *Presidential Campaigns* (New York: Oxford University Press, 1984), pp. 88-90; Richard H. Sewell, *John P. Hale and the Politics of Abolition* (Cambridge, Mass.: Harvard University Press, 1965), p. 149; Nevins, *Ordeal*, 2:26; William E. Gienapp, *The Origins of the Republican Party, 1852-1856* (New York: Oxford University Press, 1987), pp. 19, 25.

34. Frederick J. Blue, *The Free Soilers: Third Party Politics, 1848-1854* (Urbana: University of Illinois Press, 1973), pp. 232-68.

35. Nichols and Nichols, "Election of 1852," 2:948-49; Gienapp, *Origins*, pp. 32-33.

36. Nevins, *Ordeal*, 2:41, 50.

CHAPTER 3
PRESCRIPTION FOR TROUBLE:
THE ADMINISTRATION OF FRANKLIN PIERCE

1. Roy Franklin Nichols, *Franklin Pierce: Young Hickory of the Granite Hills*, rev. ed. (Philadelphia: University of Pennsylvania Press, 1958), p. 227.

2. H. Barrett Learned, "William Learned Marcy," *Dictionary of American Biography*; Nichols, *Pierce*, pp. 254-55.

3. Claude M. Fuess, "Caleb Cushing," *Dictionary of American Biography*; Nichols, *Pierce*, p. 238.

4. Allan Nevins, *Ordeal of the Union*, 2 vols. (New York: Charles Scribner's Sons, 1947), 2:47; Robert S. Cotterill, "James Guthrie," *Dictionary of American Biography*; Nichols, *Pierce*, pp. 224, 247–50.

5. Dr. Wilmer Worthington to Buchanan, 9 Nov. 1852, James Buchanan Papers, Pennsylvania Historical Society, Philadelphia; Nevins, *Ordeal*, 2:49; August Belmont to Buchanan, 5 Mar. 1853, Buchanan Papers.

6. James D. Richardson, ed., *A Compilation of the Messages and Papers of the Presidents, 1789–1902*, 11 vols. (Washington, D.C.: Bureau of National Literature and Art, 1907), 5:197–203.

7. Nichols, *Pierce*, pp. 230–36, 313.

8. Hudson Strode, *Jefferson Davis, American Patriot, 1808–1861* (New York: Harcourt, Brace and Co., 1955), p. 268; Nichols, *Pierce*, p. 356.

9. Leonard D. White, *The Jacksonians: A Study in Administrative History, 1829–1861* (New York: Macmillan, 1954), pp. 305, 510; Henry Welsh to Buchanan, 2 March 1853, Buchanan Papers.

10. Robert W. Johannsen, *Stephen A. Douglas* (New York: Oxford University Press, 1973), pp. 377–81, 467–68; Nichols, *Pierce*, pp. 254–55.

11. Nevins, *Ordeal*, 2:71–73.

12. Claude M. Fuess, *The Life of Caleb Cushing*, 2 vols. (New York: Harcourt, Brace and Co., 1923), 2:139–43.

13. Nichols, *Pierce*, pp. 254–55, 287–89; Nevins, *Ordeal*, 2:75.

14. James C. Van Dyke to Buchanan, 12 April 1855, Buchanan Papers.

15. Robert L. Scribner, "The Diplomacy of William L. Marcy: Secretary of State, 1853–1857," Ph.D. dissertation, University of Virginia, 1949, pp. 71–76; Nichols, *Pierce*, p. 279; Frederick W. Seward, *Seward at Washington, Senator and Secretary of State. A Memoir of His Life, with Selections from His Letters, 1846–1861* (New York: Derby and Miller, 1891), p. 212.

16. Strode, *Davis*, pp. 252–54; Nichols, *Pierce*, pp. 279–84.

17. White, *Jacksonians*, pp. 365–75, 391–93.

18. Ibid., pp. 173, 405–406, 409.

19. Scribner, "Diplomacy of Marcy," pp. 78–81.

20. Ibid., pp. 92–97; Merle E. Curti, "George N. Sanders—American Patriot of the Fifties," *South Atlantic Quarterly* 27 (1928): 79; Stanley T. Williams, "Nathaniel Hawthorne," Robert Spiller et al., eds., *Literary History of the United States* (New York: Macmillan, 1959), p. 418.

21. Scribner, "Diplomacy of Marcy," p. 82; Ada Sterling, ed., *A Belle of the Fifties: Memoirs of Mrs. Clay of Alabama* (New York: Doubleday, Page and Co., 1905), p. 62.

22. Scribner, "Diplomacy of Marcy," pp. 82–85.

23. H. Barrett Learned, "William L. Marcy," Samuel Flagg Bemis et al., eds., *The American Secretaries of State and Their Diplomacy*, 17 vols. (New York: Pageant Book Co., 1927–1967), 6:170; Scribner, "Diplomacy of Marcy," pp. 116–24; George Sanderson to Buchanan, 10 March 1854, Buchanan Papers; Alan Dowty, *The Limits of American Isolation: The United States and the Crimean War* (New York: New York University Press, 1971), p. 101.

24. Roy Franklin Nichols, "James Campbell," *Dictionary of American Biography*; Horace Mann to Mary Mann, 14 Feb. 1853, Horace Mann Papers, Massachusetts Historical Society, Boston; Nichols, *Pierce*, pp. 296, 351, 372, 379, 491; White, *Jacksonians*, pp. 183–85.

25. Sterling, *Clay Memoir*, pp. 70–71; Cotterill, "James Guthrie"; Nichols, *Pierce*, pp. 295, 429, 490.

26. Roy Franklin Nichols, "Robert McClelland," *Dictionary of American Biography*; Nichols, *Pierce*, pp. 489–90.

27. Strode, *Davis*, pp. 257–59; Nichols, *Pierce*, p. 502; Sterling, *Clay Memoir*, p. 68.

28. Strode, *Davis*, p. 276.

29. Ibid., p. 274; John Muldowny, "The Administration of Jefferson Davis as Secretary of War," Ph.D. dissertation, Yale University, 1959, p. 98.

30. Strode, *Davis*, p. 279; White, *Jacksonians*, p. 452.

31. Strode, *Davis*, p. 77; Muldowny, "Davis Administration," pp. 92–95; *Congressional Globe*, 33rd Cong., 1st sess., p. 1950; Wilcomb E. Washburn, *The Indian in America* (New York: Harper and Row, 1975), pp. 191–96; James C. Malin, *Indian Policy and Western Expansion, Bulletin of the University of Kansas* 22, no. 17 (Lawrence: University of Kansas, 1921), pp. 77–104; Chief Seattle's message appears in *How Shall We Live Together*, The War Resisters League Calendar for 1985 (New York: WRL, 1985).

32. William H. Goetzmann, *Army Exploration in the American West, 1803–1863* (New Haven, Conn.: Yale University Press, 1959), p. 295; Muldowny, "Davis Administration," pp. 332–33; Nevins, *Ordeal*, 2:85.

33. Goetzmann, *Army Exploration*, pp. 305–333.

34. Strode, *Davis*, pp. 287–89; Muldowny, "Davis Administration," pp. 144–47.

35. Muldowny, "Davis Administration," p. 51.

36. J. G. de R. Hamilton, "James C. Dobbin," *Dictionary of American Biography*; White, *Jacksonians*, pp. 225–26, 231, 236–37, 246–47.

37. Nichols, *Pierce*, pp. 372, 430, 491.

38. Fuess, *Life of Cushing*, 2:135–37, 180–82.

39. Fuess, "Caleb Cushing"; Nevins, *Ordeal*, 2:73–74; Fuess, *Life of Cushing*, 2:144–45, 147–50, 184–85, 198–99.

40. Fuess, *Life of Cushing*, 2:166–69, 176; Nichols, *Pierce*, pp. 462–63.

41. Fuess, *Life of Cushing*, 2:179.

CHAPTER 4
SOURCES OF DIVISION:
THE PRESIDENT AND CONGRESS

1. Larry Gara, "Slavery and the Slave Power: A Crucial Distinction," *Civil War History* 15 (1969): 5–6.

2. Albert K. Weinberg, *Manifest Destiny: A Study of Nationalist Expansionism*

in American History, reprint ed. (Gloucester, Mass.: Peter Smith, 1958), pp. 73, 85; James C. Malin, *The Nebraska Question, 1852–1854* (Lawrence, Kans.: James C. Malin, 1953), p. 18.

3. Thomas B. Alexander, *Sectional Stress and Party Strength* (Nashville: Vanderbilt University Press, 1967), pp. 85–90; Roy Franklin Nichols, *Franklin Pierce: Young Hickory of the Granite Hills* (Philadelphia: University of Pennsylvania Press, rev. ed., 1958), pp. 302–310.

4. James D. Richardson, ed., *A Compilation of the Messages and Papers of the Presidents, 1789–1902,* 11 vols. (Washington: Bureau of National Literature and Art, 1907), 5:207–226, 273–93, 327–50, 397–417; Seymour H. Fersh, "An Historical Analysis of the Changing Functions of the Presidential 'State of the Union' Message from 1790 to 1955," Ph.D. dissertation, New York University, 1955, pp. 127–29; Ada Sterling, ed., *A Belle of the Fifties: Memoirs of Mrs. Clay of Alabama* (New York: Doubleday, Page and Co., 1905), p. 59.

5. Gerald W. Wolff, *The Kansas Nebraska Bill: Party, Section, and the Coming of the Civil War* (New York: Revisionist Press, 1977), pp. 30–33; Nichols, *Pierce,* pp. 315–16.

6. Wolff, *Kansas Nebraska Bill,* pp. 33–36; Nichols, *Pierce,* pp. 316–18.

7. William C. Brown to Sumner, 28 June 1854, Charles Sumner Correspondence, Houghton Library, Harvard University; Yellow Springs, Ohio, *Free Presbyterian,* 19 July 1854; W. B. Finch to Wade, 5 Aug. 1856, Benjamin Wade Papers, Library of Congress; Chase to James T. Worthington, 2 Apr. 1855, Salmon P. Chase Papers, Library of Congress.

8. *Congressional Globe,* 33rd Cong., 1st sess., p. 1092, App., p. 50.

9. *Congressional Globe,* 32nd Cong., 2nd sess., p. 485, 33rd Cong., 1st sess., p. 1950.

10. Smith to Sumner, 4 June 1854, Sumner Correspondence; Ralph V. Harlow, *Gerrit Smith: Philanthropist and Reformer* (New York: Henry Holt and Co., 1939), pp. 255–57, 333; Octavius Brooks Frothingham, *Gerrit Smith: A Biography* (New York: G. P. Putnam's Sons, 1878), pp. 212–26.

11. Chase to Smith, 15 Dec. 1854, Chase Papers, Library of Congress; *Congressional Globe,* 32nd Cong., 2nd sess., p. 55, 33rd Cong., 2nd sess., App., p. 371; David Donald, *Charles Sumner and the Coming of the Civil War* (New York: Alfred A. Knopf, 1961), p. 270.

12. Larry Gara, "Antislavery Congressmen, 1848–1856: Their Contribution to the Debate between the Sections," *Civil War History* 32 (1986): 197–207. The antislavery congressmen were careful to distance themselves from the Garrisonian abolitionists who rejected political action and relied on agitation. While they were opposed to the expansion of slavery, they were not free of racism.

13. Helen E. Marshall, "Dorothea Lynde Dix," *Notable American Women* (Cambridge, Mass.: Harvard University Press, 1971); Frederick J. Blue, *Salmon P. Chase: A Life in Politics* (Kent, Ohio: Kent State University Press, 1987), p. 84; Richardson, *Compilation,* 5:247–56; Dorothy Clarke Wilson, *Stranger and Traveler: The Story of Dorothea Dix, American Reformer* (Boston: Little, Brown and Co., 1975), pp. 205–210; Wolff, *Kansas Nebraska Bill,* p. 117.

14. Wolff, *Kansas Nebraska Bill,* pp. 183–89; Nichols, *Pierce,* pp. 349–50, 355.

15. Nichols, *Pierce,* pp. 403–404.

16. Wolff, *Kansas Nebraska Bill,* pp. 121–23. Pierce and Tyler were the only pre-Civil War presidents to have vetoes overridden by Congress. Richard A. Watson, "Origins and Early Development of the Veto Power," *Presidential Studies Quarterly* 17 (1987): 409.

17. James C. Malin, *Indian Policy and Westward Expansion, Bulletin of the University of Kansas* 22, no. 17 (Lawrence: University of Kansas, 1921), pp. 77–104; William Christie Macleod, *The American Indian Frontier* (New York: Alfred A. Knopf, 1928), pp. 466–78.

18. For Atchison's influence see P. Orman Ray, *The Repeal of the Missouri Compromise: Its Origin and Authorship* (Cleveland: Arthur H. Clark Co., 1909), p. 219.

19. Malin, *The Nebraska Question,* pp. 18–19.

20. Allan Nevins, *Ordeal of the Union,* 2 vols. (New York: Charles Scribner's Sons, 1947), 2:93–95; William E. Gienapp, *The Origins of the Republican Party, 1852-1856* (New York: Oxford University Press, 1987), pp. 69–71.

21. Robert W. Johannsen, *Stephen A. Douglas* (New York: Oxford University Press, 1973), pp. 408–413; Hudson Strode, *Jefferson Davis, American Patriot, 1808-1861* (New York: Harcourt, Brace and Co., 1955), pp. 265–67; Nichols, *Pierce,* pp. 319–22.

22. David M. Potter, *The Impending Crisis, 1848-1861,* ed. Don E. Fehrenbacher (New York: Harper and Row, 1976), pp. 160–61.

23. Nichols, *Pierce,* pp. 323–24.

24. *Congressional Globe,* 33rd Cong., 1st sess., p. 239; Chase to E. S. Hamlin, 23 Jan. 1854, *Annual Report of the American Historical Association for the Year 1902* (Washington, D.C.: Government Printing Office, 1903), 2:256; Jacob W. Schuckers, *The Life and Service of Salmon P. Chase* (New York: Appleton and Co., 1874), pp. 140–48; Theodore C. Smith, *The Liberty and Free Soil Parties in the Northwest,* reprint ed., (New York: Russell and Russell, 1967), p. 287; Charles Desmond Hart, "The Natural Limits of Slavery Expansion: Kansas-Nebraska, 1854," *Kansas Historical Quarterly* 34 (1960): 32–50.

25. Wolff, *Kansas Nebraska Bill,* p. 61.

26. Nichols, *Pierce,* pp. 333–34; Wolff, *Kansas Nebraska Bill,* pp. 150–79; Nevins, *Ordeal,* 2:136–45; Johannsen, *Douglas,* pp. 300, 406–407, 419, 434.

27. *Congressional Globe,* 33rd Cong., 1st sess., p. 701; Chase to Theodore Parker, 5 Apr. 1854, Theodore Parker Papers, Massachusetts Historical Society, Boston; Wolff, *Kansas Nebraska Bill,* pp. 93–94; Nevins, *Ordeal,* 2:154–56.

28. Nichols, *Pierce,* p. 338; Wolff, *Kansas Nebraska Bill,* pp. 94–96; Elbert B. Smith, *Magnificent Missourian: The Life of Thomas Hart Benton* (New York: J. B. Lippincott, 1958), pp. 301-3; William N. Chambers, *Old Bullion Benton: Senator from the New West* (Boston: Little, Brown and Co., 1956), pp. 408–410; William E. Parrish, *David Rice Atchison of Missouri: Border Politician* (Columbia: University of Missouri Press, 1961), pp. 152–60; Roy Franklin Nichols, "The Kansas-Nebraska

Act: A Century of Historiography," *Mississippi Valley Historical Review* 43 (1956): 211–12.

29. Alice Felt Tyler, *Freedom's Ferment: Phases of American Social History from the Colonial Period to the Outbreak of the Civil War* (New York: Harper and Brothers, 1962), pp. 347–50; William E. Gienapp, *The Origins of the Republican Party, 1852–1856* (New York: Oxford University Press, 1987), pp. 44–60; Frank L. Byrne, *Prophet of Prohibition: Neal Dow and His Crusade* (Madison: State Historical Society of Wisconsin, 1961), p. 56.

30. Ray Allen Billington, *The Protestant Crusade, 1800–1860: A Study of the Origins of American Nativism* (New York: Rinehart and Co., 1938), pp. 380–88; Gienapp, *Origins*, pp. 60–67; J. W. Stone to Sumner, 15 Mar. 1854, E. Winslow to Sumner, 5 May 1854, Sumner Correspondence.

31. Nichols, *Pierce*, p. 388; Seth Webb, Jr., to Sumner, 14 July 1854, Sumner Correspondence; Douglas to Charles N. Lamphier, 13 Feb. 1854, Douglas to Cobb, 2 Apr. 1854, Robert W. Johannsen, ed., *The Letters of Stephen A. Douglas* (Urbana: University of Illinois Press, 1961), pp. 284, 300.

32. Nichols, *Pierce*, pp. 360–65; Gienapp, *Origins*, p. 127; Douglas to Charles N. Lamphier, 18 Dec. 1854, Johannsen, ed., *Letters of Douglas*, p. 331.

33. Giddings to Joseph Addison Giddings, 11 Jan. 1853, Joshua R. Giddings Papers, Ohio Historical Society, Columbus; Gienapp, *Origins*, p. 85; Alexander, *Sectional Stress*, p. 91.

CHAPTER 5
A POLARIZED SOCIETY:
FUGITIVE SLAVES AND BLEEDING KANSAS

1. Fred Harvey Harrington, "The First Northern Victory," *Journal of Southern History* 5 (1939): 186–89.

2. Joshua Giddings to Salmon P. Chase, 2 Nov. 1855, Salmon P. Chase Papers, Pennsylvania Historical Society, Philadelphia; James B. Stewart, *Joshua R. Giddings and the Tactics of Radical Politics* (Cleveland: Press of Case Western Reserve University, 1970), pp. 235–36.

3. Harrington, "First Northern Victory," pp. 192–93, 196.

4. Ada Sterling, ed., *A Belle of the Fifties: Memoirs of Mrs. Clay of Alabama* (New York: Doubleday, Page and Co., 1905), p. 59; Roy Franklin Nichols, *Franklin Pierce: Young Hickory of the Granite Hills*, rev. ed. (Philadelphia: University of Pennsylvania Press, 1958), pp. 436–37; James D. Richardson, ed., *A Compilation of the Messages and Papers of the Presidents, 1789–1902*, 11 vols. (Washington, D.C.: Bureau of National Literature and Art, 1907), 5:352–60.

5. Harrington, "First Northern Victory," pp. 198–204; *Congressional Globe*, 34th Cong., 1st sess., p. 335; Horace Greeley, *Recollections of a Busy Life* (New York: J. B. Ford & Co., 1868), pp. 351–52; Stewart, *Giddings*, pp. 236–37.

6. Stanley W. Campbell, *The Slave Catchers: Enforcement of the Fugitive Slave*

Law, 1850–1860 (Chapel Hill: University of North Carolina Press, 1968), pp. 84–87; Samuel Shapiro, "The Rendition of Anthony Burns," *Journal of Negro History* 44 (1959): 49.

7. Russell B. Nye, *Fettered Freedom: Civil Liberties and the Slavery Controversy, 1830–1860* (East Lansing: Michigan State University Press, 1963), pp. 265–78; Larry Gara, "The Professional Fugitive in the Abolition Movement," *Wisconsin Magazine of History* 48 (1965): 196–204; Campbell, *Slave Catchers*, pp. 151–54; Roderick W. Nash, "The Christiana Riot: An Evaluation of National Significance," *Journal of the Lancaster County Historical Society* 65 (1961): 65–91.

8. Campbell, *Slave Catchers*, pp. 87–88; Claude M. Fuess, *The Life of Caleb Cushing*, 2 vols. (New York: Harcourt, Brace and Co., 1923), 2:144–45.

9. Shapiro, "Rendition of Burns," pp. 38–39; Charles Emery Stevens, *Anthony Burns, A History*, reprint ed. (New York: Negro Universities Press, 1969), pp. 61–79, 278–79.

10. Tilden G. Edelstein, *Strange Enthusiasm: A Life of Thomas Wentworth Higginson* (New Haven, Conn.: Yale University Press, 1968), pp. 166–73; David R. Maginnes, "The Case of the Court House Rioters in the Rendition of the Fugitive Slave Anthony Burns, 1854," *Journal of Negro History* 56 (1971): 31–42. Abolitionists later purchased Burns's freedom, and he went on to attend Oberlin College.

11. John B. Allen to Sumner, 5 June 1854, George Livermore to Sumner, 1 June 1854, Sumner Correspondence, Houghton Library, Harvard University; Theodore Parker to Stephen D. Crooker, 22 June 1854, Theodore Parker Papers, Massachusetts Historical Society, Boston; Shapiro, "Rendition of Burns," p. 47.

12. Samuel May, Jr., *The Fugitive Slave Law and Its Victims* (New York: American Anti-Slavery Society, 1861), pp. 32–33; *Milwaukee Free Democrat*, 28 July 1854; Campbell, *Slave Catchers*, p. 47.

13. Campbell, *Slave Catchers*, pp. 143–44; Western Anti-Slavery Society Minute Book, 26 Aug. 1855, Library of Congress; Herbert F. Gard to Williamson, 20 Oct. 1855, Passmore Williamson Scrapbook, Chester County Historical Society, West Chester, Pa.; Passmore Williamson entry, 7 Sept. 1855, Anti-Slavery Album, Library of Congress.

14. *Cincinnati Daily Enquirer*, 22 Apr. 1855.

15. Campbell, *Slave Catchers*, pp. 144–47; May, *Fugitive Slave Law*, pp. 50–62; Western Anti-Slavery Society Minute Book, 30 Aug. to 1 Sept. 1856, Library of Congress; *Cincinnati Daily Enquirer*, 30 Jan., 2 Mar. 1856.

16. Samuel A. Johnson, *The Battle Cry of Freedom: The New England Emigrant Aid Company in the Kansas Crusade*, reprint ed. (Westport, Conn.: Greenwood Press, 1977), pp. 5–7.

17. Paul Wallace Gates, *Fifty Million Acres: Conflicts over Kansas Land Policy, 1854–1890* (New York: Atherton Press, 1966), pp. 15–59.

18. Allen Nevins, *Ordeal of the Union*, 2 vols. (New York: Charles Scribner's Sons, 1947), 2:389–90, 484–85; Wendell H. Stephenson, "Andrew Horatio Reeder" and Wilson Shannon," *Dictionary of American Biography*; Roy Franklin Nichols, "John White Geary," *Dictionary of American Biography*.

19. Nevins, *Ordeal*, 2:307–8.

20. Johnson, *Battle Cry*, pp. 26–33.

21. Nichols, *Pierce*, p. 543; Nevins, *Ordeal*, 2:428–29.

22. Nevins, *Ordeal*, 2:313–14; Alice Nichols, *Bleeding Kansas* (New York: Oxford University Press, 1954), p. 28.

23. Nichols, *Bleeding Kansas*, p. 39; Nevins, *Ordeal*, 2:387–88.

24. Nichols, *Bleeding Kansas*, pp. 35–36; Nevins, *Ordeal*, 2:417–18.

25. Johnson, *Battle Cry*, pp. 105–109; Nevins, *Ordeal*, 2:390–93.

26. Johnson, *Battle Cry*, pp. 51–79; Nevins, *Ordeal*, 2:409–11.

27. Richardson, *Messages*, pp. 352–60.

28. Nevins, *Ordeal*, 2:418–19; David J. Baker to Trumbull, 9 Feb. 1856, Lyman Trumbull Papers, Library of Congress.

29. Nevins, *Ordeal*, 2:471–72.

30. Nichols, *Bleeding Kansas*, pp. 98–103.

31. Nevins, *Ordeal*, 2:434–37; Nichols, *Bleeding Kansas*, pp. 100–109; Avery Craven, *The Coming of the Civil War*, rev. ed. (Chicago: University of Chicago Press, 1957), p. 364.

32. Sumner to Chase, 15 May 1856, Chase Papers, Library of Congress; Andrew C. McLaughlin, *Lewis Cass* (Boston: Houghton Mifflin and Co., 1891), pp. 319–20; David Donald, *Charles Sumner and the Coming of the Civil War* (New York: Alfred A. Knopf, 1961), pp. 262–63, 282–85; Nevins, *Ordeal*, 2:441–43; Craven, *Coming of the Civil War*, pp. 223–25.

33. Donald, *Sumner*, pp. 290–98, 312–47; Craven, *Coming of the Civil War*, p. 227.

34. Nevins, *Ordeal*, 2:446; Kenneth S. Greenberg, *Masters and Statesmen: The Political Culture of American Slavery* (Baltimore: Johns Hopkins University Press, 1985), p. 146; "A Friend Indeed" to Sumner, 22 May 1856, Sumner Correspondence.

35. William E. Gienapp, "The Crime against Sumner: The Caning of Charles Sumner and the Rise of the Republican Party," *Civil War History* 25 (1979): 218–45; Hebron Vincent to Sumner, 16 June 1856, Frances L. Capen to Sumner, 25 May 1856, John D. Van Buren to Sumner, 10 June 1856, Sumner Correspondence.

36. James C. Malin, *John Brown and the Legend of Fifty-six* (Philadelphia: American Philosophical Society, 1942), p. 245; Stephen B. Oates, *To Purge This Land with Blood: A Biography of John Brown* (New York: Harper and Row, 1970), pp. 132–44.

37. Nichols, *Bleeding Kansas*, pp. 127–33.

38. Ibid., pp. 144–58; Roy Franklin Nichols, "John White Geary."

39. Nichols, *Bleeding Kansas*, pp. 158–63; Nevins, *Ordeal*, 2:516.

40. Nichols, *Bleeding Kansas*, pp. 163–68.

41. Ibid., pp. 175–85.

42. Nevins, *Ordeal*, 2:455.

CHAPTER 6
FOREIGN POLICY:
LAND, TRADE, AND INFLUENCE

1. Ivor D. Spencer, *The Victor and the Spoils: A Life of William L. Marcy* (Providence, R.I.: Brown University Press, 1959), p. 235.

2. Alan Dowty, *The Limits of American Isolation: The United States and the Crimean War* (New York: New York University Press, 1971), pp. 47-48; H. Barrett Learned, "William L. Marcy," Samuel Flagg Bemis et al., eds., *The American Secretaries of State and Their Diplomacy*, 17 vols. (New York: Pageant Book Co., 1927-1967), 6:268-71.

3. Spencer, *Victor*, pp. 265-69; Robert L. Scribner, "The Diplomacy of William L. Marcy: Secretary of State, 1853-1857," Ph.D. dissertation, University of Virginia, 1949, pp. 140-47.

4. Paul N. Garber, *The Gadsden Treaty* (Philadelphia: Press of the University of Pennsylvania, 1923), pp. 43-62, 94-97; Robert L. Jenkins, "The Gadsden Treaty and Sectionalism: A Nation Reacts," Ph.D. dissertation, Mississippi State University, 1978, pp. 39-55.

5. Charles M. Brown, *Agents of Destiny: The Lives and Times of the Filibusters* (Chapel Hill: University of North Carolina Press, 1980), pp. 189-218; Jenkins, "Gadsden," pp. 136-37.

6. Learned, "Marcy," 6:274-75; Garber, *Gadsden*, pp. 115-17.

7. Jenkins, "Gadsden," pp. 162-73; Roy Franklin Nichols, *Franklin Pierce: Young Hickory of the Granite Hills*, rev. ed. (Philadelphia: University of Pennsylvania Press, 1958), p. 339.

8. Spencer, *Victor*, p. 287; Garber, *Gadsden*, pp. 130-32.

9. Garber, *Gadsden*, pp. 139-45; *Congressional Globe*, 33rd Cong., 1st sess., pp. 1541, 1561.

10. Charles C. Tansill, *The Canadian Reciprocity Treaty of 1854* (Baltimore: Johns Hopkins University Press, 1922), pp. 9-55.

11. Thomas A. Bailey, *A Diplomatic History of the American People*, 10th ed. (New York: Appleton-Century-Crofts, 1980), pp. 278-80; Tansill, *Treaty*, pp. 54-81; Nichols, *Pierce*, p. 344.

12. Scribner, "Diplomacy of Marcy," pp. 414-29, 508-18; Bailey, *Diplomatic History*, pp. 305-306.

13. Earl Swisher, "Commodore Perry's Imperialism in Relation to America's Present-Day Position in the World," *Pacific Historical Review* 16 (1947): 33-40; Arthur Walworth, *Black Ships off Japan: The Story of Commodore Perry's Expedition* (Hamden, Conn.: Archon Books, 1966), p. 230.

14. *New York Times*, 2 Feb. 1852.

15. Roger Pineau, ed., *The Japan Expedition, 1852-1854: The Personal Journal of Commodore Matthew C. Perry* (Washington, D.C.: Smithsonian Institution, 1968), p. 233; Scribner, "Diplomacy of Marcy," pp. 503-507; Ada Sterling, ed., *A Belle of the Fifties: Memoirs of Mrs. Clay of Alabama* (New York: Doubleday, Page and Co., 1905), pp. 110-11; Bailey, *Diplomatic History*, pp. 310-11; Walworth, *Black Ships*, pp. 185-93.

16. Learned, "Marcy," 6:285–87; Scribner, "Diplomacy of Marcy," pp. 436–38; John Bassett Moore, "A Great Secretary of State: William L. Marcy," *Political Science Quarterly* 30 (1915): 387.

17. Dowty, *Limits*, pp. 53–54, 76–148; Spencer, *Victor*, pp. 288–92.

18. Peter Tolis, *Elihu Burritt: Crusader for Brotherhood* (Hamden, Conn.: Archon Books, 1968), pp. 199–200; Dowty, *Limits*, pp. 124–29.

19. Learned, "Marcy," 6:237–62; Scribner, "Diplomacy of Marcy," pp. 532–44.

20. Francis Taylor Piggott, *The Declaration of Paris* (London: University of London Press, 1919), pp. 80–81, 143–49; Spencer, "Victor," pp. 381–86; Learned, "Marcy," 6:283–85.

21. Mary W. Williams, *Anglo-American Isthmian Diplomacy, 1815–1915*, reprint ed. (Gloucester, Mass.: Peter Smith, 1965), p. 148; Bailey, *Diplomatic History*, pp. 272–76.

22. Scribner, "Diplomacy of Marcy," p. 226; Learned, "Marcy," 6:222–23.

23. Dowty, *Limits*, pp. 145–47.

24. Spencer, *Victor*, pp. 309–11; Scribner, "Diplomacy of Marcy," pp. 257–59.

25. Spencer, *Victor*, pp. 311–12.

26. Williams, *Anglo-American*, pp. 179–86; James D. Richardson, ed., *A Compilation of the Messages and Papers of the Presidents, 1789–1902*, 11 vols. (Washington, D.C.: Bureau of National Literature and Art, 1907), 5:281–84.

27. Allan Nevins, *Ordeal of the Union*, 2 vols. (New York: Charles Scribner's Sons, 1947), 2:273; William O. Scroggs, *Filibusters and Financiers: The Story of William Walker and His Associates*, reprint ed. (New York: Russell and Russell, 1969), pp. 98–107.

28. Scroggs, *Filibusters*, 139–42; Brown, *Agents*, pp. 310–13.

29. Nevins, *Ordeal*, 2:405–408.

30. Scroggs, *Filibusters*, pp. 166–70, 177–95; Scribner, "Diplomacy of Marcy," pp. 290–91.

31. Scroggs, *Filibusters*, pp. 171–76, 214–15; Nichols, *Pierce*, pp. 460–63; William O. Scroggs, "William Walker," *Dictionary of American Biography*.

32. Spencer, *Victor*, pp. 376–81; Nichols, *Pierce*, pp. 492–93; Bailey, *Diplomatic History*, p. 283.

33. *New York Times*, 8 Jan. 1852; Scribner, "Diplomacy of Marcy," pp. 341–44.

34. Charles C. Tansill, *The United States and Santo Domingo, 1798–1873: A Chapter in Caribbean Diplomacy*, reprint ed. (Gloucester, Mass.: Peter Smith, 1967), pp. 172–203.

35. Dowty, *Limits*, pp. 135–39; Spencer, *Victor*, pp. 388–94; Marcy to Buchanan, 11 Sept. 1854, James Buchanan Papers, Pennsylvania Historical Society, Philadelphia; Merze Tate, *The United States and the Hawaiian Kingdom: A Political History* (New Haven, Conn.: Yale University Press, 1965), pp. 20–21.

36. Spencer, *Victor*, pp. 394–97; Osborne E. Hooley, "Hawaiian Negotiations for Reciprocity, 1855–1857," *Pacific Historical Review* 7 (1938): 135–38.

37. Roy Franklin Nichols, *Advance Agents of American Destiny* (Philadelphia: University of Pennsylvania Press, 1956), pp. 156–70; Scribner, *Victor,* pp. 449–64; Nevins, *Ordeal,* 2:180–81.

38. Nevins, *Ordeal,* 2:181–82; Scribner, "Diplomacy of Marcy," pp. 477–78.

39. Bailey, *Diplomatic History,* pp. 288–91; Nevins, *Ordeal,* 2:347–48.

40. Richardson, *Messages,* 5:198; August Belmont to Buchanan, 22 Nov. 1852, Buchanan Papers; Amos A. Ettinger, *The Mission to Spain of Pierre Soulé, 1853–1855: A Study in the Cuban Diplomacy of the United States* (New Haven, Conn.: Yale University Press, 1932), p. 165.

41. Ettinger, *Mission,* pp. 165, 482–83; Scribner, "Diplomacy of Marcy," p. 192; Amos A. Ettinger, "Pierre Soulé," *Dictionary of American Biography.*

42. A. L. Diket, *Senator John Slidell and the Community He Represented in Washington, 1853–1861* (Washington, D.C.: University Press of America, 1982), pp. 32–41; C. Stanley Urban, "The Abortive Quitman Filibustering Expedition, 1853–1855," *Journal of Mississippi History* 28 (1956): 175–84; C. Stanley Urban, "The Africanization of Cuba Scare, 1853–1855," *Hispanic American Historical Review* 37 (1957): 29–40; Scribner, "Diplomacy of Marcy," pp. 133–64; Basil Rauch, *American Interest in Cuba, 1848–1855* (New York: Columbia University Press, 1948), pp. 290–91.

43. J. A. Reinecke, Jr., "The Diplomatic Career of Pierre Soulé," *Louisiana Historical Quarterly* 15 (1932): 296–97; Spencer, *Victor,* pp. 319–22; Bailey, *Diplomatic History,* pp. 293–94; Richardson, *Messages,* 5:234–35; *Congressional Globe,* 33rd Cong., 1st sess., App., p. 417.

44. Spencer, *Victor,* pp. 320–24.

45. Ibid., pp. 324–27.

46. Philip S. Klein, *President James Buchanan: A Biography* (University Park: Pennsylvania State University Press, 1962), pp. 238–39.

47. Klein, *Buchanan,* pp. 239–40; Henry Steele Commager, ed., *Documents of American History,* 6th ed. (New York: Appleton-Century-Crofts, 1958), pp. 333–35.

48. Rauch, *American Interest,* pp. 293–95; Sidney Webster, "Mr. Marcy, the Cuban Question and the Ostend Manifesto," *Political Science Quarterly* 8 (1893): 23–24; Ettinger, *Mission,* pp. 379–81.

49. Moore, "A Great Secretary," p. 395; Ettinger, *Mission,* 397–406.

50. Urban, "Quitman Expedition," pp. 189–96; Spencer, *Victor,* pp. 342–43.

51. David M. Potter, *The Impending Crisis, 1848–1861,* ed. Don E. Fehrenbacher (New York: Harper and Row, 1976), p. 193.

CHAPTER 7
THE FINAL ACT: THE ELECTION OF 1856

1. Allan Nevins, *Ordeal of the Union,* 2 vols. (New York: Charles Scribner's Sons, 1947), 2:516.

2. Horace Greeley to Theodore Parker, 23 Mar. 1854, Theodore Parker

Papers, Massachusetts Historical Society, Boston; James Birdsall to William Seward, n.d. (postmarked Mar. 1856), Lyman Trumbull Papers, Library of Congress; George Doughty to John P. Hale, Feb. 1851, John P. Hale Papers, New Hampshire Historical Society, Concord, N.H.

3. David M. Potter, *The Impending Crisis, 1848–1861,* ed. Don E. Fehrenbacher (New York: Harper and Row, 1976), p. 193.

4. John Albree, ed., *Whittier Correspondence from the Oak Knoll Collections, 1830–1892* (Salem, Mass.: Essex Book and Print Club, 1911), pp. 126–27; G. D. A. Parks to Lyman Trumbull, 13 June 1856, and F. S. Rutherford to Trumbull, 31 Mar. 1856, Trumbull Papers.

5. D. T. Jenks to James Buchanan, 10 Dec. 1855, James Buchanan Papers, Pennsylvania Historical Society, Philadelphia.

6. Nevins, *Ordeal,* 2:393–95; Mark M. Krug, *Lyman Trumbull: Conservative Radical* (New York: A. S. Barnes and Co., 1965), pp. 94–103; Robert W. Johannsen, *Stephen A. Douglas* (New York: Oxford University Press, 1973), pp. 461.

7. Roy Franklin Nichols, *Franklin Pierce: Young Hickory of the Granite Hills,* rev. ed. (Philadelphia: University of Pennsylvania Press, 1958), pp. 388–90; William E. Gienapp, *The Origins of the Republican Party, 1852–1856* (New York: Oxford University Press, 1987), pp. 172–79.

8. Nevins, *Ordeal,* 2:397–98; Nichols, *Pierce,* pp. 390–92; John Wilson to Salmon P. Chase, 5 Feb. 1856, Chase Papers, Library of Congress.

9. Nevins, *Ordeal,* 2:402–403; Nichols, *Pierce,* pp. 426–27.

10. Chase to James W. Grimes, 27 June 1855, Chase Papers, Pennsylvania Historical Society; Gienapp, *Origins,* pp. 192–99; Frederick J. Blue, *Salmon P. Chase: A Life in Politics* (Kent, Ohio: Kent State University Press, 1987), pp. 97–100.

11. Gienapp, *Origins,* pp. 200–203; Blue, *Chase,* pp. 101–105.

12. Robert J. Rayback, *Millard Fillmore: Biography of a President* (Buffalo, N.Y.: Buffalo Historical Society, 1959), p. 396; Roy F. Nichols and Philip S. Klein, "Election of 1856," Arthur M. Schlesinger, Jr., et al., eds., *History of Presidential Elections, 1789–1968,* 4 vols. (New York: McGraw-Hill, 1971), 2:1020; Gienapp, *Origins,* pp. 260–63.

13. Nichols and Klein, "Election of 1856," 2:1021–22; Nichols, *Pierce,* pp. 466–67.

14. Nichols and Klein, "Election of 1856," pp. 1038–39; Nichols, *Pierce,* pp. 466–67; Gienapp, *Origins,* pp. 305–306; Nevins, *Ordeal,* 2:456–58.

15. Nevins, *Ordeal,* 2:467–69; Elbert B. Smith, *The Presidency of James Buchanan* (Lawrence: University Press of Kansas, 1975), p. 5; Robert W. Johannsen, ed., *The Letters of Stephen A. Douglas* (Urbana: University of Illinois Press, 1961), p. 361.

16. Nichols and Klein, "Election of 1856," p. 1039; Eric Foner, *Free Soil, Free Labor, Free Men: The Ideology of the Republican Party before the Civil War* (New York: Oxford University Press, 1970), pp. 162–63.

17. Richard H. Sewell, *Ballots for Freedom: Antislavery Politics in the United States, 1837–1860* (New York: Oxford University Press, 1976), pp. 277–79; Gienapp, *Origins,* pp. 250–51.

18. Nichols and Klein, "Election of 1856," pp. 1039–41; Gienapp, *Origins*, p. 336; James Brewer Stewart, *Joshua R. Giddings and the Tactics of Radical Politics* (Cleveland: Press of Case Western Reserve University, 1970), p. 240.

19. Blue, *Chase*, pp. 112–15; Gienapp, *Origins*, pp. 311–16.

20. Gienapp, *Origins*, pp. 316–18; William Ernest Smith, *The Francis Preston Blair Family in Politics*, 2 vols. (New York: Macmillan, 1933), 1:343–50; Philip S. Klein, "John Charles Frémont," John A. Garraty, ed., *Encyclopedia of American Biography* (New York: Harper and Row, 1974), pp. 382–84.

21. Nevins, *Ordeal*, 2:469; Gienapp, *Origins*, pp. 329–34.

22. Gienapp, *Origins*, pp. 338–46; William Herndon to Sumner, 20 June 1856, Charles Sumner Correspondence, Houghton Library, Harvard University.

23. Sewell, *Ballots*, pp. 285–89; Octavius Brooks Frothingham, *Gerrit Smith: A Biography* (New York: G. P. Putnam's Sons, 1878), pp. 172–73.

24. Foner, *Free Soil*, p. 310; Avery Craven, *The Coming of the Civil War*, rev. ed. (Chicago: University of Chicago Press, 1957), p. 378.

25. Richard H. Abbott, *Cobbler in Congress: The Life of Henry Wilson, 1812–1875* (Lexington: University Press of Kentucky, 1972), p. 85; Gienapp, *Origins*, pp. 366–67; Paul F. Boller, Jr., *Presidential Campaigns* (New York: Oxford University Press, 1985), p. 98.

26. Boller, *Campaigns*, pp. 92, 97; Allan Nevins, *Frémont: Pathfinder of the West*, 2 vols. (New York: Frederick Ungar, 1961), 2:451.

27. Rayback, *Fillmore*, pp. 406–13; Gienapp, *Origins*, p. 409.

28. Gienapp, *Origins*, pp. 401–11; Richard H. Sewell, *John P. Hale and the Politics of Abolition* (Cambridge, Mass.: Harvard University Press, 1965), p. 173.

29. Gienapp, *Origins*, pp. 413–15; Nichols, *Pierce*, p. 488; Johannsen, *Douglas*, pp. 538–39; W. H. Brown to Trumbull, 28 Feb. 1857, Trumbull Papers; Charles A. Jellison, *Fessenden of Maine: Civil War Senator* (Syracuse, N.Y.: Syracuse University Press, 1962), p. 97; Edward P. Pierce to Sumner, 4 Jan. 1857, W. H. Furness to Sumner, 9 Nov. 1856, Sumner Correspondence.

30. James D. Richardson, ed., *A Compilation of the Messages and Papers of the Presidents, 1789–1902*, 11 vols. (Washington, D.C.: Bureau of National Literature and Art, 1907), 5:397–407).

31. Nichols, *Pierce*, pp. 502–503.

32. Nichols, *Pierce*, pp. 507–21; Frank L. Klement, "Ohio and the Knights of the Golden Circle: The Evolution of a Civil War Myth," *Cincinnati Historical Society Bulletin* 32 (1974): 7–23; Frank L. Klement, "Franklin Pierce and the Treason Charges of 1861–1862," *Historian* 23 (1961): 436–48.

33. Nichols, *Pierce*, pp. 521–32.

34. Thomas A. Bailey, *Presidential Greatness: The Image and the Man from George Washington to the Present* (New York: Appleton-Century-Crofts, 1966), p. 288.

35. *New York Times*, 2 Sept. 1852; Charles Francis Adams to Sumner, 3 Sept. 1856, Sumner Correspondence; Nichols, *Pierce*, p. 529. In a final chapter entitled "Recasting a Stereotype," Roy Franklin Nichols analyzes at length the various factors contributing to Pierce's tragic life, portraying him as a victim of the times and of personal misfortunes beyond his control.

BIBLIOGRAPHICAL ESSAY

This study is based primarily on published material, though it also draws upon a variety of manuscript sources originally collected for research on the antislavery congressmen. All such sources are cited in the notes. The serious scholar will find that Franklin Pierce manuscripts are scarce. Few items in the Pierce Papers at the Library of Congress or at the New Hampshire Historical Society cover the years of his presidency. Perley Orman Ray, "Some Papers of Franklin Pierce, 1852–1862," *American Historical Review* 10 (1904–1905): 110–27, 350–70, includes relevant material from his White House years.

Of more than a half-dozen campaign biographies, Pierce's friend Nathaniel Hawthorne wrote the only one of note: *Life of Franklin Pierce* (Boston: Ticknor, Reed and Fields, 1852). The only scholarly biography is Roy Franklin Nichols, *Franklin Pierce: Young Hickory of the Granite Hills*, rev. ed. (Philadelphia: University of Pennsylvania Press, 1931, 1958), one of several of his books that were indispensable for this study. Nichols was the dean of American political historians, and his biography covers in detail all aspects of Pierce's life. Although its organization is strictly chronological and sometimes confusing, the book provides a wealth of information. Two accounts of the Pierce presidency by contemporaries are Ann Ellis Carroll's critical *Review of Pierce's Administration Showing Its Only Popular Measure to Have Originated with the Executive of Millard Fillmore* (Boston: J. French & Co., 1856) and Sydney Webster, *Franklin Pierce and His Administration* (New York: D. Appleton and Co., 1892), a pamphlet that reprints two articles by Pierce's ever-loyal secretary. Another older work, equally useful for the years of the Pierce presidency, is Allan Nevins, *Ordeal of the Union*, 2 vols. (New York: Charles Scribner's Sons, 1947), which contains a wealth of detail on every aspect of American life in the 1850s.

Additional information for the years of the Pierce presidency can be found in Avery Craven, *The Coming of the Civil War*, rev. ed. (Chicago: University of Chicago Press, 1957); Avery Craven, *The Growth of Southern Nationalism, 1848-1861* (Baton Rouge: Louisiana State University Press, 1953); and David M. Potter, *The Impending Crisis, 1848-1861*, ed. Don E. Fehrenbacher (New York: Harper and Row, 1976). Robert H. Wiebe, *The Opening of American Society from the Adoption of the Constitution to the Eve of Disunion* (New York: Alfred A. Knopf, 1984), discusses the various pressures that shaped the changes in American antebellum society. Anne Norton's *Alternative Americas: A Reading of Antebellum Political Culture* (Chicago: University of Chicago Press, 1986) deals with the emergence of sections as revealed in the literature of the period.

The picture I have drawn of life in the United States in the early 1850s is based on a career of teaching and research. A select listing of writings that provide useful information about the period includes Daniel J. Boorstin, *The Americans: The National Experience* (New York: Random House, 1965); Merle E. Curti, *The Growth of American Thought*, 2d ed. (New York: Harper and Brothers, 1951); J. C. Furnas, *The Americans: A Social History of the United States, 1597-1914* (New York: G. P. Putnam's Sons, 1969); and Arthur A. Ekirch, Jr., *The Idea of Progress in America, 1815-1860*, reprint ed. (New York: Peter Smith, 1951). Howard Zinn, *A People's History of the United States* (New York: Harper and Row, 1980), presents a provocative and unorthodox view of the times. There is no better description of the westward trek than John D. Unruh, Jr., *The Plains Across: The Overland Emigrants and the Trans-Mississippi West, 1840-1860* (Urbana: University of Illinois Press, 1979). Three useful works on early American farming are Paul W. Gates, *The Farmer's Age: Agriculture, 1815-1860* (New York: Holt, Rinehart and Winston, 1960); Robert L. Jones, *History of Agriculture in Ohio to 1880* (Kent, Ohio: Kent State University Press, 1983); and Joseph Schafer, *A History of Agriculture in Wisconsin* (Madison: State Historical Society of Wisconsin, 1922). For the land speculator see Paul Wallace Gates, "The Role of the Land Speculator in Western Development," *Pennsylvania Magazine of History and Biography* 66 (1942): 314-33, and Larry Gara, *Westernized Yankee: The Story of Cyrus Woodman* (Madison: State Historical Society of Wisconsin, 1956). Roy M. Robbins, *Our Landed Heritage: The Public Domain, 1776-1936* (Princeton, N.J.: Princeton University Press, 1942) is still useful. Two excellent syntheses of southern slavery are Kenneth M. Stampp, *The Peculiar Institution: Slavery in the Ante-Bellum South* (New York: Alfred A. Knopf, 1956), and Eugene D. Genovese, *Roll, Jordan, Roll: The World the Slaves Made* (New York: Pantheon Books, 1974). Frank L. Owsley, *Plain Folk of the Old South* (Baton Rouge: Louisiana State University Press, 1949), describes the role of the yeoman farmer who worked outside slavery.

Both Rollin G. Osterweiss, *Romanticism and Nationalism in the Old South* (New Haven, Conn.: Yale University Press, 1949), and John Hope Franklin, *The Militant South, 1800-1861* (Cambridge, Mass.: Belknap Press, 1956), discuss antebellum southern thought. Antebellum southern politics can be traced in Kenneth Greenberg, *Masters and Statesmen: The Political Culture of American Slavery* (Baltimore: Johns Hopkins University Press, 1985); William J. Cooper, Jr.,

Liberty and Slavery: Southern Politics to 1860 (New York: Alfred A. Knopf, 1983); and Cooper, *The South and the Politics of Slavery, 1828–1856* (Baton Rouge: Louisiana State University Press, 1978). Paul Finkelman, *An Imperfect Union: Slavery, Federalism, and Comity* (Chapel Hill: University of North Carolina Press, 1981) discusses the judicial war between the sections over the status of slaves in transit through the northern states.

Discussions of aspects of the industrial revolution can be found in Norman Ware, *The Industrial Worker, 1840–1860: The Reaction of American Industrial Society to the Advance of the Industrial Revolution,* reprint ed. (Gloucester, Mass.: Peter Smith, 1959); Julie A. Matthaei, *An Economic History of Women in America* (New York: Schocken Books, 1982); David A. Hounshell, *From the American System to Mass Production, 1800–1932* (Baltimore: Johns Hopkins University Press, 1984); Mitchell Wilson, *American Science and Invention: A Pictorial History* (New York: Simon and Schuster, 1954); Roger Burlingame, *March of the Iron Men: A Social History of Union through Invention* (New York: Charles Scribner's Sons, 1938); Lyon Sprague de Camp, *The Heroic Age of American Invention* (Garden City, N.Y.: Doubleday, 1961); Irvin G. Wyllie, *The Self-Made Man in America: The Myth of Rags to Riches* (New Brunswick, N.J.: Rutgers University Press, 1954); Edward Pessen, *Riches, Class and Power before the Civil War* (Lexington, Mass.: D. C. Heath and Co., 1973); and Robert H. Bremner, *From the Depths: The Discovery of Poverty in the United States* (New York: New York University Press, 1956).

George Rogers Taylor's *The Transportation Revolution, 1815–1860* (New York: Rinehart and Co., 1958), is still the best comprehensive account of the topic. Other useful works include Carter Goodrich, *Government Promotion of American Canals and Railroads, 1800–1890* (New York: Columbia University Press, 1960); Madeline S. Waggoner, *The Long Haul West: The Great Canal Era, 1817–1850* (New York: G. P. Putnam's Sons, 1958); John F. Stover, *American Railroads* (Chicago: University of Chicago Press, 1961); Harry N. Scheiber, *Ohio Canal Era: A Case Study of Government and the Economy, 1820–1860* (Athens: Ohio University Press, 1961); Arthur H. Clark, *The Clipper Ship Era* (New York: G. P. Putnam's Sons, 1910); and Louis C. Hunter, *Steamboats on the Western Rivers* (Cambridge, Mass.: Harvard University Press, 1949).

For institutional religion see Winthrop S. Hudson, *American Protestantism* (Chicago: University of Chicago Press, 1961), and *Religion in America* (New York: Charles Scribner's Sons, 1965); John Tracy Ellis, *American Catholicism* (Chicago: University of Chicago Press, 1956); Ray Allen Billington, *The Protestant Crusade, 1800–1860: A Study of the Origins of American Nativism* (New York: Rinehart and Co., 1938); Timothy L. Smith, *Revivalism and Social Reform in Mid-Nineteenth Century America* (New York: Abingdon Press, 1957); and Whitney R. Cross, *The Burned Over District: The Social and Intellectual History of Enthusiastic Religion in Western New York, 1800–1850* (Ithaca, N.Y.: Cornell University Press, 1950).

The literature of the nineteenth-century reform movements is rich and varied. The factual material in Alice Felt Tyler's *Freedom's Ferment: Phases of American Social History from the Colonial Period to the Outbreak of the Civil War* (New York: Harper and Row, 1962), is comprehensive, though many of its interpretations are quaint and out of date. Other, more recent works include Anne C. Rose, *Transcendentalism as a Social Movement, 1830–1850* (New Haven, Conn.: Yale University Press, 1981); and Robert H. Walker, *Reform in America: The Continuing Frontier* (Lexington: University Press of Kentucky, 1985). Clifford S. Griffin, *Their Brothers' Keepers: Moral Stewardship in the United States, 1800–1865* (New Brunswick, N.J.: Rutgers University Press, 1960), describes the organizations and political action of nineteenth-century Protestant reformers.

No American reform produced a larger literature than antislavery. Dwight L. Dumond's massive *Antislavery: The Crusade for Freedom in America* (Ann Arbor: University of Michigan Press, 1961), with a separately published bibliography, traces in detail the entire history of the movement from the viewpoint of an impassioned defender of political antislavery. Other useful antislavery histories include Gilbert H. Barnes, *The Antislavery Impulse, 1830–1844*, reprint ed. (New York: Harcourt, Brace and World, 1964); Merton L. Dillon, *The Abolitionists: The Growth of a Dissenting Minority* (DeKalb: Northern Illinois University Press, 1974); Martin Duberman, *The Antislavery Vanguard: New Essays on the Abolitionists* (Princeton, N.J.: Princeton University Press, 1965); Louis Filler, *The Crusade against Slavery, 1830–1860* (New York: Harper and Brothers, 1960); Lawrence J. Friedman, *Gregarious Saints: Self and Community in American Abolitionism, 1830–1870* (Cambridge, Mass.: Cambridge University Press, 1982); Louis S. Gerteis, *Morality and Utility in American Antislavery Reform* (Chapel Hill: University of North Carolina Press, 1987); Aileen Kraditor, *Means and Ends in American Abolitionism: Garrison and His Critics on Strategy and Tactics, 1834–1850* (New York: Pantheon Books, 1969); Alan M. Kraut, *Crusaders and Compromisers: Essays on the Relationship of the Antislavery Struggle to the Antebellum Party System* (Westport, Conn.: Greenwood Press, 1983); Carleton Mabee, *Black Freedom: The Nonviolent Abolitionists from 1830 through the Civil War* (London: Macmillan, 1970); Edward Magdol, *The Antislavery Rank and File: A Social Profile of the Abolitionists' Constituency* (New York: Greenwood Press, 1986); Lewis Perry and Michael Fellman, eds., *Antislavery Reconsidered: New Perspectives on the Abolitionists* (Baton Rouge: Louisiana State University Press, 1979); Benjamin Quarles, *Black Abolitionists* (New York: Oxford University Press, 1969); Leonard J. Richards, *Gentlemen of Property and Standing: Anti-Abolition Mobs in Jacksonian America* (New York: Oxford University Press, 1970); Gerald Sorin, *Abolitionism: A New Perspective* (New York: Praeger Publishers, 1972); and James B. Stewart, *Holy Warriors: The Abolitionists and American Slavery* (New York: Hill and Wang, 1976).

The following provided background material on the office of president: Clinton Rossiter, *The American Presidency*, rev. ed. (New York: New American Library, 1960); Edward S. Corwin, *The President: Office and Powers, 1787–1984*, 5th rev. ed., ed. Randall Bland, Theodore Hanson, and Jack Peltason (New York: New York University Press, 1984); Richard P. McCormick, *The Presidential Game: The Origins of American Presidential Politics* (New York: Oxford University Press, 1982); Ralph Ketcham, *Presidents above Party: The First American Presidency, 1789–1829* (Chapel Hill: University of North Carolina Press, 1984); Edward Pessen, *The Log Cabin Myth: The Social Backgrounds of the Presidents* (New Haven,

Conn.: Yale University Press, 1984); Thomas A. Bailey, *Presidential Greatness: The Image and the Man from George Washington to the Present* (New York: Appleton-Century-Crofts, 1966); Seymour H. Fersh, "An Historical Analysis of the Changing Functions of the Presidential 'State of the Union' Message from 1790 to 1955," Ph.D. dissertation, New York University, 1955; and Jeffrey Elliott Cohen, "Passing the President's Program: Presidential-Congressional Relations, 1789-1974," Ph.D. dissertation, University of Michigan, 1979. James D. Richardson, ed., *A Compilation of the Messages and Papers of the Presidents, 1789-1902*, 11 vols. (Washington, D.C.: Bureau of National Literature and Art, 1907), 5:195-426, contains the full text of all the Pierce presidential messages and proclamations. Two books by Paul F. Boller, Jr., *Presidential Campaigns* (New York: Oxford University Press, 1984), and *Presidential Wives: An Anecdotal History* (New York: Oxford University Press, 1988), provide a wealth of facts and anecdotes about all the presidents from George Washington to Ronald Reagan.

For Millard Fillmore, who preceded Pierce in the presidency, and James Buchanan, who succeeded him, see Robert J. Rayback, *Millard Fillmore: Biography of a President* (Buffalo, N.Y.: Henry Stewart, Inc., for the Buffalo Historical Society, 1959); Benson Lee Grayson, *The Unknown President: The Administration of President Millard Fillmore* (Washington, D.C.: University Press of America, 1981); Elbert B. Smith, *The Presidencies of Zachary Taylor and Millard Fillmore* (Lawrence: University Press of Kansas, 1988); Philip S. Klein, *President James Buchanan: A Biography* (University Park: Pennsylvania State University Press, 1962); and Elbert B. Smith, *The Presidency of James Buchanan* (Lawrence: University Press of Kansas, 1975).

The elections that opened and closed the Pierce administration are the subjects of Roy F. and Jeannette Nichols, "Election of 1852," in Arthur Schlesinger, Jr., et al., eds., *History of Presidential Elections, 1789-1968*, 4 vols. (New York: McGraw-Hill, 1971), 2:921-1003, and Roy F. Nichols and Philip S. Klein, "Election of 1856," 2:1007-1094 in the same volume. These articles include the full texts of the various party platforms as well as several campaign documents. Additional information may be found in Roy F. Nichols, "Some Problems of the First Republican Presidential Campaign," *American Historical Review* 28 (1923): 492-96; Eugene H. Roseboom, *A History of Presidential Elections* (New York: Macmillan, 1957); and Dean W. Burnham, *Presidential Ballots, 1836-1892* (Baltimore: Johns Hopkins University Press, 1955). The first fifty pages of Roy F. Nichols, *Disruption of American Democracy* (New York: Macmillan, 1948) contain an excellent discussion of Buchanan's election.

For the domestic policies of the Pierce administration and the executive's relations with Congress, John Muldowny, "The Administration of Jefferson Davis as Secretary of War," Ph.D. dissertation, Yale University, 1959, brings together a wealth of information on that topic, while William H. Goetzmann's *Army Exploration in the American West, 1803-1863* (New Haven, Conn.: Yale University Press, 1959) treats the Pacific railroad surveys in some detail. Indian policy during the Pierce years is treated in James C. Malin, *Indian Policy and Westward Expansion* (Lawrence, Kans.: James C. Malin, 1921), and William

Macleod, *The American Indian Frontier* (New York: Alfred A. Knopf, 1928). Leonard D. White, *The Jacksonians: A Study in Administrative History, 1829–1861* (New York: Macmillan, 1954) remains a most useful source. Biographies provide much of the material for the Pierce domestic policies. Among the more useful are Hudson Strode, *Jefferson Davis, American Patriot, 1808–1861* (New York: Harcourt, Brace and Co., 1955); William E. Dodds, *Jefferson Davis*, reprint ed. (New York: Russell and Russell, 1966); Robert W. Johannsen, *Stephen A. Douglas* (New York: Oxford University Press, 1973); Claude M. Fuess, *The Life of Caleb Cushing*, 2 vols. (New York: Harcourt, Brace and Co., 1923); Andrew McLaughlin, *Lewis Cass* (Boston: Houghton Mifflin and Co., 1891); Frank B. Woodford, *Lewis Cass* (New Brunswick, N.J.: Rutgers University Press, 1950); William E. Parrish, *David Rice Atchison of Missouri: Border Politician* (Columbia: University of Missouri Press, 1961); Rudolph Von Abele, *Alexander Stephens: A Biography*, reprint ed. (Westport, Conn.: Negro Universities Press, 1971); William Nisbet Chambers, *Old Bullion Benton: Senator from the New West* (Boston: Little, Brown and Co., 1956); Elbert B. Smith, *Magnificent Missourian: The Life of Thomas Hart Benton* (New York: J. B. Lippincott and Co., 1958); Stewart Mitchell, *Horatio Seymour of New York* (Cambridge, Mass.: Harvard University Press, 1938); Fred Harvey Harrington, *Fighting Politician: Major General N. P. Banks* (Philadelphia: University of Pennsylvania Press, 1948), and "The First Northern Victory," *Journal of Southern History* 5 (1939): 186–205; and Dorothy Clarke Wilson, *Stranger and Traveler: The Story of Dorothea Dix, American Reformer* (Boston: Little, Brown and Co., 1975).

The literature of the growth of sectional politics and the emergence of the Republican party seems unlimited. Joel H. Silbey, *The Shrine of Party, Congressional Voting Behavior, 1841–1852* (Pittsburgh: University of Pittsburgh Press, 1967), and Thomas B. Alexander, *Sectional Stress and Party Strengths: A Study of Roll-Call Voting Patterns in the United States House of Representatives, 1836–1860* (Nashville: Vanderbilt University Press, 1967), analyze congressional voting patterns in light of party loyalty and the impact of sectional issues. Joseph G. Rayback, *Free Soil: The Election of 1848* (Lexington: University Press of Kentucky, 1970) provides essential background for the Free Soil movement. Other useful works include Frederick J. Blue, *The Free Soilers: Third Party Politics, 1848–1854* (Urbana: University of Illinois Press, 1973); Stephen E. Maizlish, *The Triumph of Sectionalism: The Transformation of Ohio Politics, 1844–1856* (Kent, Ohio: Kent State University Press, 1983); William W. Freehling, *The Road to Disunion: Secessionists at Bay 1776–1854* (New York: Oxford University Press, 1990); Eugene H. Berwanger, *The Frontier against Slavery: Western Anti-Negro Prejudice and the Slavery Extension Controversy* (Urbana: University of Illinois Press, 1967); Eric Foner, *Free Soil, Free Labor, Free Men: The Ideology of the Republican Party before the Civil War* (New York: Oxford University Press, 1970); Michael Fitzgibbon Holt, *Forging a Majority: The Formation of the Republican Party in Pittsburgh, 1848–1860* (New Haven, Conn.: Yale University Press, 1969), and Holt, *The Political Crisis of the 1850s* (New York: John Wiley and Sons, 1978); Ronald P. Formisano, *The Birth of Mass Political Parties: Michigan, 1827–1861* (Princeton, N.J.: Princeton University Press, 1971); Theodore Clarke Smith, *The Liberty and Free Soil Parties in the Northwest* (New York: Longman's Green and Co., 1897), and *Parties and Slavery, 1850–1859* (New York: Harper and Brothers, 1906).

William E. Gienapp, *The Origins of the Republican Party, 1852–1856* (New York: Oxford University Press, 1987) provides an essential source for the politics of the Pierce years. The title of Richard Sewell's very fine book, *Ballots for Freedom: Antislavery Politics in the United States, 1837–1860* (New York: Oxford University Press, 1976), highlights his interpretation of sectional politics. Biographical studies were also useful, especially the following: James Brewer Stewart, *Joshua R. Giddings and the Tactics of Radical Politics* (Cleveland: Press of Case Western Reserve University, 1970); H. L. Trefousse, *Benjamin Franklin Wade: Radical Republican from Ohio* (New York; Twayne Publishers, 1963); Charles A. Jellison, *Fessenden of Maine: Civil War Senator* (Syracuse, N.Y.: Syracuse University Press, 1962); Octavius Brooks Frothingham, *Gerrit Smith: A Biography* (New York: Putnam and Sons, 1909); Richard H. Sewell, *John P. Hale and the Politics of Abolition* (Cambridge, Mass.: Harvard University Press, 1965); Richard H. Abbott, *Cobbler in Congress: The Life of Henry Wilson, 1812–1875* (Lexington: University Press of Kentucky, 1972); Ernest A. McKay, "Henry Wilson: Unprincipled Know-Nothing," *Mid-America* 46 (1964): 29–37; Mark M. Krug, *Lyman Trumbull: Conservative Radical* (New York: A. S. Barnes and Co., 1965); Frederick J. Blue, *Salmon P. Chase: A Life in Politics* (Kent, Ohio: Kent State University Press, 1987); Reinhard E. Luthin, "Salmon P. Chase's Political Career before the Civil War," *Mississippi Valley Historical Review* 29 (1943): 517–40; Glyndon G. Van Deusen, *William Henry Seward* (New York: Oxford University Press, 1967); and David Donald, *Charles Sumner and the Coming of the Civil War* (New York: Alfred A. Knopf, 1961).

Stanley W. Campbell's *The Slave Catchers: Enforcement of the Fugitive Slave Law, 1850–1860* (Chapel Hill: University of North Carolina Press, 1968) emphasizes the early success in administering the law. Larry Gara, *The Liberty Line: The Legend of the Underground Railroad* (Lexington: University of Kentucky Press, 1961), treats the civil liberties issue of the fugitive slave question, as does Russell B. Nye, *Fettered Freedom: Civil Liberties and the Slavery Controversy, 1830–1860* (East Lansing: Michigan State University Press, 1963). Samuel May, Jr., *The Fugitive Slave Law and Its Victims* (New York: American Anti-Slavery Society, 1861), details virtually all the fugitive slave incidents. For the Anthony Burns case see Emery Stevens, *Anthony Burns, A History*, reprint ed. (New York: Negro Universities Press, 1969); Jane H. and William H. Pease, *The Fugitive Slave Law and Anthony Burns: A Problem in Law Enforcement*, ed. Harold M. Hyman (Philadelphia: J. B. Lippincott, 1975); David R. Maginnes, "The Case of the Court House Rioters in the Rendition of the Fugitive Slave Anthony Burns, 1854," *Journal of Negro History* 56 (1971): 31–42; and Samuel Shapiro, "The Rendition of Anthony Burns," *Journal of Negro History* 44 (1959): 34–51. Thomas D. Morris, *Free Men All: The Personal Liberty Laws of the North, 1780–1861* (Baltimore: Johns Hopkins University Press, 1974), discusses those laws as a moderate response to the violence of the southern slave codes.

Any study of the Kansas-Nebraska Act and its aftermath must start with Roy F. Nichols, "The Kansas-Nebraska Act: A Century of Historiography," *Mississippi Valley Historical Review* 43 (1956): 187–212. Two other significant works are Gerald W. Wolff, *The Kansas Nebraska Bill: Party, Section, and the Coming of the Civil War* (New York: Revisionist Press, 1977), and Joan E. Lampton, "The Kansas-Nebraska Act Reconsidered: An Analysis of Men, Methods and Motives," Ph.D. dissertation, Illinois State University, 1979. Frank Hodder emphasizes the railroad interests of Stephen A. Douglas in "The Railroad Background of the Kansas-Nebraska Act," *Mississippi Valley Historical Review* 12 (1925): 3–22, and in other articles, as does James C. Malin in numerous articles and his definitive work, *The Nebraska Question, 1852–1854* (Lawrence, Kans.: James C. Malin, 1953). P. Orman Ray assigned a major role to Senator David Atchison in *The Repeal of the Missouri Compromise: Its Origin and Authorship* (Cleveland: Arthur H. Clark Co., 1909). The work of the Emigrant Aid Company is the subject of Samuel A. Johnson, *The Battle Cry of Freedom: The New England Emigrant Aid Company in the Kansas Crusade* (Lawrence: University of Kansas Press, 1954); Ralph V. Harlow, "The Rise and Fall of the Kansas Aid Movement," *American Historical Review* 41 (1935): 1–25; and Louise Barry, "The Emigrant Aid Company Parties of 1854," and "The New England Aid Company Parties of 1855" in *Kansas Historical Quarterly* 12 (1943): 115–55, 227–68. Paul Wallace Gates emphasized the vital importance of land policy in Kansas Territory in *Fifty Million Acres: Conflicts over Kansas Land Policy, 1854–1890* (New York: Atherton Press, 1966). James C. Malin's *John Brown and the Legend of Fifty-six* (Philadelphia: American Philosophical Society, 1942), raises disturbing questions for those who would ennoble Brown, while Benjamin Quarles, *Allies for Freedom: Blacks and John Brown* (New York: Oxford University Press, 1974), gives a much different view. Stephen B. Oates, *To Purge This Land with Blood: A Biography of John Brown* (New York: Harper and Row, 1970), tends to confirm the Malin thesis. Civil conflict in Kansas is the subject of Alice Nichols, *Bleeding Kansas* (New York: Oxford University Press, 1954), and Jay Monaghan, *Civil War on the Western Border, 1854–1865* (Lincoln: University of Nebraska Press, 1955). The importance of Charles Sumner's speech on Kansas and the attack on him that followed is treated in William E. Gienapp, "The Crime against Sumner: The Caning of Charles Sumner and the Rise of the Republican Party," *Civil War History* 25 (1979): 218–45.

The complexities of foreign relations during the years of the Pierce administration have also inspired far more books than it is possible to list. Albert K. Weinberg, *Manifest Destiny: A Study of Nationalist Expansionism in American History*, reprint ed. (Gloucester, Mass.: Peter Smith, 1958), remains a basic work for the background of expansionism. Other useful books are Norman A. Graebner, *Empire on the Pacific: A Study in American Continental Expansion* (New York: Ronald Press, 1955); Reginald Horsman, *Race and Manifest Destiny: The Origins of American Racial Anglo-Saxonism* (Cambridge, Mass.: Harvard University Press, 1981); Thomas R. Hietala, *Manifest Design: Anxious Aggrandizement in Late Jacksonian America* (Ithaca, N.Y.: Cornell University Press, 1985); Frederick

Merk, *Manifest Destiny and Mission in American History: A Reinterpretation* (New York: Alfred A. Knopf, 1963).

For the contributions of William Marcy see Ivor D. Spencer, *The Victor and the Spoils: A Life of William L. Marcy* (Providence, R.I.: Brown University Press, 1959); H. Barrett Learned, "William L. Marcy," in Samuel Flagg Bemis et al., eds., *The American Secretaries of State and Their Diplomacy*, 17 vols. (New York: Pageant Book Co., 1927–1967), 6:145–294; Robert L. Scribner, "The Diplomacy of William L. Marcy: Secretary of State, 1853–1857," Ph.D. dissertation, University of Virginia, 1949; John Bassett Moore, "A Great Secretary of State: William L. Marcy," *Political Science Quarterly* 30 (1915): 377–96. The imperialists of derring-do are the subject of Merle Curti's "Young America," *American Historical Review* 32 (1926): 34–55, and "George N. Sanders—American Patriot of the Fifties," *South Atlantic Quarterly* 27 (1928): 79–87.

Commodore Perry's historic mission is treated in Arthur Walworth, *Black Ships off Japan: The Story of Commodore Perry's Expedition* (Hamden, Conn.: Archon Books, 1966), and Roger Pineau, ed., *The Japan Expedition, 1852–1854: The Personal Journal of Commodore Matthew C. Perry* (Washington, D.C.: Smithsonian Institution, 1968). Earl Swisher discusses some implications of the Perry expedition for twentieth-century policy in "Commodore Perry's Imperialism in Relation to America's Present-Day Position in the World," *Pacific Historical Review* 16 (1947): 30–40.

Both Paul Garber, *The Gadsden Treaty* (Philadelphia: Press of the University of Pennsylvania, 1923), and Robert L. Jenkins, "The Gadsden Treaty and Sectionalism: A Nation Reacts," Ph.D. dissertation, Mississippi State University, 1978, deal with the Pierce administration's relations with Mexico. The Anglo-American rivalry in Latin America is traced in Mary W. Williams, *Anglo-American Isthmian Diplomacy, 1815–1915*, reprint ed. (Gloucester, Mass.: Peter Smith, 1965), as well as in Richard W. Alstyne, "British Diplomacy and the Clayton-Bulwer Treaty, 1850–1860," *Journal of Modern History* 11 (1936): 149–83, and Alstyne, ed., "Anglo-American Relations, 1853–1857," *American Historical Review* 42 (1937): 491–500. The role the filibusters played is detailed in Charles H. Brown, *Agents of Destiny: The Lives and Times of the Filibusters* (Chapel Hill: University of North Carolina Press, 1980); William O. Scroggs, *Filibusters and Financiers: The Story of William Walker and His Associates*, reprint ed. (New York: Russell and Russell, 1969); Laurence Greene, *The Filibuster: The Career of William Walker* (Indianapolis, Ind.: Bobbs-Merrill, 1937); and Robert E. May, *John A. Quitman: Old South Crusader* (Baton Rouge: Louisiana State University Press, 1985).

Much has been written about the Pierce administration's preoccupation with Cuba. Some useful works are Basil Rauch, *American Interests in Cuba, 1848–1855* (New York: Columbia University Press, 1948); Philip S. Foner, *A History of Cuba and Its Relations with the United States*, 2 vols. (New York: International Publishers, 1962); Henry L. Janes, "The Black Warrior Affair," *American Historical Review* 12 (1907): 280–98; C. Stanley Urban, "The Abortive Quitman Filibustering Expedition, 1853–1855," *Journal of Mississippi History* 28

(1956): 175–96, and "The Africanization of Cuba Scare, 1853–1855," *Hispanic American Historical Review* 37 (1957): 29–45; Amos A. Ettinger, *The Mission to Spain of Pierre Soulé, 1853–1855: A Study in the Cuban Diplomacy of the United States* (New Haven, Conn.: Yale University Press, 1932); J. A. Reinecke, Jr., "The Diplomatic Career of Pierre Soulé," *Louisiana Historical Quarterly* 15 (1932): 281–329; and Sydney Webster, "Mr. Marcy, the Cuban Question and the Ostend Manifesto," *Political Science Quarterly* 8 (1893): 1–32.

Other foreign policy matters are covered in Charles C. Tansill, *The United States and Santo Domingo, 1798–1873: A Chapter in Caribbean Diplomacy,* reprint ed. (Gloucester, Mass.: Peter Smith, 1967), and *The Canadian Reciprocity Treaty of 1854* (Baltimore: Johns Hopkins University Press, 1922); Francis Taylor Piggott, *The Declaration of Paris* (London: University of London Press, 1919); Donald F. Warner, *The Idea of Continental Union: Agitation for the Annexation of Canada to the United States, 1849–1893* (Lexington: University of Kentucky Press, 1960); Alan Dowty, *The Limits of American Isolation: The United States and the Crimean War* (New York: New York University Press, 1971); Charles Edward Hill, *The Danish Sound Dues and the Command of the Baltic: A Study of International Relations* (Durham, N.C.: Duke University Press, 1926); and Osborne E. Hooley, "Hawaiian Negotiations for Reciprocity, 1855–1857," *Pacific Historical Review* 7 (1938): 128–46. Roy F. Nichols, *Advance Agents of American Destiny* (Philadelphia: University of Pennsylvania Press, 1956), includes good background material on the guano controversy.

INDEX

211